*Fruit of*
# LIES WOMEN BELIEVE:
## AND THE TRUTH THAT SETS THEM FREE

---

"This study has changed my life—I wish I had it as a young woman instead of at age seventy, but better late than never."

"We just finished a weekly Bible study using this book at a nearby women's prison. Many of the women there shed tears and told us repeatedly, 'If only someone had taught us the Truth when we were outside!' But God is using them as missionaries behind bars now, and many ladies are eager to hear the truth of God's Word and repent and believe."

"God is using this book as a tool to heal a disastrous marriage."

"I taught this book in a small group, and by the end of the study one of the (older) ladies commented that she would not have divorced if she had been aware of these truths when she was younger."

"I bought *Lies Women Believe* during a particularly hard time in my life. I have been a believer for a long time but had a rebellious spirit. This book ministered to me the way a godly friend would. I rededicated my life to the Lord."

"*Lies Women Believe* literally changed my life. I am an orphan, and this book is like a sister to me."

"I teach a Bible study for postabortive women, and I have used *Lies Women Believe* over and over again. It is a much-needed resource. These women have believed so many lies, including that abortion would solve their crisis pregnancy."

"*Lies Women Believe* was one of the most impacting books (next to the Bible) in my early walk as a Christian. It opened my eyes to the truth of Scripture and the true nature of how God designed us as women!"

"I went through *Lies* with some friends soon after it came out (I was a mom of young teens then), and it impacted me so much I wanted to share it with others. I have led three groups of young women in their twenties through the book, and three groups of high school girls through *Lies Young Women Believe*. I still use principles from the book in my daily life, and it's the first study I recommend to others."

"I believe this is the only Christian book for women in Bosnia. Because the people are poor, each book sold is getting read many times."

"*Lies Women Believe* changed my life. I had no idea how much I had bought into the world's lies. The Lord used this book to open my eyes to His truth. I have now led five different groups of women through it, and every time it has impacted me. And wow, what a difference it has made in other women's lives. This book needs to be taught in every church across the world."

"To say this book has been eye opening is an understatement. There are so many lies that have controlled me and kept me in bondage my entire life! Now, with the help of my precious Jesus, I am breaking the ties that bind me and finding freedom in the Truth!"

"I am a converted frazzled, exhausted, joyless, anxious woman, who—because I recognized that I was being deceived by the lies of Satan when I read *Lies Women Believe* over three years ago—am now filled with joy, peace, and contentment. I was living as if I did not really believe the truth in the Word. Now I am confident in who I am in Christ. He is working in my life to rearrange me from the inside out, and I am so excited to share this freedom with other women, I'm about to burst. I've told everybody, 'You have to read this book!'"

# LIES
## *Women*
# BELIEVE

---

### AND THE TRUTH THAT SETS THEM FREE

---

## NANCY DeMOSS
## WOLGEMUTH

MOODY PUBLISHERS

CHICAGO

Unless otherwise indicated, Scripture quotations are from the ESV® Bible (The Holy Bible, English Standard Version®), copyright © 2001 by Crossway, a publishing ministry of Good News Publishers. Used by permission. All rights reserved.

Scripture quotations marked CSB®, are taken from the Christian Standard Bible®, Copyright © 2017 by Holman Bible Publishers. Used by permission. Christian Standard Bible®, and CSB® are federally registered trademarks of Holman Bible Publishers.

Scripture quotations marked NIV are taken from the Holy Bible, New International Version®, NIV®. Copyright © 1973, 1978, 1984, 2011 by Biblica, Inc.™ Used by permission of Zondervan. All rights reserved worldwide. www.zondervan.com The "NIV" and "New International Version" are trademarks registered in the United States Patent and Trademark Office by Biblica, Inc.

Scripture quotations marked NASB are taken from the *New American Standard Bible*®, © Copyright 1960, 1962, 1963, 1968, 1971, 1972, 1973, 1975, 1977, 1995 by The Lockman Foundation. Used by permission.

Scripture quotations marked NKJV are taken from the *New King James Version*. Copyright © 1982 by Thomas Nelson, Inc. Used by permission. All rights reserved.

Scripture quotations marked PHILLIPS are taken from The New Testament in Modern English, copyright © 1958, 1959, 1960 J.B. Phillips and 1947, 1952, 1955, 1957 The Macmillian Company, New York. Used by permission. All rights reserved.

The testimonies in this book are true. Unless both the first and last name are given, individuals' names and minor details of their stories have been changed to maintain anonymity.

Italics in Scripture references indicate author emphasis.

Published in association with the literary agency of Wolgemuth & Associates.

Edited by Anne C. Buchanan
Interior design: Smartt Guys design
Cover concept: Amjad Shahzad
Cover design: Erik M. Peterson
Cover images: Front cover photo of apple with bite copyright © 2014 by eli_asenova/iStock (475190475). All rights reserved. Back cover illustration of apple tree copyright © 2014 by WesAbrams/iStock (487774771). All rights reserved.
Author photo: Nathan Bollinger

ISBN: 978-0-8024-1836-4

We hope you enjoy this book from Moody Publishers. Our goal is to provide high-quality, thought-provoking books and products that connect truth to your real needs and challenges. For more information on other books and products written and produced from a biblical perspective, go to www.moodypublishers.com or write to:

Moody Publishers
820 N. LaSalle Boulevard
Chicago, IL 60610

1 3 5 7 9 10 8 6 4 2

*Printed in the United States of America*

**TO MY MOTHER**

*who taught me to recognize
many of the lies women believe
and who knows the beauty and power
of the Truth*

# CONTENTS

 FOREWORD

ELISABETH ELLIOT (1926–2015) *was a beloved role model, mentor, and spiritual mother to many in my generation. We were initially spellbound by her chronicles of the life and death of Jim Elliot, her first husband, who was martyred at the age of twenty-eight by the Huaorani tribe in Ecuador. In subsequent years, she continued to speak into our lives through her many books, her speaking ministry, and* Gateway to Joy, *her daily radio program that was a rich source of biblical wisdom and practical encouragement.* Revive Our Hearts, *the ministry I am blessed to serve, began in 2001 as the successor to Elisabeth's program. How thankful I am for this sweet legacy.*

*Although we met on a few occasions, I did not have the privilege of knowing Elisabeth well. But I admired her from a distance, and her straightforward, thought-provoking teaching significantly influenced my life and thinking as a young woman.*

*When I first wrote* Lies Women Believe, *I asked Elisabeth if she would be willing to write a foreword. I felt that she, more than anyone else I could think of, embodied the heart and essence of this message. I was honored and grateful when she agreed to do so.*

*Fast-forward fifteen years. I wept when I received the news that Elisabeth had gone to be with the Lord. Her eternal gain was our temporal loss. Though she is no longer serving Christ here on earth, we have retained her foreword in this revised edition of* Lies. *It is my hope that a new generation of women will be inspired to read her books, follow her Master, hold firmly to the Truth, and, like Elisabeth, touch their world with Christ-saturated wisdom and grace.*

NANCY DeMoss WOLGEMUTH (2018)

NANCY LEIGH DEMOSS, a woman of compassion and keen insight, has had the courage to plumb the depths of women's illusions and delusions, of their hopes, fears, failures, and sorrows, so much of which might have been avoided were it not for lies propagated thirty or more years ago—such as "You can have it all," "Don't get caught in the compassion trap," "Anything men can do we can do better," etc.

But of course the lies began long before that. The woman God gave to the first man, Adam, listened to the Whisperer: Hath God said? Eve listened to the snake in the garden. Then, instead of protecting her from the lies being propagated, her husband said, in effect, "If this is what the little lady wants, this is what the little lady should have." Consequently, sin entered into the world and death by sin. Eve refused what was given, usurped what was not given, and said, in effect, "My will be done."

Thanks be to God, there is redemption. A humble village girl in Nazareth was visited by an angel, who delivered a startling message. Mary was to become the mother of the Son of God. Although she was greatly troubled, she received the message. "I am the Lord's servant," she responded. "May it be to me as you have said."

It is my prayer that the Spirit of God will direct you as you read this greatly needed book. "The essence of true salvation," the author writes, "is not a matter of profession or performance; rather it is a transformation: 'If anyone is in Christ, he is a new creation; the old has gone, the new has come!'"

ELISABETH ELLIOT (2001)

PREFACE TO THE UPDATED
& EXPANDED EDITION

rom a marketing perspective, there might have been a better title
for this book. After all, it can be a little awkward to hand a woman a
book with *Lies Women Believe* in large print on the cover and say, "You
really need to read this!"

But the Lord has been pleased to give this message a warmer reception
and a broader reach (including translations into twenty-six languages)
than I ever could have anticipated—a testimony, I believe, to the longing
in women's hearts to experience the freedom of walking in the Truth.

So why this new edition?

- Our world has been shaken by seismic cultural shifts since *Lies*
  was first released in 2001. For example, social media as we know
  it today did not exist back then. And certain sexual issues and
  themes that were peripheral twenty years ago now touch most
  of our lives in personal ways. I've added an entire chapter on lies
  about sexuality and made some other needed updates.

- Over these years, by God's grace, I've grown in my walk with
  the Lord, my understanding of His Word, and my appreciation
  for how the gospel intersects with all of life, and there are some
  things I would say differently today than I did back then. I'm
  grateful for this opportunity to reflect those changes.

- Hundreds, perhaps thousands, of women have provided feed-
  back on this message in conversations, letters, emails, and online
  reviews. Some have expressed their disagreement with particular
  points. I've tried to listen carefully and humbly. Their input has
  helped me to clarify and fine-tune my message in places and to

express it in a way that I trust is both faithful to the Scripture and sensitive to women in various life circumstances.

- I've had the joy of meeting women who first read this book years ago when they were younger. They have shared how this message opened their eyes to deception, and the sweet fruit they are enjoying years later, as a result of learning to build their lives on the foundation of Truth.

I cannot think of any greater way to invest this season of my life than by encouraging a new generation of women to know and embrace Christ and His Word. My prayer is that they will point those coming behind them to the Truth that will set them free.

- I was in my early forties and single when I first wrote *Lies*. As this version releases, I am close to the sixty-year marker and (wonder of wonders!) in my third year of marriage. In God's providence, I am experiencing the beauty and power of the Truth in fresh ways. At selected points in this book, I've added thoughts or illustrations from my older/married vantage point.

(My book *Adorned: Living Out the Beauty of the Gospel Together*[1] more fully reflects this season of my life, and addresses in greater depth some of the topics I've touched on in *Lies*. I hope you'll consider *Adorned* as a follow-up to this book.)

And a few more notes:

- This has been a team effort. On pages 303–304 I've thanked those who played various roles. I particularly want to acknowledge Mary Kassian and Dannah Gresh for their assistance in developing portions of this expanded version.

- To get the most out of this book, you'll want to go through it with a friend or a group of women. The *Lies Women Believe Study Guide*[2] includes suggestions for going deeper into God's Word and "making it personal," as well as questions for group discussion.

- You'll find additional resources at **LiesWomenBelieve.com**, including an extensive list of recommended resources on many of the topics found in this book. You'll also find information about other books in this family: *Lies Young Women Believe* (coauthored with Dannah Gresh), *Lies Girls Believe* and *A Mom's Guide for Lies Girls Believe* (both by Dannah Gresh), and *Lies Men Believe* (by Robert Wolgemuth, whom I'm blessed to call my husband!).[3]

Finally, I'd love to pray for you as you embark on this journey.

*Thank You, Father, for making Your truth known to us*
*through Your Word*
*and in Your Son, Jesus Christ.*

*And thank You for the woman who holds this book in her hand.*

*Whatever her age or marital status,*
*however much or little she may have experienced of You in the past,*
*whatever her current circumstances and challenges may be . . .*

*I ask You to make Yourself known to her as she reads this book.*
*May she experience the freedom and joy of walking in the Truth.*
*And may You use her as an instrument of Grace and Truth in the lives of others.*

*For Jesus' sake and in His holy Name, I pray.*
*Amen.*

*B*anished from Eden, wearing clothes of animal skins, her husband frustrated with her, on her way to being the mother of the first murdered child—and the mother of his killer—Eve must have felt very low.

Alone.

Defeated.

A failure.

How hard it must have been to walk with Adam east of Eden into a world in which it was a struggle just to stay alive. How hard it must have been to have known a paradise and then to be told to leave it.

What must Eve have wanted the most at that moment?

What would *you* have wanted?

I believe that with all her heart Eve wished she could have taken back the instant just before she bit into the forbidden fruit—when her arm was still outstretched toward the limbs of the Tree of the Knowledge of Good and Evil and escape was still possible.

She ached to do things over, to have done things right the first time.

And haven't we all been there?

We've experienced defeats and failures, trouble and turmoil.

We know what it is to battle a selfish heart, a shrewish spirit, anger, envy, and bitterness.

Some of our failures may not be so extreme as Eve's. They're not catastrophic, public events. Maybe they're just "small" lapses. But they still reveal how far our hearts are from where they ought to be. And we ache to do things over, to have lives of harmony and peace.

Whenever I lead a women's conference, I ask the women to fill out prayer cards so our prayer team can intercede for them during the weekend. Over the years I have read through many of those cards my-self. I have often found myself tearful over what has been expressed on them, heavyhearted over the reality so many Christian women are experiencing.

- *Women whose marriages are hanging by a thread*
- *Women whose hearts ache for their children*
- *Women who are overwhelmed with past failures and wounds*
- *Women with intense personal struggles*
- *Women filled with doubts and confusion about their walk with God*

These women are real women. Some of them have been in church all their lives. Some of them attend your church and mine. They serve in the children's ministry and on the worship team. Some attend small group every week—they may even be Bible study leaders. When you ask how they're doing, they may smile and say, "Fine." You might never suspect the turmoil and pain lying buried under their seemingly serene demeanor.

And these are not isolated instances. I'm not talking about a few ex-treme, dysfunctional women living on the margins. After all, who among us doesn't have something going on in or around us that makes us feel perplexed, frightened, or broken?

Our culture is experiencing an epidemic of "soul-sickness"—not just among women "out there" in the world, but among those of us in the church. I think you'd agree that at any given time, many of us could be described by one or more of the following words:

| | | | |
|---|---|---|---|
| *frazzled* | *defeated* | *confused* | *uptight* |
| *exhausted* | *discouraged* | *angry* | *fearful* |
| *overwhelmed* | *ashamed* | *frustrated* | *lonely* |

*. . . and yes, even suicidal*

*Suicidal?* I suspect you and I would be stunned to learn how many people in any audience of Christian women have contemplated ending their own life—some of them within recent weeks or months. Just recently I visited with a woman who has a responsible position in a Christian ministry and who has battled suicidal thoughts throughout her life. I have no doubt that someone who is reading this paragraph has come to the end of her rope. Maybe it's you. Maybe you feel it just isn't worth going on. Let me say to you, dear one, that there *is* hope! Reading this book won't make your problems go away, but I believe it will point you in the direction of Someone who can help. Please, please, keep reading.

*Spiritual bondage* is another phrase that comes to mind when I think of many Christian women. In fact, I'd go so far as to say that the majority of women I know (including myself at times), are not free in one or more areas of their lives.

For example, many women live under a cloud of personal guilt and condemnation. They are not free to enjoy the grace and the love of God.

Many are enslaved to their past. Whether the result of their own failures or the failures of others, their past hangs like a huge weight around their neck. They carry it everywhere they go, unable to break free from the burden.

Others are in bondage to what the Bible calls the "fear of man"—they are gripped by fear of rejection, fear of what people think of them, and a longing for approval. Still others are emotional prisoners, enslaved by worry, fear, anger, depression, and self-pity.

One of the greatest areas of captivity women express is in relation to food. I have heard this from women of all sizes and shapes. Some can't stop eating. Some can't make themselves eat. All are in prison.

I don't want to suggest that all women are a mess (although we all have moments when that's the case!). But I am saying that many among us are struggling deeply—dealing with issues that require more than superficial solutions and remedies.

When we turn to the Scriptures, we are reminded that God didn't intend for it to be this way. We read the words of Jesus in the gospel of John and know that God has something better for us:

> I came that they may have life and have it abundantly.
>
> —John 10:10

As you look at your life, would you say you are experiencing the abundant life Jesus came to give? Or do you find yourself just existing, coping, surviving?

I'm not asking if you have a trouble-free life. In fact, some of the most winsome, joyful women I know are women who are living in painfully difficult marriages; women who have wept at the graveside of a son or daughter; women who have been diagnosed with cancer or are caring for an elderly parent with Alzheimer's. But somehow, in the midst of the problems and the pain, they have discovered a source of life that enables them to walk through the valley with peace, confidence, and wholeness.

What about you? Do you relate to some of the women whose stories I shared above? Are there areas of spiritual bondage in your life?

What if I told you that instead of being miserable, frustrated, and enslaved, you could be

| | | |
|---|---|---|
| *free* | *confident* | *joyous* |
| *gracious* | *content* | *peaceful* |
| *loving* | *stable* | *radiant* |

These words describe the kind of woman I long to be. I'm guessing you feel the same way.

Most likely, you know other women who are living in captivity, though they claim to have a relationship with Christ. Would you like to learn how to show them the pathway to freedom?

I'm not talking about a magic formula that will make problems vanish; I'm not offering any shortcuts to an easy life, nor am I promising the absence of pain and difficulties. Life is hard—there's no way around that. But I am talking about walking through the realities of life—things like rejection, loss, disappointment, wounds, and even death—in freedom and true joy.

You say, "That's what I want! I want it for myself; I want it for other women I know. Where do we begin?"

Through years of interacting with women about our burdens and concerns and searching the Word of God for wisdom, I have come to a simple but profound conclusion about the root of most of our struggles:

> You and I have been lied to.
> We have been deceived.

In the pages that follow, I invite you to take a walk with me back to where all our problems began: the Garden of Eden, the first home of Adam and Eve—a perfect, ideal environment. What took place in that setting has a huge bearing on each of our lives today.

I want you to see how a lie was the starting place for all the trouble in the history of the universe. Eve listened to, believed, and acted on that lie. In some sense every problem, every war, every wound, every broken relationship, every heartache goes back to one simple lie.

As lies have a way of doing, that first lie grew and spun off more lies. Eve believed the lie, and we, the daughters of Eve, have followed in her steps—listening to, believing, and acting on one lie after another. (Throughout this book, you will find fictionalized entries from "Eve's Journal." They are intended to suggest some of the lies Eve may have been vulnerable to at different seasons of her life. Her journal may even read a bit like yours or mine at points.)

There is no end to the kinds of deception that humans have fallen for since the Garden of Eden. My goal in this book is to expose a handful of those lies for what they really are. Some of the lies we will consider are so widely believed that you may find it difficult to recognize them as lies. But the "best" lies—the most effective ones—are those that look the most like the Truth. And the "newest" lies are the oldest ones.

In addition to exposing some of the lies commonly believed by Christian women, I want to unmask the one who tells us those lies. Satan poses as an "angel of light" (2 Cor. 11:14). He promises happiness and pretends to have our best interests at heart. But he is a deceiver and a destroyer; he is determined to dethrone God by getting us to side with him against God. I want you to see how Satan may have used some subtle lies or even half-truths to deceive and destroy you or those you love.

But we must do more than identify the Deceiver and his lies. I want to introduce you to the power of the Truth and to show you how believing and acting on the Truth is our means to freedom—not just survival or escape—but true, glorious freedom in the midst of this fallen, broken, hurting world.

Over the course of four decades of speaking and writing ministry, countless women have shared their story with me, in person or in writing. Many of them have been transparent about some of the lies they have believed and how their lives have been affected. And many have shared how they have learned to reject those lies and are enjoying the freedom that comes with embracing God's Truth. These women provided the impetus for this book. Throughout these pages, I've included some of their testimonies. I hope they will help you recognize lies you may have fallen for and encourage you to replace those lies with the Truth found in God's Word and in Christ, the Living Word.

One day, as I was putting the finishing touches on the first edition of this book, I was out walking, meditating on James chapter 5. The last two verses in particular caught my attention:

> If anyone among you wanders from the truth
> and someone brings him back,
> let him know that whoever brings back a sinner
> from his wandering
> will save his soul from death
> and will cover a multitude of sins.
>
> —James 5:19–20

From the time this book was first released, it has been my desire that the Lord would use it to help bring back women who have wandered away from the path of Truth, and that He would set them free to walk in His grace, forgiveness, and abundant life. In His kindness and mercy, He has been pleased to do just that.

That said, I know some will find it difficult to swallow parts of what I've written. (More than one woman has told me she reacted to something she came across in this book by throwing it across the room.) I have no desire to stir up controversy or to wound anyone unnecessarily; but when any of us veers off from the Truth, in small or large ways, we need more than political correctness and nice, polite thoughts. Sometimes radical surgery—a reorientation of our entire way of thinking and living—is required to deal with our diseased hearts and make us whole. Sometimes the Truth hurts. It is rarely popular. But I would not be loving or kind if I failed to share with you the Truth that can set you and me free.

The liberating power of the Truth was evident in two encounters I had with women some time ago.

> *I'm free! I had given up hope that it was possible, but God has set me free from years of spiritual bondage.*

Those were the words of a young wife at an informal gathering as she began sharing with me what God had been doing in her life. She told me that she had been masturbating ever since she was thirteen years old:

> *I tried and tried to stop; I did everything I knew to do—including Bible study, prayer, and being accountable to a friend—but I kept failing. When I blew it, I would confess my sin and ask God's forgiveness, but deep in my heart, I knew I would fall again. I just couldn't stop.*

This woman had been a Christian for years, and she and her husband were active in Christian ministry. But she had never been able to shake the enormous frustration and guilt she felt within.

She became more animated as she described the process that led to the release she had longed to experience:

*I finally got up the courage to ask a godly older woman for help. She encouraged me to ask God what lies I had been believing. I honestly didn't think I was believing any lies, but when I began to pray about it, God opened my eyes and showed me specific areas where I had been deceived. Those lies had kept me in bondage for over ten years! Once I saw the Truth, I repented of believing the lies and asked God to take back the ground I had allowed Satan to have in that area of my life.*

Her countenance told the story of what happened next. She continued:

*From that point, I have been totally free from this sin that had such a hold on my life. Plus, God is giving me victory in other areas where I have been tempted in the past. I can't begin to express the joy and freedom I have been experiencing. The Truth is so incredibly powerful!*

I witnessed the power of the Truth in another situation as I talked to a woman who had become emotionally involved with one of the pastors of her church. When I first became aware of the situation, I called her at work because I didn't know how much her husband knew. Since she was a receptionist for her company, I knew we might not have long to talk.

After identifying myself and affirming her for having the courage to share her predicament, I got right to the point, which I introduced with a word picture: "If I looked out the window in the middle of the night and noticed that my neighbors' house was on fire, I would run next door and do whatever I had to do to get their attention and get them out of danger. I wouldn't worry that they might be annoyed with me for waking them up in the middle of the night. I wouldn't be concerned about hurting their feelings."

Then I said to this woman, "I'm deeply concerned for you; I know you're in a really difficult situation. I know you feel trapped and that your emotions are in a tailspin. But I have to tell you that you're in a burning house—you're in grave danger. Because this is a desperate situation, I'm going to do whatever I can to warn you about the danger you're in and to help you get out of that burning house before it's too late."

Tearfully I begged this woman to realize the truth of what was happening in her life. I pleaded with her to take immediate, drastic steps to extricate herself from the dangerous situation she had allowed herself to get into.

As we talked, God turned on the light in this woman's heart. I can't take any credit for what happened in the days ahead—"For it is God who works in you, both to will and to work for his good pleasure" (Phil. 2:13). But what a joy it was to watch this dear woman embrace the Truth about her choices and about God's will for her life, marriage, and relationships. As she took one difficult step after another, the grace of God enabled her to move on past her emotions, old habits, and deeply ingrained (but false) ways of thinking. She began to walk in the Light. And in the Light she found a whole new way of life—the pathway of freedom and blessing.

That's how it is with Truth, and that's what I want for you.

$$\approx$$

For a dozen years or more, I have been part of a group of eight women who have built a sweet friendship around our common love for Christ and His Word. Though we live in two different countries (six states and provinces), we have made it a point to stay connected through many changing seasons, keeping each other updated on the happenings in our lives. We share and celebrate our deepest joys and victories. And we have grown to trust each other enough to share our deepest fears, failures, and unfulfilled longings. At times, in our periodic gatherings and conference calls, we have laughed together until it hurt. And we have cried together until it hurt.

We all have a more or less public profile. You may have seen our smiling, touched-up photos on ministry websites, conference promotions, and book jackets. But I can tell you this: not one of us *feels* polished or put together. To the contrary, each of us feels weak, inadequate, and needy.

Each of us has broken pieces and parts—past and present. And each of us has areas of our life where we battle the consequences of believing lies about God, about ourselves, or about our circumstances—to name a few.

What an incredible gift it has been to help each other bring those areas of deception into the light and then to watch the Spirit graciously, persistently use His Truth to renew our minds and bring us into a place of greater freedom. And out of that freedom we are able to encourage each other in meaningful ways as the need arises. What a sweet, healing, freeing cycle of grace God has allowed this precious circle of friends to experience together.

My hope in writing (and now updating) this book is that I can be a true friend to you, as these women and so many others have been to me, and that as you and I circle up together, God will touch every area of your life that is in need of restoration and grace.

The journey we're about to take will not always be easy. It can be difficult—even painful—to identify and root out those areas of deception that have placed us in captivity. But I know a Good Shepherd who loves you dearly, who laid down His life for you, and who will take you by the hand and lead you into green pastures and by quiet waters if you will let Him.

> For freedom Christ has set us free; stand firm therefore,
> and do not submit again to a yoke of slavery.
>
> —Galatians 5:1

> Come to me, all who labor and are heavy laden,
> and I will give you rest. Take my yoke upon you, and learn from me,
> for I am gentle and lowly in heart,
> and you will find rest for your souls.
> For my yoke is easy, and my burden is light.
>
> —Matthew 11:28–30

SECTION ONE

# FOUNDATIONS

*My head is spinning. I hardly know where to start. This day started out so per-fectly—like every other day we've ever had. As we always do, Adam and I got up early to take a walk with God. Those walks have always been the highlight of our day.*

*This morning, no one said anything for a while. We just enjoyed being to-gether. Then God started singing. It was a love song. When He got to the chorus, we started to sing with Him—first Adam's deep voice, then mine joined in. We sang songs about love and stars and joy and God. Finally, we all sat down un-der a big shade tree near the middle of the garden. We thanked God for being so good; we told Him all we wanted to do was to make Him happy and to find our happiness in Him. It was such a sweet time—it always was when the three of us were together.*

*I don't know how to explain what happened next. All of a sudden we heard a voice we'd never heard before. I turned and there, looking right at me, was the most beautiful creature I had ever seen. He talked directly to me. He made me feel important, and I found myself wanting to hear what he had to say.*

*I'm not sure what happened to God at this point. It wasn't like He left us. I think I just kind of forgot He was there. In fact, for a while I forgot Adam was there too. I felt as if I were alone with this dazzling, mysterious creature.*

*The conversation that followed is indelibly etched in my mind. He asked me questions—questions I'd never thought about before. Then he offered me some things I had never had before, things I'd never thought I needed. Independence—from God and from Adam. Position—I had always looked up to God and Adam, but this creature said they would look up to me. Knowledge—of mysteries known only to God. Permission—to eat the fruit from the tree in the middle of the garden.*

*At first I just listened and looked. In my heart I pondered, I questioned, I de-bated. Adam had reminded me many times that God had said we were not to eat the fruit from that tree. But the creature kept looking into my eyes and talking in*

that soothing voice. I found myself believing him. It felt so right. Finally I surrendered. I reached out, cautiously at first. Then I took it. I ate it. I handed it to Adam.
He ate it. We ate together—first me, then him.

Those next moments are a blur. Sensations deep down inside that I've never
had before. New awareness—like I know a secret I'm not supposed to know. Ela-
tion and depression at the same time. Liberation. Prison. Rising. Falling. Confident. Afraid. Ashamed. Dirty. Hiding—I can't let Him see me like this.

Alone. So alone.

Lost.

Deceived.

# CHAPTER ONE

# TRUTH...OR *Consequences*

"Become a World-Class Violinist Instantaneously."

"How to Play the Piano . . . Instantly!"

"'Instant Health' at the Flip of a Switch!" (ad for a kitchen appliance).

"Melt 10 Lbs. in 10 Minutes! . . . a Workout So Easy, You Do It in Your Pajamas!"

"Delivers So Much Peace of Mind It Should Be Covered under Your Health Plan" (ad for a popular car).

"Look Better and Feel Younger in Just Minutes a Day . . . the Key to a Healthier, Happier Life" (ad for an oxygen chamber, price tag: $3,999.95).

*Y*ou've no doubt seen these kinds of outlandish claims on social media ads or at the checkout line in the supermarket. They've been around as long as there has been advertising.

And then there are the endless, more subtle, variations. Is it just me, or does it seem that "gluten free" is stamped on everything from celery bags to milk cartons today? Advertisers trying to get us to purchase their product based on a hollow promise. (I'm pretty sure celery and milk have always been gluten free!)

Our culture is riddled with deception. Sometimes it's easy to see through the falsehood (as in the claim that one can become a world-class violinist instantaneously). Unfortunately, however, deception is not always easy to detect.

Deception in advertising appeals to our natural human longings. We *want* to believe that somehow, mysteriously, those unwanted pounds really could melt away in just ten minutes—no sweat, no discipline, no cost, no effort, no pain. That's why we buy the pills, the diet drink powders, and the exercise equipment promoted on Internet ads.

A clever and cunning pitchman whose intention was to change Adam and Eve's thinking about God and His ways designed the first advertising campaign. Satan's objective was to drive a wedge between God and His creatures. He rightly assumed that the man and woman were not likely to support anything that appeared to be an all-out assault on God. He knew that, instead, he would have to subtly trick them, to deceive them, to seduce them by making an offer that appeared to be reasonable, desirable, and not entirely "anti-God."

Satan deceived Eve through a clever combination of outright lies, half-truths, and falsehoods disguised as truth. He began by planting seeds of doubt in her mind about what God had actually said ("Did God really say . . . ?" [Gen. 3:1 CSB]).

Next he led her to be careless with the Word of God and to suggest that God had said something that, in fact, He had not said. God had said, "Do not *eat* the fruit of the tree." However, Eve quoted God as saying, "Neither shall you *touch* it" (v. 3).

Satan deceived Eve by causing her to question the goodness, love, and motives of God. His implication was: "Has God put restrictions on your freedom? Sounds like He doesn't want you to be happy."

The Truth is that God had said, "You are *free* to eat from any tree of the garden" (2:16 CSB)—except one.

The Truth is that God is a generous God.

In that entire, vast garden, God had posted only one Keep Out sign: "Do not eat from the Tree of the Knowledge of Good and Evil." Furthermore, the one restriction God imposed was in the best interests of the couple and was intended to guarantee their long-term blessing and happiness. God knew that when they ate of that tree, they would die; their relationship with Him would be severed; they would become slaves—to Satan, sin, and self.

The Serpent further deceived Eve by lying to her about the consequences of choosing to disobey God. God had said, "In the day that you eat of it you shall surely die (2:17). Satan countered, "You will *not* surely die" (3:4). He flatly contradicted what God had already said.

The devil seduced Eve by offering her all kinds of benefits if she would just eat the forbidden fruit (3:5). He promised that a whole world of knowledge and experience would open up to her ("Your eyes will be opened"). He assured her that she would be equal with God—that is, that she could be her own god ("You will be like God").

Finally, he promised that she would be able to decide for herself what was right and wrong ("knowing good and evil"). God had already told Adam and Eve what was right and what was wrong. But Satan said, in essence, "That's His opinion. But you're entitled to your own opinion—you can make your own decisions about what's right and wrong."

Satan deceived Eve by causing her to make her decision based on what she could see and on what her emotions and her reason told her to be right, even when it was contrary to what God had already told the couple:

> When the woman saw that the tree was good for food,
>     and that it was a delight to the eyes,
>   and that the tree was to be desired to make one wise,
>     she took of its fruit and ate.
>
> —Genesis 3:6

Eve took the bite. But instead of the promised rewards, she found herself with a mouth full of worms—shame, guilt, fear, and alienation. She had been lied to—she had been deceived.

As seventeenth-century Puritan pastor Thomas Brooks put it,

Satan promises the best, but pays with the worst; he promises honor, and pays with disgrace; he promises pleasure, and pays with pain; he promises profit, and pays with loss; he promises life, and pays with death.[1]

From that first encounter in the garden to the present day, Satan has used deception to win our affections, influence our choices, and destroy our lives. In one way or another, every problem we have in this world is the fruit of deception—the result of believing something that simply isn't true.

Satan holds out the glittering promise of "real life," knowing full well that those who respond to his offer will certainly die (Prov. 14:12).

So why do we fall for his deception? Why do we go for the lure? For starters, Satan's lies don't come at us overtly, through talking serpents. Rather, they may be attractively disguised in a *New York Times* bestseller, a popular mommy blog, a movie, a TV show, or a catchy hit song. They may also surface subtly in a classroom with a brilliant professor or in sincere advice from a relative or friend, a therapist, or even a Christian writer, teacher, or counselor.

Day after day, we are bombarded with countless forms of deception that make their way into our minds, lobbed at us not only by our tireless enemy, the devil, but by this fallen world system in which we live and by our own sinful, weak flesh, all of which are at odds with God and the Truth and seek to seduce us.

Regardless of the immediate source, anytime we receive input that is not consistent with the Word of God, our antennae should go up. What we read or hear may sound right, may feel right, may seem right—but if it's contrary to the Word of God, it *isn't* right. If we could only see that the forbidden fruit—fruit that looks so ripe and tastes so sweet in the first moment—ultimately leads to death and destruction.

## THE STRATEGY OF DECEPTION

Deception was—and still is—crucial to Satan's strategy. According to Jesus, it is the devil's very nature to deceive:

[The devil] was a murderer from the beginning,
and does not stand in the truth, because there is no truth in him.
When he lies, he speaks out of his own character,
for he is a liar and the father of lies.

—John 8:44

For reasons we don't fully understand, Satan chose to target the woman for his initial deception. Twice in the New Testament the apostle Paul reminds us that it was the woman who was deceived: "The serpent deceived Eve by his cunning" (2 Cor. 11:3); "Adam was not the one deceived, but the woman was deceived" (1 Tim. 2:14).

Some theologians believe there was something in the way Eve was created that made her more vulnerable. Others suggest that because God had placed her under the headship of her husband, once she stepped out from under that spiritual covering and protection, she was more easily deceived. Or perhaps it was because of Eve's softer, relational, responsive makeup that she was willing to engage with the Serpent.

Whatever the reason, the Deceiver approached and deceived the woman, and she fell for the ploy. She then seduced her husband to sin with her, and together they led the whole human race into sin (though Adam, as her head, was held ultimately responsible).

Since that day, every man and woman who has ever lived has been born with a propensity to sin and has been deceived by Satan's lies. He knows that if we buy into his deception, we will influence others around us to sin, and our sinful choices will set a pattern for subsequent generations to follow.

Sometimes, as was the case with Eve, Satan deceives us directly. And sometimes he uses other people as instruments of deception.

In the fifth chapter of Ephesians, Paul warns, "Let no one deceive you with empty words" (v. 6). Repeatedly, he challenges God's people to speak Truth to one another. When we are not honest with each other, we help the Enemy out, acting as his agents, deceiving and destroying each other.

According to the Scripture, we can even be deceived by spiritual leaders—those who have been entrusted with the responsibility of shepherding God's flock and communicating the Truth to His people. Through the prophet Ezekiel, God addressed those leaders who were abusing their calling and their followers by failing to speak the Truth:

> Because with the lies you have made the heart
> of the righteous sad. . . ;
> you have strengthened the hands of the wicked,
> so that he does not turn from his wicked way to save his life.
>
> —Ezekiel 13:22 NKJV

This description isn't limited to Old Testament spiritual leaders. There are respected "Christian leaders" and influencers today of whom the same might be said. They may not intend to deceive their followers—in fact, they may not even realize they are being deceptive.

Nonetheless, they "strengthen the hands of the wicked" by promising God's blessing and grace to people who do not qualify because of their willful disobedience and unrepentant hearts. Their teachings help people justify . . .

- rage ("You're just being honest about your feelings")
- selfishness ("If you don't look out for yourself, no one else will")
- irresponsibility ("Your problems and your reactions have all been caused by others")
- infidelity ("God wants you to be happy—it's OK to divorce your mate and marry someone you really love")

At the same time, they make "the righteous" feel "sad" or guilty . . . for taking responsibility for their own sinful choices, for demonstrating a servant's heart, and for being faithful to their vows. They may also mislead their followers by preaching the law of God without pointing to Christ, who alone can fulfill the law. Doing this can leave people without hope and under chronic guilt and condemnation of works- or performance-based religion.

## OPEN YOUR EYES

Many of us have unthinkingly exposed ourselves to deception, oblivious to the fact that we are being deceived. That is the very nature of deception.

One of my goals in this book is to urge Christian women to open their eyes and begin to evaluate what is going on around them—to wake up to the deception that is so pervasive. So much of our lifestyle is rooted in ways of thinking that simply are not true. The result is a house built on sinking sand. One lie leads to another and another and another.

It's tempting to mindlessly accept whatever we hear and see. We listen to music, radio, and podcasts; read blogs, magazines, and social media; watch movies; listen to advice; and respond to advertisements without asking ourselves:

- "What's the message here?"
- "Is it really true?"
- "Am I being deceived by a way of thinking that is contrary to the Truth?"

Satan's promise to Eve was tantalizing: "Your eyes will be opened, and you will be like God, knowing good and evil" (Gen. 3:5). Who could resist such an amazing offer?

The forbidden fruit was "*good* for food . . . a *delight* to the eyes . . . to be *desired* to make one wise" (v. 6). If it hadn't seemed so attractive, do you think Eve would have fallen for the offer? If that fruit had been rotten and crawling with worms, would she have considered disobeying God? Probably not. What makes Satan's offers so alluring and so deceptive is that they look so right.

The problem is that Eve didn't stop to evaluate what was really happening. She didn't take time to discern Truth from error. She didn't stop to consider the cost and the consequences of what she was about to do. If Eve could have imagined the ugly, painful, deadly consequences of her choice—in her own life, in her relationship with God, in her marriage, in her children, in her children's children, and (through the sin of her husband, who joined her in disobeying God) in every human being that would ever live on the planet—do you think she would have listened to Satan's lie and disobeyed God? I doubt it.

But how often do we make choices without stopping to consider the consequences that may follow? Many of us simply live our lives, responding to the people, circumstances, and influences around us—eating what we crave at the moment, buying the latest deals that pop up in our social media feeds, adopting the latest fads, and embracing the lifestyles, values, and priorities of our friends. It all looks so good; it feels so right; it seems so innocent. But we end up in abusive relationships, head over heels in debt, angry, frustrated, trapped, and overwhelmed. We have been deceived. We have fallen for a lie.

In an unforgettable example of this kind of deception, a mother of seven young children (five of them adopted) told me she was carrying on an illicit relationship with a man she had met on the Internet; she was seriously thinking of leaving her husband for this other man. As we met together one night at a mall (while her husband watched the kids), she acknowledged that what she was doing was wrong. "But," she said of the other man, "he's so good to me and to my children."

For sure, there were issues in her marriage that had left her sad, emotionally thirsty, and vulnerable to the attention of another man. She felt that she had a chance to exchange sadness for happiness, that perhaps she would find a shortcut to solve the pressures and challenges she faced at home. But as I listened, it became clear to me that leaving her marriage would only set her up for new and greater problems.

As we talked over the next couple of hours, I begged her to realize that this man was not truly interested in her or her children. If he were, he would not be breaking up her marriage. If he really loved her, he would not be leading her to violate God's law. I gently explained that the road she was on, though it seemed so appealing, would not lead to the freedom and happiness she was seeking. I tried to help her see that she was being deceived and that her only hope was to believe and embrace the Truth. The long pathway of confession, counseling, prayer, and recommitment to her marriage and children would not be easy. But it would lead to a beauty that could not possibly be found in pursuing a shortcut.

## THE PROGRESSION FROM DECEPTION TO SPIRITUAL BONDAGE

In the chapters that follow, we'll examine some of the most common and destructive lies women believe, but first let's take a look at how we become deceived and how deception leads to captivity.

Generally speaking, people don't fall into spiritual bondage overnight. They don't just wake up one morning and discover that they are addicted to food or have a temper they can't control. There's a progression that leads to enslavement, and it begins when we . . .

### Listen to a lie.

That's how it all began in the Garden of Eden. Eve *listened* to the lies told her by Satan. I'm confident she had no idea where those lies would ultimately lead her and her family. Perhaps it didn't seem particularly dangerous just to *listen* to the Serpent—to hear him out, to see what he had to say. Listening in itself wasn't disobedience. But—and here's the key—listening to a viewpoint that was contrary to God's word put Eve in a dangerous position that led to disobedience, which in turn led to physical and spiritual death.

Listening to things that are not true is the first step toward spiritual bondage. That's why I believe it is so important to carefully monitor the input we allow into our minds and hearts.

My parents both came to know Jesus as young adults. From the time they married, they were eager to establish a Christ-centered home, based on the solid foundation of His Word. They didn't have the advantage of the many helpful resources that are available to Christian parents today. However, God gave them the wisdom and resolve to cultivate a climate in our home that was conducive to spiritual hunger and growth. My six younger siblings and I couldn't help but be "infected" by their love for Christ, His Word, His people, and His kingdom. They were intentional about surrounding us with spiritually nurturing influences, and they were equally intentional about protecting us from influences that could be harmful to young hearts or could desensitize us to sin.

This approach to child rearing did not always make sense to us when we were kids. But how I thank the Lord today that my parents had the courage to say, "We are not going to knowingly allow our children's lives to be shaped by the lies promoted in this world." They earnestly desired that we would grow up to love the Word and the ways of God, that our hearts would be quickened by the Truth, and that we would embrace it for ourselves. Once they released us from that protected environment into the world, they prayed we would continue to walk in the Truth and to recognize and reject anything that was deceptive and untrue.

Today, as an older woman, I still have to guard my mind—to carefully choose the input I allow into my life and to reject that which promotes ungodly thinking. The world's deceptive way of thinking comes to us through so many avenues—television, magazines, movies, music, friends, and social media, to name a few. A steady diet of these influences will shape our view of what is valuable, beautiful, and important.

There are no harmless lies. We cannot expose ourselves to the world's false, deceptive way of thinking and come out unscathed. Eve's first mistake was not eating the fruit; her first mistake was listening to the Serpent.

Listening to counsel or ways of thinking that are not according to the Truth is the first step in developing wrong beliefs that will ultimately place us in spiritual bondage. And once we have listened to the lie, the next step toward captivity is that we . . .

### Dwell on the lie.

First we listen to it. Then we dwell on it. We begin to consider what the Enemy has said. We mull it over in our minds. We engage the Enemy in conversation. We contemplate that he may be right, after all. The process can be likened to farming or gardening. First the soil is cultivated—we open ourselves up to input that is contrary to God's Word. Then the seed is sown—we listen to the lie. Next the seed is watered and fertilized—we dwell on the lie.

And then, if we allow our minds and hearts to dwell on things that are not true, sooner or later, we will . . .

## Believe the lie.

At this point the seed that has been sown begins to take root and grow. That's exactly what happened with Eve. First she listened to the Serpent's sales pitch. Then she considered it and engaged him in further discussion about it. Before long she believed that what he had told her was true—in spite of the fact that it clearly contradicted the Truth of what God had said. And once she believed the lie, the next step was a small one. Listen to the lie, dwell on it, believe it, and sooner or later you will . . .

## Act on the lie.

Now the seed that has been sown, watered, and fertilized and has taken root begins to produce fruit. Beliefs produce behavior. Believing things that aren't true produces sinful behavior.

What we believe will be seen in the way we live. Conversely, the way we behave will invariably be based on what we believe to be true—not what we *say* we believe, but what we actually believe. "As [a man] *thinks* in his heart, so *is* he" (Prov. 23:7 NKJV).

The important thing to remember is that *every act of sin in our lives begins with a lie.* We listen to the lie; we dwell on it until we believe it; then finally we act on it.

Now watch what happens next. We reject the Truth and violate the Word of God one time in what seems to be just a little matter. However, the next time we are tempted, we find that it's easier to sin, and the next time it's easier still. We don't just sin once; we sin again and again and again until a groove has been worn in our hearts—a sinful pattern. Before we realize what has happened, we're trapped. A sinful stronghold has been established. Satan threw out the bait, we took it, and now he has reeled us in and made us his catch.

Don't miss how the progression got started:

> ### Every area of bondage in our lives can be traced back to a lie.

A seed is sown. It is watered and fertilized. It takes root. Finally it produces fruit—not just a single piece of fruit, but an entire harvest of spiritual bondage, destruction, and death.

## MOVING FROM CAPTIVITY TO FREEDOM

Most of us have areas of our lives where we are held captive because we have listened to, believed, and acted on lies. How can we escape and begin to move toward freedom in those areas? Here are three steps to keep in mind as we begin to deal more specifically with some of the lies that lead to spiritual bondage and the Truth that sets us free.

**1.** *Identify the area(s) of spiritual bondage or sinful behavior.* Chances are, you already know what some of these are, but there may be others that are not as obvious. We're going to look at some common ones throughout this book. But right now ask God to start showing you specific areas where you are not free. The Scripture says, "Whatever overcomes a person, to that he is enslaved" (2 Peter 2:19). Can you pinpoint any issues in your life that have overcome you?

- Are there areas where you are in physical bondage (overeating, disordered eating, substance abuse)?

- Are you in emotional bondage (anxiety, fear, depression, chronic emotional disorders)?

- Are you in bondage to sexual sin (masturbation, pornography, lust, fornication, homosexuality)?

- Is financial bondage (overspending, greed, stinginess) an issue in your life?

- Are there sinful habits that plague you (anger, lying)?

- Are you in bondage to the need for approval?

- Are you hooked on TV, computer games, social media, romance novels, or erotica ("sexy" stories designed to arouse)?

God may bring other areas of bondage to your mind. Once you identify those areas, don't just try to eliminate them. That's likely to be futile. In fact, you may have already tried to deal with these behaviors, failed, and been tempted to give up.

If you want to get rid of poisonous berries growing on your property, it's not enough to go out and pick all the berries off the bush. More will quickly grow back in their place. The only way to permanently get rid of the poisonous fruit is to pull the bush out from the roots. That's why this next step is so important.

**2. *Identify the lie(s) at the root of that bondage or sin pattern.*** What lies have you listened to, believed, and acted on? The answer to that question may not be immediately apparent—roots are generally hidden beneath the surface, and lies, by their very nature, are deceptive. We need the Lord to help us see what we have been believing that is not true.

In the pages that follow, we will identify forty-five lies that are representative of the countless different lies we may have allowed to take root and produce fruit in our lives. Ask God to show you which of the Enemy's lies you have bought into—whether the ones in this book or others He brings to mind—and to help you repent of believing them.

Once you identify the specific lies you have believed, what next?

**3. *Replace the lie(s) with the Truth.*** This is so important. Satan is a formidable enemy. His primary weapon is deception. His lies are powerful. But there is something even more powerful than Satan's lies—and that is the Truth. Once we identify the lies that have put us in spiritual bondage and repent of believing those lies, we have an effective weapon to overcome deception—the weapon of Truth!

Each lie must be countered with Truth. Where we have listened to, dwelt on, believed, and acted on lies, we must begin to listen to, meditate on, believe, and act on the Truth. That is how we can move from spiritual bondage to true freedom—by the power of the Spirit of God. This process won't always be easy, but He will give us the grace we need each step of the way. And what joy we will experience as the lies are exposed, chains are broken, and we begin walking in the Truth.

As Jesus declared, it is the Truth that "will set you free" (John 8:32).

Remember the woman who was thinking about leaving her husband and children for a man she had met on the Internet? She had grown up in a Christian home and graduated from a Christian college. She knew a lot of Truth in her head. But at the time we first connected, she was deeply deceived and blinded. The Enemy had done a number on her thinking, and she was not ready or willing to listen to the Truth.

Long story short, over the next few years she continued going her own way and making one foolish choice after another, for which she and her family paid dearly. But God in His mercy continued to pursue her, just as He pursued Adam and Eve in the garden. Years later, this woman wrote and updated me on her journey:

> Broken, feeling utterly worthless and alone, I finally began to seek Him again. I started reading my Bible, attending church, and praying. The change in my heart was nearly instantaneous. I pressed on, driven by the seeds of Truth planted in my soul.
>
> The Lord miraculously and amazingly started removing the scales from my eyes! The God I thought I knew suddenly revealed Himself as vastly more mysterious and powerful than ever before. At the same time, He showed me the great depths of His love, compassion, and mercy. He was not only what my tired, weary soul had been craving; He was so much more!
>
> Today He reassures me that He sees me as holy, perfect, and unstained through the blood of Jesus Christ. After nearly thirty-six years of running, I understand that all along He just wanted me to find my solace in Him. He has amazingly rebuilt all that I sought to destroy in my defiance. I now know that God's love is irresistible.

We have a redeeming God who is making all things new. He is redeeming and making this woman new. And He wants to do the same with you and me, whatever our history may be, whatever lies we may have believed, and whatever consequences we may have experienced. His grace and love truly are irresistible.

# LIES *Women* BELIEVE

# CHAPTER TWO

# LIES WOMEN BELIEVE...
## ABOUT *God*

*I'm so confused. Yesterday morning I was so sure about a lot of things. Now I don't know who—or what—to believe. I've never had reason to doubt that God loved me. I had a thousand reasons to believe He is good. I never wondered if He was telling us the truth. I trusted Him. I believed what He said.*

*Now, for some reason, He doesn't seem like the same God who walked and talked and sang with us every morning. If He is so good, why didn't He stop me from talking to the beautiful creature or eating the fruit? Why did He make the fruit look so good? Why did He put that tree there anyway? And why did He care if we ate that fruit?*

*He seems so far away. I'm afraid of Him. He said we would die if we ate from that tree. I'm not even sure what it means to die; but it seems like an awfully harsh punishment—hardly fair, especially for a first offense. Today He told us we have to leave Eden. Why couldn't He have given us a second chance? Does He really care what happens to us?*

*This whole thing is such a mess. Why doesn't God do something?*

As we begin to identify some of the lies women believe, we need to remember that the list in this book is by no means exhaustive. Satan is a master deceiver, and his lies are endless. There are countless other lies that could have been included in this book.

*our choices, our priorities, our response to pain reveals what we really believe*

Further, entire books have been written on many of these subjects. My goal is not to give a comprehensive treatment of what in some cases are major issues, but rather to give a broad overview of the kind of thinking that I see undermining the lives and homes of women—lies that are at the root of much of the spiritual bondage we experience.

Of course, no one believes *all* of these lies. Our enemy knows where each of us is most vulnerable to being deceived (James 1:14), and that's where he will likely target his attack.

You may look at some of the lies I've chosen and think: "I sure don't believe *that*." One of Satan's strategies is to blind us to the lies we have bought into—to make us assume that because we *know* the Truth, we also *believe* the Truth. But the way we actually live—our choices, our priorities, our response to pain—reveals what we really believe.

For instance, it's one thing for me to say I believe that God is sovereign, loving, good, all-sufficient, and wise. But when I respond to the stresses and pressures of life with fear or resentment or manipulative behavior, my response indicates I'm believing things about God that aren't true—that He is not truly good or wise or in control, at least in this situation.

So as we consider these lies, it's not enough to ask, "Do I believe this lie?" We must also ask, "Do I *live* as though I believe this lie?"

A number of the lies listed in this book are particularly deceptive because they are half-truths rather than outright lies. That makes them even more subtle and dangerous. The fact is, a half-truth will put you in captivity just as surely as a whole lie.

Some of the issues we will address are controversial, even among believers. In some cases, you may find yourself thinking, "I don't believe that's a lie" or "I can't agree with her on that."

Let me appeal to you not to get tripped up by a handful of particular issues where you may have a genuine disagreement. I am simply presenting what I understand the Scripture to teach. I am not the final word on any of these matters; Jesus and His Word are "the Truth." My objective is not for you to agree with everything I say but to motivate you to seek out the

48

Truth as it is revealed in the Word of God and to examine and evaluate every area of your life in light of that Truth.

I've chosen to start by dealing with lies that women believe about God because what we believe about God is foundational to what we believe about everything else. Twentieth-century author and pastor A. W. Tozer made this point in the opening line of his classic book, *The Knowledge of the Holy* (a must read!):

> What comes into our minds when we think about God is the most important thing about us.[1]

It's true. If we have wrong thinking about God, we will have wrong thinking about everything else. What we believe about God determines the way we live. If we believe things about Him that aren't true, we will eventually act on those lies and end up in various types of bondage.

## 1. *"God is not really good."*

Few women who identify as Christians consciously believe this lie. Most of us would never say, "God is not really good." We know better. Theologically, intellectually, we know that God is good. But deep in many of our hearts, there lurks a suspicion that He may not really be good—at least, that He has not been good to *us*.

I believe this lie is at the core of much of our wrong thinking about God. In essence, this is the lie Satan used to seduce Eve back in the garden. God had blessed the man and woman and created a whole paradise for their enjoyment. He had given them the freedom to partake of the fruit on every tree except one.

If you have any doubt about the goodness of God, go back and reread the first two chapters of Genesis. There you see a personal, generous, good God. Everything He made was good—a reflection of His goodness.

When Satan wanted to tempt the woman to rebel against God, he did so by planting in her mind that seed of doubt about God's goodness: "Did God actually say, 'You shall not eat of any tree in the garden'?"

(Gen. 3:1). The implication was that "God must not be good. If He were, He would not have denied you something you really wanted."

When turbulence, disappointment, or pain comes into our lives, when we lose people we love, when things don't go as we had hoped or planned, Satan tempts us to wonder, "Is God really good? If He were, how could He have let this happen?" or "Why would He have kept this [good thing] from me?"

Though we may never say it outright, we may particularly feel these doubts when we compare our circumstances with the experience of others around us:

- "God is good to others, but He doesn't want good for me."
- "God may fight for others, but He doesn't have *my* best interests at heart."
- "God may delight in blessing others, but He seems to enjoy seeing me suffer."

And when we look around at this fallen world, where wars, terrorism, sex trafficking, and natural disasters are a reality, we may be especially likely to fall for the Deceiver's negative pitch: "How could a truly good God let the Holocaust take place? Or 9/11 and other terrorist attacks? What about mass shootings?"

Once we doubt the goodness of God, it becomes easy for us to feel justified in making our own decisions about right and wrong.

The Truth is, God *is* good. Whether or not His choices seem good to us, He is good. Whether or not we feel it, He is good. Whether or not it seems true in my life or yours, He is still good.

And God doesn't gain any pleasure from our suffering. In fact, because He loves us, He suffers when we suffer. He is not removed from our suffering, but is compassionate toward us.

> Then the LORD said, "I have surely seen the affliction of
> my people who are in Egypt
> and have heard their cry because of their taskmasters.
> I know their sufferings."
>
> —Exodus 3:7

I will never forget the first crisis in my life where I consciously found refuge in the Truth of God's goodness. I had spent the weekend of my twenty-first birthday at home, visiting my parents and my six younger siblings. On Saturday afternoon, my parents took me to the airport to catch a flight to Virginia, where I was serving on the staff of a local church.

When I landed in Lynchburg, I received a call from my mother telling me that my father had had a heart attack and had instantly gone to be with the Lord. There had been no warning. No time to say final good-byes. My forty-year-old mother was left a widow with seven children, aged eight to twenty-one.

Over the next few days and in the weeks and months that followed, the tears flowed freely. Each of us had shared a close relationship with this extraordinary husband and father. Everyone who knew Art DeMoss felt an enormous sense of loss when he was taken to heaven.

But in that moment when I first learned of my dad's homegoing, the Lord did something especially gracious for me—He reminded me of the Truth. Before there was any other conscious thought, before there were tears, He brought to mind a verse I had read not many days earlier. Paraphrased, the verse reminds us: "God is good, and everything He does is good" (Ps. 119:68).

My dad had spent the first twenty-one years of my life teaching me this Truth. Now, at a crucial moment, the Truth proved to be a fortress for my heart. I missed my dad terribly—I still do at times. I never knew him in my adult life. There are so many things I wish we could talk about. But I knew then, and I know now, that God is good and that everything He does is good, even when I can't understand His ways.

## 2. *"God doesn't love me."*

This lie is often related to the previous one. Again, few of us would actually admit to believing this; we know we are supposed to believe that God loves us. But for many of us there is a disconnect between what we know intellectually and what we feel emotionally. And therein lies one of our problems: we trust what our feelings tell us is true rather than what God's Word declares to be true.

We look around at our relationships—a forlorn marriage, rejection by a spouse, grown children who don't call or come to visit, approaching forty with not a man in sight—and our feelings tell us, "Nobody loves me—not even God. He may love the world. He may love everyone else. But He doesn't really love me." We might never say this aloud, but that is what we *feel* to be true. So the seed of a lie is planted in our minds, we dwell on the lie until we believe it to be true, our behavior eventually reflects what we really believe, and ultimately those false beliefs end up enslaving us.

Perhaps you can relate to "Victoria's" background:

*I come from a difficult and distant family in which love was always conditional. As a result, it was hard for me to believe God could really love me unconditionally. That brought undue condemnation whenever I would make a mistake and sin—not that sin is anything to be overlooked, but I did not believe God would forgive me.*

It's no small matter to accept the lie that "God doesn't love me." The implications affect every other area of our lives and relationships. Tiny little seeds, allowed to take root in our minds, grow up to produce a great big harvest.

The Truth is, God *does* love us. Whether or not we feel loved, regardless of what we have done or where we have come from, He loves us with an infinite, incomprehensible love.

God loves you and He loves me—not because of anything good or wonderful about us, but because He *is* love. His love for us is not based on anything we have ever done or ever could do for Him. It is not based on our performance. We do not deserve His love and could never earn it.

The Scripture says that when I was His enemy, *He loved me.* You say, "How could you have been God's enemy when you were a little girl?" According to the Bible, from the moment I was born, I was ungodly, a sinner, God's enemy, and deserving of His eternal wrath (Rom. 5:6–10). In spite of my alienation from Him, He loved me and sent His Son to die for me. He loved me in eternity past; He will love me for all of eternity future. There is nothing I could do to make Him love me any less or any more. The same is true for you.

My friend Melana Monroe faced a long, hard battle with breast cancer. At one point in her journey, she shared how her husband's response to her double mastectomy gave her a deeper comprehension of the incredible love of God:

> We wept and trembled when he took my bandages off the first time. I was so ugly, scarred, and bald. I was in intense grief that I could never be a whole wife to him again. Steve held me tightly and with tears in his eyes said, "Melana, I love you because that is who I am."
>
> I instantly recognized Christ in my husband. As His bride, we are also eaten up with cancer—sin—and are scarred, mutilated, and ugly, but He loves us because that is who He is. No comeliness in us draws Christ's attention; it is only His essence that draws Him to us.

### 3. *"God is just like my father."*

A dear friend of mine struggled for years to believe that God (or, for that matter, her husband or anyone else) really loved her. She knew what the Bible had to say about God's love. Her husband had never given her any reason to doubt his love. She had many friends who cared for her deeply. But emotionally she was stuck. She just couldn't seem to rest in the truth she knew in her head. As we explored this "blockage" in her heart, I learned that my friend's father had deserted his family when she was a teen, leaving her haunted by fear, insecurity, and deep trust issues.

Sadly, my friend's struggle is not uncommon.

A woman who led a small-group study of this book shared that a group member named "Beth" had approached her privately at the end of a session and confessed that she had believed this lie that "God is just like my father." Beth's dad had never forgiven her for getting pregnant and having an abortion when she was young, so she assumed her heavenly Father wouldn't either.

As women, our view of God is often influenced by the men we have known—particularly our fathers. Our perception of God can be positively or negatively shaped by those men. I am blessed and deeply grateful to have had a loving, faithful, involved father. This has made it easier for me to trust my heavenly Father and to receive His love. How I wish that every woman could say the same.

However, many women have had just the opposite experience. Your father may have been distant, absent, critical, overbearing, harsh, abusive, or unable to express love. If so, the idea of God being your Father may make you cringe. You may relate to these women:

> I had a stepfather who was cruel to me, and it is very hard to accept that God is not like him.

〜

> My dad is a Christian and a good guy, but I have never heard much encouragement from him. For instance, when I would help him paint, I would say, "Does this look okay?" hoping to hear, "Hey, that looks really nice!" But he would only say, "Try not to _____ [whatever]." Maybe that is why I imagined God finding fault instead of loving me unconditionally and accepting me.

If you have been wounded by a father—or another man you trusted—you may find it difficult to trust God. You may even be afraid of Him or angry with Him. But the Truth is, God is different from any man we have ever known (see Num. 23:19). The wisest, kindest earthly father is but a pale reflection of our heavenly Father. The God of the Bible is infinitely more devoted and pure and loving than even the most wonderful father. That is why it is so important that we not allow our view of God to be determined by other men, for at their very best they are flawed representations of God.

When we turn to the Scripture, we get to know what God is really like. We also get to know Jesus, who is the "radiance of God's glory and the exact representation of his being" (Heb. 1:3 NIV) and who consistently referred to God as His Father too. The God we see in the Bible is compassionate, tender, merciful. He cares deeply for his children, protects them, and has their best interests at heart.

That doesn't mean He gives us everything we want—no wise father would do that for his children. It doesn't mean we can always understand His decisions—He is far too great for that. It doesn't mean He never allows us to suffer pain—He sees the bigger picture and values our growth and our sanctification more than He values our comfort.

A teaching making its way through some circles in the Christian world today is that parental discipline withdraws love and is unnecessary and ineffective. But Scripture tells us that God is a wise and loving Father who "disciplines us for our good, that we may share his holiness" (Heb. 12:10).

So regardless of how we feel or what we think, the Truth is:

> You're a good good Father
> It's who you are
> You are perfect in all of your ways
> It's who you are
> And I'm loved by you[2]

For years, I longed for my friend whose father had abandoned his family to experience this truth and to be assured in the depths of her soul of her Father's love. That assurance did not come quickly. But over the course of time, as she learned to counsel her heart with the truth of the Father's Word, her doubts and fears gradually began to be displaced and replaced with faith. I will never forget the day she said to me, "I can't say exactly when or how it happened, but I thought you'd want to know that over the past several months, I've realized that *I really do believe God loves me.*" My heart breathed, "Thank You, thank You, Father, for making Yourself known to this daughter of Yours!"

### 4. "God is not really enough."

- "Christ is all I need, all that I need."
- "Your grace is enough. Your grace is enough.
  Your grace is enough for me."[3]
- "In Christ alone my hope is found;
  He is my light, my strength, my song."[4]

*Y*ou've probably sung these or similar songs in a church service. But when you walk out the church doors and into the rough-and-tumble world, do you really believe what you've been singing?

As with the first three lies, few of us would admit or even be aware of believing that God is not enough for us. But the way we live reveals the depth of our deception. When it comes down to it, we don't believe God's Word is truly sufficient to deal with our problems. Oh, it can deal with everyone else's problems; but it doesn't speak to *our* issues, *our* needs, *our* relationships, *our* situations.

Do you really believe that if you have God you have enough? Or are you more like "Sure, I need God. But I need Him *plus* close friends; I need Him *plus* good health; I need Him *plus* a husband; I need Him *plus* children; I need Him *plus* a job that pays enough." Do you truly believe God is enough, or do you find yourself turning to other things and people—food, shopping, friends, hobbies, vacations, job, family—to fill the empty places of your heart?

Asaph was a gifted singer, poet, and worship leader in the tabernacle choir in King David's era. At times, however, he struggled to understand why those who did not honor the Lord seemed to have more material blessings and fewer problems. The apparent injustice tormented and paralyzed him—until he looked up and was reminded that the prosperity of the ungodly was short-lived and that in Jehovah he had all he needed for time and eternity. His conclusion is a bedrock assurance for your heart and mine in every season and circumstance we may face on earth:

> Whom have I in heaven but you?
> And there is nothing on earth that I desire besides you.
> My flesh and my heart may fail,
> but God is the strength of my heart and my portion forever.
>
> —Psalm 73:25–26

I've heard it said this way: *"You'll never know that Christ is all you need, until He's all you have. And when He's all you have, you'll find out that He truly is all you need."*

So let's keep singing those songs, reminding ourselves and others that His grace really is enough and that all our hope truly is found in Christ alone.

## 5. *"God's ways are too restrictive."*

Over and over again, the Scripture teaches that God's laws are good and that they are for our good. Obedience is the pathway to blessing and freedom. But Satan places in our minds the idea that God's laws are burdensome, unreasonable, and unfair and that if we obey Him we'll be miserable. In the garden, he caused Eve to focus on the one limitation God had placed on her. The Deceiver's motto is "Have it your way. No one has the right to tell you what you can or cannot do."

If we're honest, many of us can identify with "Sarah":

*I felt that putting restrictions on my behavior was depriving me of pleasure and of what was good. I ate whatever I wanted, whenever I wanted it, and in whatever quantities I wanted because I felt punished by saying no.*

I've often wondered why food is such an issue with so many women. It has been a major battleground in my own life. I'm convinced it has something to do with Genesis 3. After all, the very first temptation and the very first sin involved *food*. Food is a good thing, a God-created thing, a gift from our Creator, who loves us. But Eve was tempted to elevate this good gift above the God who had given it to her. She was willing to trade in her relationship with Him for an appetizing snack.

The single limitation God put on Eve was one too many for her. Like Sarah, she felt that following God's instructions would deprive her "of pleasure and of what was good." She felt she would be missing out on something desirable "by saying no." So what did she do? (Remember—beliefs determine behavior.) Like Sarah, she ate whatever she wanted.

We are free to choose our own way, just as Eve was free to eat the forbidden fruit. We can throw off God's restrictions and do what we want. But there is one thing we're not free to choose, and that is the consequences of our actions.

We have said that believing and acting on a lie will ultimately lead to bondage, but that the truth will set us free. Listen to the rest of Sarah's testimony:

> When I understood that true freedom comes from obedience, I was freed from my bondage to food. I lost sixty-five pounds, as well as the depression I had experienced.

Sarah was determined to eat what she wanted, whenever she wanted, and in whatever quantities she wanted. Sounds like freedom, doesn't it? But wait—according to her testimony, her "freedom" was short-lived. She ended up in "bondage to food," gained sixty-five unwanted pounds, and became depressed. Not until she discovered that "true freedom comes from obedience" and began to act on that truth were her chains shattered.

You may chafe against God's will for your life in other areas—restraining your tongue or your spending habits, abstaining from sex until marriage, refusing to fuel an online or workplace connection with a man other than your husband, or loving a prodigal child.

we are free to choose our own way
we are not free to choose consequences of our actions

As I've been working on the updated version of this book, a dear friend has been walking through a difficult and painful journey. She is trying to unravel a situation in which she was horribly sinned against, then ended up believing lies that led to her making sinful choices herself. With the help of a godly counselor, she is discovering the power of the Truth and the grace of God to turn ashes to beauty and to redeem our worst predicaments. But the process is messy and complex, with no simple solutions nor quick fixes. She wrote to me recently:

> There's no way to deal with this without hurting a lot of people. That is terribly grieving to me. This is a big part of why God gives us the instructions He does. Departing from them inevitably leads to brokenness and hurting ourselves and others. It's more than just a matter of obedience and submission; His ways are not arbitrary. When He says something is wrong, that reveals how much He cares for us! It's not just bad because He says so; it's also bad because its unintended consequences spread like a disease. By giving us direction, He aims to protect us from those consequences.

God's commands are a reflection of His holiness and His grace. They are intended for our good and our blessing. Far from being restrictive, they are actually liberating. Paul reminds us that "the law is holy, and the commandment is holy and righteous and good" (Rom. 7:12). Jesus is the only human being who has ever perfectly fulfilled the law of God. And no one knows better than He the joy that comes from saying yes to God's ways:

> You have loved righteousness and hated wickedness;
> therefore God, your God, has anointed you with the oil of
> gladness beyond your companions.
>
> —Hebrews 1:9

The trouble, of course, is that we are incapable of keeping God's commandments, so they cannot save us. That's why we need Jesus. He took on

Himself the penalty for our lawbreaking and offers to credit us with His law-keeping so that we, too, might be anointed with the "oil of gladness." When we accept that offer, it's as if we had never broken one of God's laws. And that, my friends, is true freedom.

"Amazing grace, how sweet the sound!"

### 6. *"God should fix my problems."*

This way of thinking is deceptive on two counts.

First, it reduces God to a cosmic genie who exists to please and serve us—a hired servant who comes running to wait on us every time we ring the bell. This lie sets us up for disillusionment and disappointment with God. If we have any problems that haven't been fixed, then apparently God has not come through for us.

Second, this thinking suggests that the goal in life is to be free from all problems—to get rid of everything that is difficult or unpleasant. Our society is conditioned to think that we should not have to live with problems—that every problem must be "fixed."

- Don't like your boss? Quit and get another job.
- Don't like your pastor's style of preaching? Find another church.
- Can't afford a newer car? Borrow.
- Men don't notice you? Flirt and dress in a way that attracts their attention.
- Your husband is insensitive, consumed by sports, and doesn't romance you the way he did when you were dating? Find a man at work (or at church) who cares and is willing to listen.

From this way of thinking, it's an easy jump to the so-called gospel of prosperity. It's so tempting for us to believe we can just pray and believe in God, and *presto*, all our problems will vanish . . .

- We'll have plenty of money in the bank.

- Our friend will be cured of cancer.

- We won't be lonely anymore.

- Our marriage will be salvaged.

- Our rebellious children will get right with God.

- We'll get instant victory over sin so we won't have to struggle with bad habits anymore.

- We'll be happy and healthy.

No wonder so many Christian women are angry, resentful, and frustrated! They thought that if they accepted Jesus and went to church and tried to live a "good Christian life," they wouldn't have all these problems. No wonder they feel deceived. They *were* deceived, but not by God.

Living an obedient life does spare us from many problems that are the natural consequences of a life lived apart from God and His ways. But that doesn't mean that those who follow Christ will be exempt from problems. The Truth is, life is hard. We live in a fallen world. Even those who have been redeemed live in earthly bodies and have to deal with the realities of temptation, sin (both our own and others'), disease, loss, pain, and death. Being a Christian—even a mature believer—does not wrap us up in some sort of celestial cocoon where we are immune to pain. Not until God makes a new heaven and new earth will we be totally free from the ravages of sin. Until then there will be tears, sorrows, pressures, and problems.

But—and here's the good news—God is not removed or detached from our problems. He doesn't just sit up in heaven and watch to see if we will manage to survive. No, the God of the Bible is "a very present help in trouble" (Ps. 46:1). That doesn't mean He waves a magic wand and makes all our problems disappear. But it does mean He uses pressures and problems to mold and shape our lives and to make us like His Son, Jesus, who "learned obedience through what he suffered" (Heb. 5:8). And through it all, His presence provides the comfort, strength, and tailor-made grace we need to endure.

No one really wants to have to deal with suffering and heartache. But our wise, loving heavenly Father says, "I have a good, beautiful purpose in all of this. I want to use your pain and your problems to change you and to reveal My grace and power to the world."

Dr. G. Campbell Morgan is one of my favorite Bible teachers of the last century. One of his statements has stayed with me for many years. It reminds us of the importance of seeing God as He really is:

> The supreme need in every hour of difficulty and distress is for a fresh vision of God. Seeing Him, all else takes on proper perspective and proportion.[5]

When our focus is fixed on our circumstances, our problems, other people, or ourselves, God will seem to be small in comparison, distant, or not there at all. But when we lift up our eyes, though they may be filled with tears, and behold Him, "the things of earth will grow strangely dim in the light of His glory and grace."[6]

That's the Truth that sets us free.

| THE LIE | 1. God is not really good. |
|---|---|
| THE TRUTH | • God is good, and everything He does is good.<br>Psalms 31:19; 34:8; 100:5; 106:1; 119:68; 136:1; Ephesians 1:3–14<br><br>• God never makes mistakes.<br>Isaiah 46:10; Romans 8:28–39 |

| THE LIE | 2. God doesn't love me. |
|---|---|
| THE TRUTH | • God's love for me is infinite and unconditional.<br>John 15:13; Romans 5:8; 8:32, 38–39; Ephesians 3:14–19; 1 John 4:7–10<br><br>• I don't have to perform to earn God's love or favor.<br>Ephesians 1:4–6<br><br>• God always has my best interests at heart.<br>Psalm 21 |

| THE LIE | 3. God is just like my father. |
|---|---|
| THE TRUTH | • God is exactly what He has revealed Himself to be in His Word.<br>John 1:1; Hebrews 1:3<br><br>• God is infinitely more wise, loving, generous, and kind than any earthly father could ever be.<br>Hebrews 12:9–10 |

| THE LIE | 4. God is not really enough. |
|---|---|
| THE TRUTH | • God is enough. If I have Him, I have all I need.<br>Psalms 23:1; 73:23–26; Colossians 2:9–10 |

| | |
|---|---|
| **THE LIE** | **5. God's ways are too restrictive.** |
| **THE TRUTH** | • God's ways are best.<br>Deuteronomy 6:24–25; Joshua 1:8<br><br>• God's restrictions are always for my good.<br>James 1:19–27<br><br>• Resisting or rebelling against God's ways brings conflict and heartache.<br>Psalm 68:6; Proverbs 15:32–33 |
| **THE LIE** | **6. God should fix my problems.** |
| **THE TRUTH** | • In this world, we will have problems and pain.<br>Romans 8:21–22; John 16:33<br><br>• Our pain and heartaches are purposeful and will ultimately be for our good and His glory.<br>2 Corinthians 4:17; Job 23:10<br><br>• God has an eternal purpose He is fulfilling in the midst of my suffering.<br>Romans 5:3–4; James 1:2–4<br><br>• No matter what difficulty I may be facing, God's grace is sufficient for me.<br>2 Corinthians 12:7–10 |

# CHAPTER THREE

# LIES WOMEN BELIEVE...
## ABOUT *Themselves*

*These past few weeks have been the hardest of my life. I really wish there were some-one I could to talk to. Adam and I haven't exactly been on the best of terms since we had to move. I don't know if he'll ever trust me again. In a way, I can't blame him. I've really wrecked his life. I feel so stupid. Adam just doesn't understand the effect that creature had on me. He was so irresistible—I felt like I couldn't help myself.*

*I keep reliving that moment when I first looked down and realized I was naked. Then I glanced over at Adam and realized he was thinking the same thing. For the first time since we met, I couldn't look him in the eyes. We had never be-fore felt awkward around each other. Now we feel that way a lot of the time. Even though God gave us real clothes to replace those useless fig leaves, I still feel so . . . exposed—not just on the outside, but even more on the inside.*

*I never used to think about how I looked to Adam. I always knew that he loved me and thought I was the most beautiful thing God had ever made. Now I find myself wondering if he really loves me and finds me attractive. Does he wish God hadn't given me to him?*

Some time ago, I developed a problem with one of my eyes. It be-came irritated whenever I put in my contact lens. At first I assumed I was having an allergy attack, which I tried to treat with medication. However, the problem persisted. Not only did it cause me pain, it also distorted my vision; I couldn't see through the lens clearly. The irritation became so intense that I had to remove the lens for a few days until I could get an appointment with my eye doctor.

When he examined my eye, he explained that my problem was definitely not allergies. In fact, the problem was not with my eye at all, but with the contact lens. Somehow it had been damaged—the curve had been flattened—and the misshapen lens was rubbing against my eye. In order to restore my vision, the damaged lens had to be replaced with a new one.

In much the same way, a distorted or damaged view of God will distort the way we see everything and everyone around us. We may think the irritation and turmoil within our souls is due to annoying people or frustrating circumstances, when the real problem is that we are seeing things through a damaged lens—a belief based on a lie.

What we believe about God is crucial because that's the lens through which we view everything else in our life. And one of the areas that is particularly impacted by our view of God is our view of ourselves. If we don't see Him as He really is—if we believe things about Him that aren't true—invariably, we will have a distorted view of ourselves.

If we have an impoverished view of God, we will become impoverished ourselves. If we have constructed in our minds a god who is weak, powerless, and not in control of every detail of the universe, we will see ourselves as being helpless and will be overwhelmed by the storms and circumstances around us. If our god is worthless, we will see ourselves as being worthless.

If we have believed lies about God, in other words, chances are we will also believe lies about ourselves. In this chapter we'll look at some of these.

### 7. *"I'm not worth anything."*

Prior to writing this book, I surveyed several hundred women about these lies. Nearly half of the women indicated that this is a lie they have believed. It is a powerful lie, as you can see from the kinds of stories they shared:

*For the longest time I thought I was not worth anything. Even after I was saved, I thought I was equal to pond scum. This threw me into depression. I began to isolate myself and, as a result, was not living the life of joy that God had intended for me.*

*I lie in bed most nights scrolling through my phone and feeling miserable. Everyone else seems to have prettier homes, better-behaved children, fancier vacations, and better hair than me. I know that social media doesn't tell the whole story. Even so, I feel the need to have constant reassurance from those around me of my value because I feel worthless! If people really knew me, they'd agree.*

*Because of the hurt in my marriage, I felt that I was useless and that nobody, not even God, could love me. I just didn't measure up, and since I have always felt I had to be perfect to be loved, then obviously God would not love me either.*

In many cases, these feelings of worthlessness are the result of believing things we have heard from other people; we allow the opinions of others to determine our view of ourselves and our sense of worth. Sometimes the input of others is accurate and helpful. But not always.

If, for some reason, the person we are listening to is looking through a defective lens, his or her vision will be distorted. Some of us have lived all our lives in an emotional prison because we have accepted what a false, broken "mirror" said to us about ourselves.

Sometimes, a single sentence heard as a child can haunt and plague a person for years. That is what happened to "Mindy":

*I have a memory of being about six and being told I had no right to live and I should have never been born. I don't remember who said it, but I do remember my mother just standing there and not doing anything about it. I became very withdrawn, and it was extremely difficult to talk to people.*

*By the time I was to start seventh grade, it was decided I be-
longed in special education. I was accepted into the classes, but
there wasn't room, so I went to the normal junior high school. I
never believed I belonged there.*

*I believed I was stupid, not normal, and I should be locked away
somewhere. In junior high, I had no friends, and people went out
of their way to hurt me. As a result, I withdrew even more, became
very depressed, and wanted to go to sleep and never wake up.*

Mindy's story poignantly illustrates the progression through which
people become imprisoned by deception. First, as a child, this woman was
told a terrible, destructive lie, and she listened to it. Then, rather than
countering the lie with the Truth, she dwelt on the lie until she believed
it was actually true. Ultimately she acted on the lie ("I withdrew . . ."), until she found herself enslaved to the lie: "[I] became very depressed, and
wanted to go to sleep and never wake up."

Now, as a six-year-old, Mindy may have had no way of recognizing
or dealing with the lie she was told. Not until years later was she able to
work through her feelings of worthlessness by countering the lies with
the Truth. But her story still illustrates that what we believe about ourselves determines how we live. If we believe and act on lies, we will end up
in personal and spiritual bondage.

We all desire affirmation; we naturally crave the approval of others.
We instinctively seek to balance the scales of the negative input we receive from others. Social media feeds this craving: we interpret every tech-
nological "ping" (like, share, smiley face) to mean we are accepted. But
for many women, no number of positive strokes or pings can outweigh
those negative, hurtful expressions that have led them to believe they are
worthless. No amount of affirmation is enough.

I've known women who can get a hundred compliments about how
they look or their accomplishments, but if one family member offers a
criticism, they are devastated. Why? Because they are letting others determine their worth. They are allowing their value to be up for a vote.

This may look like:

- feeling a constant need to post polished versions of our lives on social media in order to satisfy our cravings for likes, shares, and followers,
- agreeing to serve in areas where we're not gifted or for which we don't have the bandwidth at the moment, in order to gain approval from others,
- basing our feelings of worth on any given day on what others say or don't say about our performance.

There's a wonderful verse in 1 Peter that shows us how Jesus' sense of worth was determined not by what others thought of Him, good or bad, but by the Truth as expressed by His heavenly Father: He was "rejected by men but in the sight of God chosen and precious" (2:4). I Peter

Jesus was *rejected by men*—those He had created for Himself, those He loved and for whom He laid down His life. But that is not what determined His value. He was *chosen by God*. That is what made Him precious. That is what determined His worth.

It's conceivable that someone who didn't recognize or appreciate fine art would toss a masterpiece into the trash. Would that make the painting any less valuable? Not at all. The true worth of the art would be seen when an art collector spotted the painting and said, "That is a priceless piece, and I am willing to pay any amount to acquire it."

When God sent His only Son, Jesus, to this earth to bear your sin and mine on the cross, He put a price tag on us—He declared the value of our souls to be greater than the value of the whole world. The question is, whose opinion are we going to accept? Believing a lie will put us in prison. Believing the Truth will set us free.

### 8. *"I need to love myself more."*

*Y*ou need to learn to love yourself" is often the world's prescription for those who are plagued with a sense of worthlessness. It doesn't take many social media clicks to hear this message. Here are a few actual posts:

- "22 ways to love yourself more"
- "Baby, love yourself like you're not waiting for someone else to do it."
- "You are enough!"
- "How to love yourself first"

This message comes through loud and clear in blogposts and best-selling books (some by Christian authors) that seem to elevate loving self above loving others.

As with much deception, the lies represented in these kinds of pieces are not always the polar opposite of the Truth; they may be distortions of the Truth. According to God's Word, if you are a child of God, the Truth is:

- You are created in the image of God. (Gen. 1:27)
- He loves you, and you are precious to Him. (Eph. 2:4; 1 John 3:1)

However, we don't bestow our worth on ourselves. Nor do we experience the fullness of God's love by telling ourselves how lovable we are. To the contrary, Jesus taught that it is in losing our lives that we find them. The message of self-love can quickly put people on a lonely, one-way path to misery.

How often have we heard someone say, "I've never liked myself" or "She just doesn't love herself"? According to the Scripture, the Truth is that we *do* love ourselves—immensely. When Jesus tells us to love our neighbors as ourselves, the point is not that we need to learn to love ourselves so that we can love others. Jesus is saying we need to give others the same attention and care we naturally give ourselves.

If I get a toothache, I immediately look for a way to identify the problem and get rid of it. If I didn't "love myself," I would ignore the pain. But when someone else has a toothache, it's easy to be indifferent to her need—to assume that's her problem. At some level, we naturally love ourselves; but it's not natural to love others well, especially those who have wronged or wounded us in some way.

In Ephesians 5, Paul applies this concept to marriage. Husbands, he says, are to "love their wives as [they instinctively love] their own bodies. . . . For *no one ever hated his own flesh*, but nourishes and cherishes it, just as Christ does the church" (vv. 28–29).

We are constantly looking out for ourselves, keenly sensitive to our own feelings and needs, always conscious of how things and people affect us. More often than not, the reason we get hurt so easily is not that we hate ourselves but that we love ourselves. We want to be accepted, cherished, and treated well. Truth be told, we care deeply about ourselves.

So for most of us, our need is not to learn to love ourselves more, but to learn to deny ourselves so we can do that which does not come naturally—to love God and others selflessly.

Our most common malady is not having a low view ourselves, but having a low view of God. Our problem isn't so much a poor self-image as it is a poor God-image.

To be sure, I've known some women whose spirits have been crushed by unkind parents, teachers, spouses, or others who have repeatedly ignored them, belittled them, ridiculed them, or cast them in a negative light. They feel invisible, worthless, and unloved. You may be one of those women. How I long for you to know that you matter and that you are dearly loved and cherished. But I would gently suggest that what you need most is not to learn to love yourself more, but to recognize and receive the incredible love God has for you and the value He places on you as a woman created in His own image.

As we believe and receive God's love, we can be set free from self-loathing, comparison, and self-absorption. And then we can become channels through whom His love can flow out to others.

## 9. *"I can't help the way I am."*

This is another lie that puts many people in lifelong bondage. It's a lie we've all believed at one time or another. Perhaps you can relate to one of these women:

*The lie I believed was "You'll be just like your parents. It's heredi-tary—you can't help it." My dad was a minister while I was growing up. He and my mom turned away from God and the church. I be-lieved that a person could not remain faithful to God forever—that because my parents didn't, I wouldn't either.*

*I have excused my laziness and lack of discipline, believing that I can't help the way that I am.*

We see things about ourselves that we wish were different or that we know are not pleasing to the Lord. But rather than accept personal responsibility for our own choices, attitudes, and behavior, we have 101 reasons for why we are the way we are:

- "Our house is so tiny, everything gets on my nerves."
- "My job is so stressful, I can't help being irritable with my kids when I get home."
- "It's that time of the month; I just can't handle the pressure at work."
- "My family never dealt with problems; we just stuffed every-thing and pretended nothing was wrong. To this day, I can't really confront issues."
- "My mother was never a real mother to me. I've never had a model to show me how to raise my kids."
- "My family was dysfunctional and unreliable, so I've never been able to get close to people or trust them."

Now it's true that living in this fallen world really does affect us. But the unspoken implication of these kinds of statements is often that we are merely victims who can't help but react to wounds inflicted on us by others.

However, as we reflect on Eve's story, we discover that it was not parents or a spouse or a child who accounted for the first woman's misery. It was not a man who ruined her life. Nor could Eve blame her environment. In fact, talk about an environment where it should have been easy to succeed and be happy! Adam and Eve had no financial problems, no problems at work, no pollution, no unpleasant neighbors, and no weeds to pull. They didn't even have in-law problems!

The troubles Eve encountered in her marriage, her family, and her environment began when she chose to listen to, believe, and act on the Serpent's lie. That choice placed her in captivity and brought pain and misery to her life, her family, and every generation that was to follow.

Of course, unlike Eve, we do have sinful neighbors, parents, in-laws, and spouses. We live in a fallen world, and our lives can be profoundly impacted by our circumstances, our past, and wrongs done to us by others. But allowing those issues to become our identity is a trap that can keep us stuck.

Believing this lie—"I can't help the way I am"—can reduce us to assuming we are helpless victims of people and circumstances that we can't change and over which we have no control. The suggestion is that someone or something else is responsible for who we are—that we are like marionettes, destined to be controlled by whoever or whatever is pulling our strings.

This lie leaves us without hope that we can ever be any different. And if we believe we can't help the way we are, we will never change. We'll go on living in spiritual bondage. And if we believe we are doomed to fail, to keep on sinning or to be miserable, we *will* fail. We *will* keep on sinning, and we *will* be unhappy, frustrated women.

The Truth is that we *do* have a choice. God's grace can empower us to make good, wise choices. We can be changed by the power of His Spirit.

Once we know and embrace the Truth, we can break free from the chains of our past, our circumstances, and even our deeply ingrained habits.

As we learn to view our difficulties from God's perspective and respond to them by His grace, even the most troubled past or challenging circumstances can actually be transformed into a fresh, hope-filled future (see Jer. 29:11).

## 10. *"I have my rights."*

*I*n a sense, this lie is at the heart of the one that started all the others!

The Serpent taunted Eve with the suggestion that she was somehow being shortchanged by God, that she was entitled to more than what He saw fit to give her.

That seed, first planted in Eve's heart, became deeply rooted in the human race and has been springing up in the hearts of men and women ever since.

"I've got a right" has been a driving force behind endless wars, revolutions, demonstrations, protests, strikes, lobbying efforts, political movements, shouting into camera lenses, rioting in the streets, lockdowns, social media wars, rants on the blogosphere, nasty church splits, acrimonious divorces, and more.

This is not to imply that there are no legitimate means of speaking out against injustice or taking action to redress social evils. Our God hears the cry of the poor and needy; He cares for the oppressed, and He expects His people to share His concerns and to execute justice on behalf of the vulnerable and the mistreated.

But it is human nature to be self-seeking and demanding, to feel entitled to more than we have. And it seems that the more human rights we have, the more entitled we feel.

Back in the mid-twentieth century, women were told that demanding their rights was the ticket to happiness and freedom. After all, "if you don't stand up for your rights, no one else will!"

Those early days of the women's lib movement may seem to you to be a thing of the distant past. After all, haven't its objectives been achieved? But the mindset it produced in our Western culture is still very much present.

And here's the curious thing: even in those parts of the world that are enjoying wealth, prosperity, and human rights unparalleled in history, people don't seem to be much, if any, happier. To the contrary, incivility, rancor, and discord are on the rise. The selfish demanding of rights is more likely to bring increased discontent and unhappiness than deep, lasting satisfaction.

Day after day, I hear from women who acknowledge that "standing up for their rights" has not brought the promised benefits:

> The mindset that "I have my rights" has caused many unnecessary arguments and much unhappiness in our marriage.

>      ⌁

> When I stand up for my rights and demand my way, I am temporarily happy, but the pit of despair soon follows.

The fact is, successful relationships and healthy cultures are not built on the *claiming* of rights but on the *yielding* of rights. Even our traffic laws reflect this principle. You'll never see a sign that says, "You have the right of way." Instead, the signs instruct us to yield the right of way. That is how traffic flows best; it is also how life works best.

Nonetheless, the idea of claiming rights is in the air we breathe. The turmoil and rebellion of the 1960s was birthed out of a philosophy that promoted rights. This philosophy has subtly permeated our entire culture. It creeps into our conversations. It has shaped the way we view all of life. Today it is assumed that

- we have a right to be happy, understood, respected, and loved
- we have a right to a certain standard of living, to an equitable wage and decent benefits
- we have a right to companionship and romance

- we have a right to be valued by our husband and appreciated by our children

- we have a right to a good night's sleep

And most important, if any of our rights are violated, we have a right to be angry. We have a right to rant on social media. We have a right to insist on our rights!

The Old Testament prophet Jonah illustrates the natural human tendency to claim rights and become angry when those "rights" are violated. When God called him to go to Nineveh, Jonah felt he had a right to dislike the Ninevites. After all, they were a vicious people, greatly feared by the surrounding nations. Jonah felt he had a right to minister where he wanted to minister. He had a right to see the Ninevites judged by God.

When God acted differently from the way Jonah thought He should, "it displeased Jonah exceedingly, and he was angry" (Jonah 4:1). He became so angry that he begged God to take his life.

When the Lord responded to Jonah, He didn't coddle Jonah's wounded feelings or try to stroke his ego. Instead, He confronted the pouting prophet with the issue of rights: "The LORD said, 'Do you do well to be angry?'" (v. 4).

Jonah refused to answer the question. Instead, he went to the outskirts of Nineveh, built a temporary shelter, and sat down to wait and see if God would change His mind and destroy the city. Out of His loving-kindness and mercy, "the LORD God appointed a plant and made it come up over Jonah, that it might be a shade over his head, to save him from his discomfort. So *Jonah was exceedingly glad because of the plant*" (v. 6).

Can you see how Jonah's emotions were controlled by whether or not he thought his expectations and rights were being fulfilled? When God was merciful to the pagans Jonah detested, Jonah became disgruntled and irate. And when God provided the convenience of a shelter from the hot eastern sun, Jonah was ecstatic.

His happiness was short-lived, however, for the next morning God sent a worm that chewed the vine until it withered. Then He sent a scorching wind and a hot sun to burn down on Jonah until he became faint. Once again the depressed prophet begged to die. And once again God challenged Jonah's rights: "Do you do well to be angry for the plant?" (v. 9). Jonah responded, "Yes, I do well to be angry, angry enough to die" (v. 9).

Jonah felt he had the right to control his own life and environment, to have things go the way he wanted them to go, and to be angry when they didn't. His insistence on his rights caused him to become emotionally unstable, isolated, and estranged from God.

The sad thing is that Jonah's story sounds a lot like my own at times. All too often I find myself annoyed and perturbed when things don't go my way. A decision someone makes at the office, a rude driver on the freeway, a long line at the checkout counter, a thoughtless word spoken by a family member, a minor offense (real or perceived) by my husband, a friend who fails to come through on a commitment, a phone call that wakens me when I've just fallen off to sleep—if I am staking out my rights, even the smallest violation of those rights can leave me feeling and acting moody, uptight, and angry.

The only way to get off that kind of spiritual and emotional roller coaster is to *yield* our rights to the One who ultimately holds all rights. That's not something we do once and for all. Each new hurt, each new offense, is a fresh opportunity to surrender our rights and to respond in the spirit of Christ,

> who, though he was in the form of God,
> did not count equality with God a thing to be grasped,
> but emptied himself, by taking the form of a servant.
>
> —Philippians 2:6–7

Paradoxically, it is in that posture of humility and yieldedness that we find ourselves lifted up. That's where we discover that all that is His has become ours . . . through His willingness to lay down His rights (see Phil. 2:6–8; 1 Peter 5:6; 1 Cor. 3:21–23).

## 11. *"Physical beauty matters more than inner beauty."*

This message is one our culture preaches in earnest to girls and women, beginning in earliest childhood. It comes at us from virtually every angle: television, movies, music, books, social media, digitally enhanced advertisements. In nearly perfect unison, these media paint for us a picture of what really matters. And what matters most for women, they insist, is beauty—physical beauty. Even parents, siblings, teachers, and friends sometimes add unwittingly to the chorus. "Darling" children get oohs, aahs, and doting attention while less attractive, overweight, or gangly kids may be the objects of unkind comments, indifference, or even overt rejection. Those negative reactions can replay themselves endlessly in women's minds long past their childhood.

In a sense, our preoccupation with external appearance can be traced all the way back to the first woman. Do you remember what it was that appealed to Eve about the forbidden fruit?

> When the woman saw that the tree was good for food,
> *and that it was a delight to the eyes*, and that the tree was to
> be desired to make one wise, she took of its fruit and ate, and she
> also gave some to her husband who was with her, and he ate.
>
> —Genesis 3:6

The fruit had a functional appeal (it was "good for food"). It also appealed to Eve's desire for wisdom. But equally important was the fact that it was "a delight to the eyes"—it was physically attractive. The Enemy succeeded in getting the woman to value physical appearance more highly than less visible qualities such as trust and obedience.

The problem wasn't that the fruit was beautiful—God had made it that way. Nor was it wrong for Eve to enjoy and appreciate the beauty of God's creation. But she got into trouble when she allowed her craving for external, physical beauty to overrule her obedience to God's Word. And interestingly, from that moment on, she and her husband saw themselves and their physical bodies through different eyes. They became self-conscious and ashamed of their naked bodies—bodies that had been masterfully formed by a loving Creator. They immediately sought to cover up their bodies, afraid to risk being seen by one another.

The priority Eve placed on physical appearance is a pattern her sons and daughters are prone to follow. And the deception that physical beauty is to be esteemed above beauty of heart, spirit, and life leaves both men and women feeling unattractive, ashamed, embarrassed, and hopelessly flawed.

Ironically, the pursuit of physical beauty is invariably an unattainable, elusive goal—always just out of reach. Even some of the most glamorous, admired women admit to being dissatisfied with their physical appearance. One Hollywood darling said of herself: "I think I'm kind of weird-looking. If I could change the way I look, I'd like to have longer legs, smaller feet, a smaller nose."[1]

One might ask, how much damage can it do to place too much value on physical, external beauty? Let's go back to our premise: what we believe ultimately determines how we live. If we believe something that is not true, sooner or later we will act on that lie, and believing and acting on lies leads us into captivity.

*I believed that outward beauty (my body) was all that was valuable about me to anyone, especially men. I chose to take advantage of that to get the attention I so desperately craved.* I became a sexual addict.

*I have a beautiful sister whom I adore, but I am plain. I have always believed myself to be inferior and thought I must perform to be accepted by others. I see that the beautiful people get the breaks in life. I just accept that I won't, and* I am in bondage to my perception of my appearance.

*All my life I have believed that my self-worth was based on my appearance, and of course I never looked like the world said I should, so I have always had a low self-worth. I developed eating disorders, am a food addict, and struggle in my marriage with the perception that I am not attractive and that my husband is always looking at other women who are attractive to him.*

Each of these women believed something about beauty that is not true. What they believed impacted the way they felt about themselves and caused them to make choices that placed them in bondage in a variety of ways. Comparison, envy, competitiveness, promiscuity, sexual addictions, eating disorders, immodest dress, flirtatious behavior—the list of attitudes and behaviors that can flow out of a false view of beauty is long.

What can set us free from this captivity? Only the Truth! God's Word reminds us of the transitory nature of physical beauty and the importance of pursuing lasting, inner beauty:

> Charm is deceitful, and beauty is vain,
> but a woman who fears the LORD is to be praised.
>
> —Proverbs 31:30

> Do not let your adorning be external—the braiding of hair
> and the putting on of gold jewelry, or the clothing you wear—but
> let your adorning be the hidden person of the heart with the
> imperishable beauty of a gentle and quiet spirit, which in God's
> sight is very precious. For this is how the holy women who
> hoped in God used to adorn themselves.
>
> —1 Peter 3:3–5

These verses do not teach, as some might think, that physical beauty is somehow sinful or that it's wrong to pay attention to our outward appearance. That is just as much a deception as the lie that places an overemphasis on external beauty. Nowhere does the Scripture condemn physical beauty or suggest that the outward appearance does not matter. What is condemned is taking pride in God-given beauty, giving excessive attention to physical beauty, or tending to physical matters while neglecting matters of the heart.

Some who manage to avoid that pitfall fall into an opposite extreme, by having an aversion to attractiveness in their dress, appearance, and physical surroundings. But that, too, proves to be a lie when seen in the light of Scripture.

As Christian women we have a high and holy calling to reflect the beauty, order, excellence, and grace of Christ, to let others see the difference He makes in our lives. We are children of God, daughters of the King, the bride of Christ. He made us women. It is a good thing to beautify the setting where He has placed us and the bodies He has given us. But let's not forget that all of that is just a frame for the true masterpiece—the portrait of Christ we want others to marvel at.

Those of us who are married have even more reason to find the right balance in this matter. The "virtuous wife" of Proverbs 31 is physically fit and well dressed (vv. 17, 22). She is a complement to her husband. But a wife who makes no effort to care for her physical appearance will reflect negatively on both her husband and her heavenly Bridegroom.

When the apostle Paul wrote to Timothy about how things ought to be in the church, he took time to address the way women dress. His instructions show the balance between the inner heart attitude of a woman and her outer attire and behavior. Paul exhorts women to

adorn themselves in modest apparel, with propriety and moderation, not with braided hair or gold or pearls or costly clothing, but, which is proper for women professing godliness, with good works.

—1 Timothy 2:9–10 NKJV

The words translated "adorn" and "modest" in this text mean "orderly, well-arranged, decent"; they speak of "harmonious arrangement."[2] Our outward appearance as Christian woman should reflect a heart that is pure and well ordered—not drawing attention to ourselves by being extravagant, extreme, or indecent. In everything, our goal is to reflect the beauty of Christ and to make the gospel attractive to our world.

## AGING GRACEFULLY

I distinctly remember that no sooner had I turned forty than I started receiving catalogs promoting products guaranteed to combat the effects of aging. They promised me younger, clearer skin; fewer wrinkles; no more dark shadows; more energy; prettier nails and hair; and improved eyesight and hearing. The implication was that, as I got older, what mattered most was looking and feeling younger.

Well, that was some two decades ago. The fact—then and now—is that I *am* getting older, and in this fallen world that means my body is slowly deteriorating. I look in the mirror and see lines that weren't there twenty years ago. My hair started turning gray in my early twenties, and I've long since changed the hair color on my driver's license to "gray." I struggle with my distance vision, and I don't have the physical stamina I had at thirty.

But I refuse to buy into the lie that those things are ultimate tragedies or that my biological clock can somehow be reversed. I'm not trying to hasten my physical decline, but neither am I going to get obsessed with fighting off the inevitable. And as I get older, I want to focus on those things that God says matter most—things like letting His Spirit cultivate in me a gracious, wise, kind, loving heart.

Regardless of what potions and products I might be able to purchase, I know there is a process taking place in my physical body that will not be reversed this side of eternity. To believe otherwise is to be deceived. But I also know that "the path of the righteous is like the light of dawn, which shines brighter and brighter until full day" (Prov. 4:18). That means there is a dimension of life that can grow richer and fuller even as our outer bodies are decaying.

The fact is, if we devote our time and energy to staying thin, glamorous, and youthful looking, we may achieve those objectives—for a while.

But if we neglect to cultivate the inner beauty and character that are pleasing to God and last forever, we will end up with unnecessary regret.

Oh, and let's not forget the promise that awaits us as women who belong to God—the hope of seeing our Savior, "who will transform our lowly body to be like his glorious body" (Phil. 3:21). That's something worth waiting for!

## 12. *"I should not have to live with unfulfilled longings."*

This is another lie that has worked its way into the way we think and live. Our society has bought into the philosophy that there is (or ought to be) a remedy (preferably quick and easy) for every unfulfilled longing.

We're encouraged to identify our longings and do whatever is necessary to get those "needs" met. So . . . if you want something you can't afford, charge it. If you crave romance, dress or act in a way that will get men to notice you. If you're lonely or bored in your marriage, reach out to that old boyfriend on Facebook.

The next time you're in the grocery store, take a quick look at the women's magazines at the checkout counter. Or just pause to see what you're scrolling through on social media. No matter where you look, you're confronted with offers that promise to satisfy every imaginable longing:

- "24 Signs You've Found Your Soul Mate"
- "3-Day Detox Program for clean energy, weight loss, and bright skin"
- "25 Secrets to Looking Young"
- "Indulge Yourself: Instant Long Hair; Goof-proof Self-tanning"
- "The Little Health Habit That Keeps You Thin, Improves Your Skin, and Ups Your Energy"
- "How to Invest in Yourself"

- "The Easy Life: Fun Jobs, Cool Dresses, Wild Fantasies, and Smart Solutions"

Somewhere, somehow, there's a way to fulfill your longings—it may be

- a how-to book
- a romance novel
- a cruise
- a new romantic relationship
- a new hairstyle, wardrobe, house, or job
- a deep-dish pizza dripping with melted cheese
- a picture-perfect home

At best, this way of thinking leaves women still unfulfilled, still grasping, still searching for something to fill the inner emptiness. At its worst, it causes deep heartache. This lie fuels anxiety, resentment, and depression. It causes women to trade in their virginity for a warm body and the promise of companionship. It can lead a married woman to seek fulfillment in the arms of a man at work who claims to care about her feelings. It can lead a young woman down the aisle of a church to exchange wedding vows for all the wrong reasons. And one day it may lead that same woman down the aisle of a divorce court—all in an effort to satisfy deep, unfulfilled inner longings.

"Carmen" shares where this lie led her:

*Believing that I should not have to live with unfulfilled longings, I got what I wanted when I wanted it. Clothes, trips to Europe, or weekends away—put on credit cards or financed some way, until I had approximately $7,000–10,000 in debt by the time I was twenty-two.*

"Eileen's" story also illustrates the depths of emotional and personal destruction that can result from believing this lie:

*I was not sexually fulfilled in my marriage, and I believed it was my husband's fault. I blamed him and sought another man to satisfy me sexually. I called it love, knowing it was lust, but believing that my husband owed me sexual fulfillment. It was great for a while, but when it unraveled, the guilt, the shame, and the destruction left a patch of hurt and pain too great and not worth whatever pleasure I may have felt for such a brief moment.*

How can the Truth set us free from the chains of this deception?

First, we have to recognize that *we will always have unfulfilled longings this side of heaven* (Rom. 8:23). In fact, if we could have all our longings fulfilled down here, we would easily be satisfied with the status quo, and our hearts would never long for a better place.

It's important to understand that our inner longings are not necessarily sinful in and of themselves. What *is* wrong is when we make idols out of those things we long for—when we demand that our longings be fulfilled here and now or insist on meeting those longings in illegitimate ways.

God created the sexual drive. Sex is a good gift (Gen. 2:24–25; Prov. 5:18–19; 1 Cor. 7:3–5). It's not wrong to fulfill the desire for sexual intimacy as long as we do so in God's timing and in His way—within a covenantal marriage between a man and a woman. However, the world tells us that we have the right to fulfill our sexual drive regardless of how, when, where, or with whom.

Food, too, is a good gift (Ps. 145:15; 1 Tim. 4:3–4). It's not wrong to have physical hunger, nor is it wrong to eat. What is wrong is when we stuff ourselves in an effort to satisfy emotional and spiritual longings.

Likewise, it's not wrong to long to be married or to have children, but it's a mistake to expect marriage or motherhood to meet our deepest needs.

We can be honest with God about what we desire. But until He provides the legitimate context to fulfill those desires, we have to learn to be content with unfulfilled longings.

In addition, we need to realize that *the deepest longings of our hearts cannot be filled by any created person or thing.* This is one of the most liberating truths I have discovered in my own spiritual journey. For years, I looked to people and circumstances to make me happy. Time after time, when they failed to come through, I would find myself disgruntled and disappointed.

Every created thing is guaranteed to disappoint us. Things can burn or break or be stolen or get lost. People can move or change or fail or die. It took the loss of some of my dearest friends some years ago to awaken me to the Truth that I would always live in a state of disappointment if I was looking to people to satisfy me at the core of my being.

I have talked with many single women—some of them godly, committed believers—about their struggle with loneliness and their longing for God to bring them a husband. On occasion I find myself reminding these precious women of something they already know in their head—that marriage is not necessarily a cure for loneliness. We all know married women who struggle with a deep sense of loneliness and isolation. The fact is, there is no man on the face of the earth who can satisfy the deepest longings of a woman's heart. God has made us in such a way that we can never be truly satisfied with anything or anyone less than Himself (Pss. 16:11; 34:8-10).

Whether married or single, we must recognize that it is not wrong to have unfulfilled longings—they do not make us any less spiritual. We must learn to accept those longings, surrender them to God, and look to Him to meet the deepest needs of our hearts.

Those of us who grew up under the ministry of Elisabeth Elliot remember that she often spoke of this matter of unfulfilled longings. In her devotional book *A Lamp unto My Feet*, she explained how these longings can actually become "material for sacrifice":

> I had been praying for something I wanted very badly. It seemed a good thing to have, a thing that would make life even more pleasant than it is, and would not in any way hinder my work. God did not give it to me. Why? I do not know all of His reasons, of course. The God who orchestrates the universe has a good many things to consider that have not occurred to me, and it is well that I leave

them to Him. But one thing I do understand: He offers me holiness
at the price of relinquishing my own will.

"Do you honestly want to know Me?" He asks. I answer yes.
"Then do what I say," He replies. "Do it when you understand it;
do it when you don't understand it. Take what I give you; be willing not to have what I do not give you. The very relinquishment
of this thing that you so urgently desire is a true demonstration of
the sincerity of your lifelong prayer: 'Thy will be done.'"

So instead of hammering on heaven's door for something
which it is now quite clear God does not want me to have, I make
my desire an offering. The longed-for thing is material for sacrifice. Here, Lord, it's yours. He will, I believe, accept the offering.
He will transform it into something redemptive. He may perhaps
give it back as He did Isaac to Abraham, but He will know that I
fully intend to obey Him.[3]

We have seen that a flawed view of God results in a flawed view of
ourselves and that deception in either of these crucial areas affects the
way we live. Inevitably, believing lies about God or about ourselves will
also lead to being deceived about sin.

| THE LIE | 7. I'm not worth anything. |
|---|---|

| THE TRUTH | • My value is not determined by what others think of me or what I think of myself. My value is determined by how God views me.<br>Psalm 139:1–18; Ephesians 1:3–8; 1 Peter 2:4<br><br>• God paid the ultimate price to purchase me for Himself.<br>John 3:16, Romans 5:6–8<br><br>• If I am a child of God, I am His cherished possession and treasure.<br>Romans 8:15–17; Ephesians 1:18; 1 Peter 2:9 |
|---|---|

| THE LIE | 8. I need to love myself more. |
|---|---|

| THE TRUTH | • By faith, I need to receive God's love for me.<br>Galatians 2:20; Romans 8:31–39; 1 John 4:16<br><br>• God wants me to experience His love and to let Him love others through me.<br>Matthew 16:24-26; John 15:12; Ephesians 5:29 |
|---|---|

| THE LIE | 9. I can't help the way I am. |
|---|---|

| THE TRUTH | • If I am a child of God, I can choose to obey God.<br>Romans 6:1–14; 8:1–2<br><br>• I am responsible for my own choices.<br>Deuteronomy 30:19; Joshua 24:15<br><br>• I can be changed through the power of God's Spirit.<br>Galatians 5:16; Philippians 2:13 |
|---|---|

| THE LIE | 10. I have my rights. |
|---|---|
| THE TRUTH | • Claiming rights will put me in spiritual bondage.<br>Jonah 4; Psalm 37:1–11; Luke 6:46<br><br>• Yielding rights will set me free.<br>John 6:38; Hebrews 10:7 |

| THE LIE | 11. Physical beauty matters more than inner beauty. |
|---|---|
| THE TRUTH | • At best, as long as we are on this earth, physical beauty is temporal and fleeting.<br>Proverb 31:30<br><br>• The beauty that matters most to God is that of my inner spirit and character.<br>1 Samuel 16:7; 1 Timothy 2:9; 1 Peter 3:3–5 |

| THE LIE | 12. I should not have to live with unfulfilled longings. |
|---|---|
| THE TRUTH | • I will always have unfulfilled longings this side of heaven.<br>Romans 8:23, 25; Ephesians 3:11; Hebrews 11:13–16<br><br>• The deepest longings of my heart cannot be filled by any created person or thing.<br>Psalms 16:11; 73:25<br><br>• If I will accept them, unfulfilled longings will increase my longing for God and for heaven.<br>Deuteronomy 8:3; Psalm 34:8–10; Philippians 3:20–4:1 |

# CHAPTER FOUR

# LIES WOMEN BELIEVE...
## ABOUT *Sin*

*It's been six months since we left Eden. I wish we could put this all behind us. Adam still blames me for the whole mess. I know I shouldn't have listened to the Serpent. But Adam was right there with me. Why didn't he do something? And it's not like he didn't eat the fruit too.*

*At the time, I honestly didn't think it was such a big deal. Now I have this over-whelming sense of guilt—how could I have done this to God after all He had done for us? Will we ever be able to have the same kind of relationship we used to have? Whenever I try to talk to Him, I feel like there is this great big wall between us.*

*One thing I hadn't counted on was how totally unnatural it would be to obey God once I ate that fruit. For example . . . until that day, whenever I got hungry I would eat; when I was full I stopped. Now I have this constant craving for food. Once I start eating I can't stop, even when I know I should.*

*That's not the only area where I get out of control. My tongue gets me in so much trouble, especially on days like yesterday! It was that time of the month, and I wasn't feeling well, and I found myself snapping at Adam about every little thing. I hate it when I act this way. I don't like being moody and uptight. But sometimes I feel like I just can't help myself.*

When the Romeros first got Sally as a family pet, she was only one foot long. Eight years later she had grown to eleven and a half feet and weighed eighty pounds. Then on July 20, 1993, Sally, a

Burmese python, attacked fifteen-year-old Derek, strangling the teenager until he suffocated to death.

In one fatal moment, the creature that had seemed so docile and harmless was exposed as a deadly beast. The "pet" the unsuspecting family had brought into their home, cared for, and nurtured turned on them and proved to be a destroyer. But in a sense, no one should have been surprised at the turn of events, for in the end the python merely did what was its nature to do.

So it is with sin. Though it may entertain us, play with us, sleep with us, and amuse us, its nature never changes. Inevitably it will rise up to strangle and devour those who befriend it.

All deception is deadly. But no lies are more deadly than those we believe about God and about sin. The enemy of our souls tries to convince us that God is not who He says He is and that sin is not what He says it is. The picture he paints diminishes the goodness and the holiness of God as well as the sinfulness of sin. He makes God out to be not so good and makes sin out to be not so evil.

Photographs can be enhanced in such dramatic ways today that the ugliest image can be made to look beautiful. And that's what Satan does with sin. He cleverly Photoshops the image to make something that is hideous and deformed appear to be a work of beauty and art.

But dressing sin up cannot change its essential nature. Like the python that seemed so innocent and tranquil, there comes a point when its true, deadly nature is exposed.

Satan used deception in the garden to pull off a revolt that turned out to be more costly than anyone could have imagined. The lies he tells us today are essentially the same as the lies he told the first woman.

### 13. *"I can sin and get away with it."*

This may be the most fundamental lie Satan tells us about sin. God had said to Adam, "If you eat the fruit of this tree, you will die." The command was clear: "Don't eat." The consequence for disobedience was equally clear: "You will die."

After Satan raised a question in Eve's mind about the goodness of God in giving such a mandate and whether God in fact had the right to control her life, he proceeded to challenge the consequence. He did so with a direct, frontal attack on the word of God: "The serpent said to the woman, *'You will not surely die'*" (Gen. 3:4).

Three times in Psalm 10 the writer indicates that the people often disobey God because they believe they can get away with it:

> He says in his heart, "I shall not be moved;
> throughout all generations I shall not meet adversity.". . .
>
> He says in his heart, "God has forgotten,
> he has hidden his face, he will never see.". . .
>
> Why does the wicked renounce God
> and say in his heart, "You will not call to account"?
>
> —Psalm 10:6, 11, 13

The Enemy causes us to believe:

- "There will be no judgment on my sin."
- "I won't reap what I sow."
- "The choices I make today will not have consequences."
- "I can play with fire and not get burned."

Once again we may not consciously believe these things. We may even intellectually reject this kind of thinking. But when we choose to sin, it is invariably because we tell ourselves this lie.

And so we entertain ourselves with romance novels, TV, music, and websites that promote worldly philosophies and legitimize profanity, immodesty, and immoral behavior, never stopping to contemplate that in so doing

- we are desensitizing our conscience and developing a tolerance for sin

- we are increasing our appetite for sin and diminishing our hunger for holiness

- we are erecting a barrier in our fellowship with God

- we are programming our minds to think the world's way (and how we think will ultimately determine how we live)

- we are increasing the likelihood that we will actually act out the things we are seeing and hearing

- we are developing an unbiblical view of sexuality that is not honoring to God and may destroy our present or future marriage

We choose to hold a grudge against someone who has wronged us, ignoring the fact that sooner or later, our bitterness will

- destroy our capacity to think rationally

- make us miserable and emotionally unstable

- affect our bodies in such ways as chronic tiredness, loss of energy, headaches, muscle tension, and intestinal disorders

- keep us from being able to experience God's forgiveness for our sins

- make us hard to live with and cause people not to want to be around us

We flirt with a nice guy at work or someone we meet online, refusing to let ourselves believe that . . .

- what begins as a few compliments or playful emojis can easily progress to a full-blown emotional affair

- we will need to lie or cover up our choices to keep them from our spouse

- we are planting seeds of infidelity in our minds and emotions

- we are making it impossible for our own husband to please us because reality cannot compete with fantasy

- even if we don't commit adultery with him, we may be setting ourselves up for future moral failure

- we may end up estranged from our mate, our children, our in-laws, and our God

We must keep reminding ourselves that Satan is a liar. The things God calls "sin," Satan repeatedly tells us are

| | |
|---|---|
| *fun* | *no big deal* |
| *safe* | *meeting our needs* |
| *innocent* | *unavoidable* |
| *desirable* | |

But the Truth is that sin is none of those things. To the contrary, God's Word tells us that

- sin is dangerous, deadly, and destructive

- we will reap what we sow

- every choice we make today will have consequences

- sooner or later the consequences of our sin will catch up with us

- "sin when it is fully grown brings forth death" (James 1:15)

Unfortunately, we don't always make the connection between our natural, fleshly choices and the unintended consequences in our lives—whether now or down the road.

## THE DELIGHTS OF SIN

Satan's deception goes a step further than telling us we can get away with sin. In the garden he suggested to Eve, "Not only can you disobey

God and avoid negative consequences; there are also some terrific benefits you'll experience if you eat this fruit."

> God knows that when you eat of it your eyes will be opened,
> and you will be like God, knowing good and evil.
>
> —Genesis 3:5

He was saying, in effect, that whatever consequences you may reap are worth the pleasure and benefits you'll receive from having it your way. Eve believed him, and so do we. After all, if we didn't think there was some joy to be had from sinning, why would we choose to sin? No doubt that's why an advice columnist for *Self* magazine suggests, "An affair can help you survive a disappointing marriage and occasionally it gives a woman the energy . . . necessary to leave a bad one."[1]

There's a sense in which Satan is right about the "positive" results of sin. According to Hebrews 11:25, sin does bring pleasure—for a short time. Ultimately, however, sin exacts a devastating toll. *There are no exceptions.*

I have a friend who keeps in his billfold a list of sin's consequences:

- Sin steals joy. (Ps. 51:12)
- Sin removes confidence. (1 John 3:19–21)
- Sin brings guilt. (Ps. 51:3)
- Sin gives Satan the upper hand. (2 Cor. 2:9–11)
- Sin quenches God's Spirit. (1 Thess. 5:19)
- Sin brings physical damage. (Pss. 38:1–11; 31:10)
- Sin causes an ache in the soul. (Ps. 32:3–4)
- Sin breaks God's heart. (Eph. 4:30)
- Sin opens the door to other sins. (Isa. 30:1)
- Sin breaks fellowship with God. (Isa. 59:1–2)

- Sin produces fear. (Prov. 28:1)

- Sin makes me its slave. (John 8:34; Rom. 6:16)

When he's tempted to disobey God in some matter, my friend pulls out that list and reads it. He asks himself, "Is this a price I really want to pay? Is this a price I can afford to pay?"

Sometimes the consequences of our sin are not seen until months or years down the road; sometimes they don't show up until the next generation; and some consequences will be delayed until we stand before God at the judgment seat. That's why we persist in thinking we have somehow managed to get away with our sin. As we read in Ecclesiastes, "When the sentence for a crime is not quickly carried out, people's hearts are filled with schemes to do wrong" (8:11 NIV).

One of God's purposes in delaying final judgment is to give us time to repent. He is "patient toward [us], not wishing that any should perish, but that all should reach repentance" (2 Peter 3:9). Nonetheless, the day of reckoning will come. And when it does, each of us will wish with all our heart that we had turned from every sin and chosen the pathway of obedience.

After years of toying with sin and enjoying its "pleasures," King Solomon ultimately came to the conviction that:

> Though a sinner does evil a hundred times and prolongs his life,
> yet I know that it will be well with those who fear God,
> because they fear before him. . . .
>
> The end of the matter; all has been heard.
> Fear God and keep his commandments,
> for this is the whole duty of man.
> For God will bring every deed into judgment,
> with every secret thing, whether good or evil.
>
> —Ecclesiastes 8:12; 12:13–14

## 14. *"My sin isn't really that bad."*

Those of us who have grown up in good, moral homes and been active in church all our lives may be particularly susceptible to this deception. Perhaps you've not ever thought of being a prostitute or having an abortion or living a homosexual lifestyle. You may never have used profanity or embezzled money. From all appearances, you look the part of a "good Christian."

If we begin to compare our sins to the sins of others, we easily fall prey to the lie that our sin isn't all that bad. Don't be deceived. That's the warning of the apostle Paul:

> Do you not know that the unrighteous will not
> inherit the kingdom of God?
> Do not be deceived: neither the sexually immoral, nor idolaters,
> nor adulterers, nor men who practice homosexuality, nor thieves,
> nor the greedy, nor drunkards, nor revilers, nor swindlers
> will inherit the kingdom of God.
>
> —I Corinthians 6:9–10

Did you notice that slander (reviling) and greed—things we may not think are all that serious—get slipped right in there with what some might think of as the "biggies"—immorality, idolatry, homosexuality, and drunkenness?

Our sins of wasting time, self-protection, talking too much, eating or drinking too much, indulging a sharp tongue or a critical spirit, overspending, fear, worry, acting out of selfish motives, or complaining may not seem all that major to us. We may not even consider them to be sins at all—preferring to think of them as weaknesses, struggles, or personality traits.

Eve easily could have viewed her sin this way. After all, she didn't leave her husband; she didn't curse God or deny His existence. All she did, when you think about it, was to take one bite of something God told her not to eat.

What was the big deal?

The big deal was that God said, "Don't," and Eve said, "I will."

That one, simple act of eating something God said was off-limits produced enormous consequences—in her body; in her mind, will, and emotions; in her relationship with God; and in her marriage. That one "little" sin influenced her husband to sin, which resulted in the entire human race being plunged into sin. Like a rock thrown into a pond, the ripples caused by sin go on and on.

If only we could see that every single sin is a big deal, that every sin is an act of rebellion and cosmic treason, that every time we choose our way instead of God's way, we are revolting against the God and King of the universe.

As John Bunyan put it, "One leak will sink a ship; and one sin will destroy a sinner."

Or as Bunyan's contemporary, Jeremy Taylor, said, "No sin is small. No grain of sand is small in the mechanism of a watch."

Robert and I live in a house with white siding—at least it looks white most of the year. However, when the snow falls in the winter, all of a sudden our house looks dingy and yellow. What may look "clean" when we compare ourselves to other sinners takes on a whole different cast when seen next to the perfect holiness of God.

The way to see the Truth about sin is to see it in the light of who God is. When we gaze upon the brilliance of His untarnished holiness, we become acutely aware of the hideousness of our sin.

The Puritans of the seventeenth and eighteenth centuries were known for their commitment to holiness and obedience. From all outward appearances, there is little for which they could be faulted. But as you read their writings, you discover that *they* thought of themselves as great sinners. Because they walked in close communion with God, they cultivated a sense of the horror of their sin, no matter how insignificant it might seem to others. This perspective comes out in the kind of prayers they prayed:

Unmask to me sin's deformity,
    that I may hate it, abhor it, flee from it . . .
Let me never forget that the heinousness of sin
    lies not so much in the nature of the sin committed,
        as in the greatness of the person sinned against.[2]

## 15. *"God can't forgive what I've done."*

This lie and the previous one—"My sin is not that bad"—represent two opposite ends of the spectrum. If we're not tempted to believe one, there's a good chance we may be tempted to believe the other. Both are equally deceptive, and both lead to spiritual bondage.

When I speak on the subject of forgiveness, someone will often tell me, "I've never been able to forgive myself for what I've done." Now, the Bible never speaks of the need to forgive ourselves. But I think what many of these women are really saying is that they have never been able to *feel* forgiven for what they have done.

They are still carrying a sense of guilt and shame over their failure. Though they may *know* that God can forgive them, deep down they do not *believe* they are truly, fully forgiven. They find it difficult to accept God's mercy and forgiveness. They feel that in order to be restored into favor and fellowship with God, they need to do something more to atone for their sin; to do "penance," to somehow be good enough to make up for the wrong they have done.

The problem is that a lifetime of "good deeds" is not sufficient to deal with the guilt of even one sin against a holy God. Like a stubborn stain that no dry cleaner can remove, sin makes a stain that cannot be washed away by any amount of human effort. There is only one "solution" that can deal with the guilt of our sin:

What can wash away my sin?
Nothing but the blood of Jesus;
What can make me whole again?
Nothing but the blood of Jesus.

Nothing can for sin atone,
Nothing but the blood of Jesus;
Naught of good that I have done,
Nothing but the blood of Jesus.[3]

The Truth about both of these lies—"My sin isn't really that bad," and "God can't forgive what I've done"—is revealed at Calvary. In Psalm 85:10 (NKJV), we find a beautiful description of the Lord Jesus and what He did for us on the cross:

Mercy and truth have met together;
Righteousness and peace have kissed.

It was at Calvary that God's mercy and love for sinners and the Truth of His holy hatred for sin found a meeting place. At Calvary, God heaped upon Jesus all the punishment for all the sin of the world. At the same time He offered peace and reconciliation to sinners who had been estranged from Him.

The cross shows us in the starkest possible terms what God thinks of our sin. It reveals the incredible cost He paid to redeem us from those "weaknesses" that we trivialize in our minds. The cross also displays brilliantly the love and mercy of God for even the "foremost" of sinners (1 Tim. 1:15).

## 16. *"It's not my fault!"*

*I*f we go back to the Garden of Eden, it becomes apparent that this idea that we are not responsible for our own actions is one of the oldest forms of deception.

After Adam and Eve ate the forbidden fruit, God came to hold them accountable for what they had done. (This is a recurring theme throughout the Scripture—that we will give account to God for every deed we have done.) Notice that God did not approach them as a family unit. He didn't ask, "What have y'all [plural] done?" Neither did He ask Adam and

Eve to explain each other's behavior. He didn't ask Adam, "What did Eve do?" Nor did He ask Eve, "What did your husband do?" He approached first Adam, then Eve, and asked each one individually, "What have *you* [singular] done?"

God's question to Adam was pointed and specific: "Have *you* eaten of the tree of which I commanded you not to eat?" (Gen. 3:11). Likewise, God asked Eve, "What is this that *you* have done?" (v. 13). God was asking for a simple admission of the Truth.

As the account unfolds, we see that Adam and Eve both chose to play the blame game rather than take personal responsibility for their actions. When God asked what had happened, Adam answered, "The woman whom you gave to be with me, she gave me fruit of the tree, and I ate" (v. 12). And Eve's response was similar: "The serpent deceived me, and I ate" (v. 13).

Both responses were technically accurate. Eve *was* the woman God had given to Adam, and she *had* given the fruit to her husband. The Serpent *had*, in fact, deceived Eve. However, both responses were really ways of sidestepping God's question. By shifting the blame to another, Adam and Eve were attempting to diminish their own responsibility in the matter.

God was not asking them what someone else had done to make them sin. He was asking them to take responsibility for their own behavior. Regardless of what had influenced them, their choice was still theirs.

Adam and Eve may have been the first, but they certainly weren't the last in what has become a long, unbroken line of blame shifters. The game that began in the garden is one we have all played. In fact, we are naturally proficient at it, as illustrated by these testimonies:

*By constantly* blaming others, blaming circumstances, and blaming God, *I found myself totally irresponsible for my life, my sins, and my choices—and then I was trapped and felt helpless and out of control.*

*I used to believe that I was chronically depressed* due to being a victim. *When I began to realize that much of my depression was*

*caused by my choice to be angry, I began to take responsibility for
my sin and found freedom.*

~

*I had an ungodly relationship with a male coworker. I relied on
him for emotional support and affection because my husband
was keeping secrets from me, using pornography, and not "being
there" for me.* In my eyes, my husband's behavior had pushed me
into this relationship. *I was giving myself a reason and an excuse
that "it was not as bad as what he was doing."*

When we are angry, anxious, annoyed, impatient, or fearful, our natural inclination is to try to shift at least some of the responsibility onto
the people or circumstances that "made" us that way.

I'll never forget the testimony a middle-aged woman gave during a
women's conference I was leading. She introduced herself by saying that
she had been a therapist for twenty-two years. Her next words were deeply
penetrating. Brokenly, she said, "I want to repent before You, my God,
and before you, my sisters, for leading you astray and for telling you lies—
for not encouraging you to accept personal responsibility for your own
choices and for your responses to the behavior of others. I'm so sorry!"

This is not to discount or deny the ways we may have been wronged
or wounded by other people or by difficult circumstances. Nor is it to
suggest that we are responsible for the sins of others. It is only to say that
we cannot be truly free until we humbly acknowledge our own responsibility for any ways we may have sinned against God or others.

The Enemy tells us that if we accept full responsibility for our choices,
we'll be plagued with unnecessary guilt. But the Truth is that only by accepting full responsibility for our own actions and attitudes can we ever be
fully free from guilt. As one writer said,

Sin is the best news there is, the best news there could be in our
predicament.

Because with sin, there's a way out. There's the possibility of
repentance. You can't repent of confusion or psychological flaws

inflicted by your parents—you're stuck with them. But you can repent of sin. Sin and repentance are the only grounds for hope and joy.[4]

## 17. *"I can't live in consistent victory over sin."*

Anyone who has been a Christian for any length of time can probably relate to the frustration expressed by "Hylie":

*There are so many sins that control my life. How will I ever be free? I feel like I am a hopeless case. I want so badly to get rid of these sins, but they continue to rule my flesh. I feel embarrassed to come to God with these things over and over again. When I pile them all together, it seems even more hopeless. How do I stay free from this lie? I want to be changed.*

These words remind me of the apostle Paul's heart cry:

So I find it to be a law that when I want to do right,
evil lies close at hand. For I delight in the law of God,
in my inner being, but I see in my members another law waging
war against the law of my mind and making me captive to the law
of sin that dwells in my members. Wretched man that I am!
Who will deliver me from this body of death?

—Romans 7:21–24

More than half of the women I surveyed about their beliefs before writing this book, acknowledged they had bought into the lie that they could not live in consistent victory over sin. It's easy to see how this can keep believers in bondage.

As we see in the passage above, any person who is a true child of God has been given a new nature—a nature that desires to obey God. Deep down, every true believer *wants* to live a life that is pleasing to God (1 John 5:3; 2 Cor. 5:9).

However, according to the Scripture, even after we are born again, our "flesh" (our natural inclinations) continues to wage war against the Spirit of God living within us.

The Spirit says: Forgive.
The flesh says: Hold a grudge.

The Spirit says: Exercise self-control.
The flesh says: It's okay to blow your top. After all, you need to vent.

The Spirit says: Give that money to someone in need.
The flesh says: Spend that money on yourself.

The Spirit says: Spend some time in the Word and prayer.
The flesh says: You've had a long day; binge watch Netflix until the middle of the night. Then sleep in tomorrow.

The Spirit says: Hold your tongue. What you are about to say is not kind or necessary.
The flesh says: Tell it like it is!

Every time we choose to give in to the flesh rather than yielding to the Spirit of God, we allow sin to gain mastery over us. On the other hand, every time we say yes to the Spirit, we give Him greater control of our lives.

When we make repeated choices to obey sin rather than God, we establish habit patterns that are extremely difficult to break—we choose to live as sin's slaves. For a while we may find ourselves trying to do right, then failing, trying and failing, trying and failing. That's when the devil begins to convince us that it can never be any different, that we will always be enslaved to that sinful habit. We think, *What's the use? I'm just going to blow it again! I'm going to be defeated by this for the rest of my life.* So we give up.

What has happened? We've bought into the lie that we cannot walk in consistent victory over temptation and sin. Though their specific issues were different, that's what happened to these women:

*I struggled with being attracted to women in a way that I clearly knew was wrong. As hard as I fought within myself, my thoughts just got worse and worse.* I didn't think I could control my thoughts. *I knew I wasn't pure before God, but I couldn't seem to clean myself up.*

*My temper has been out of control for so long. I feel like I've always been angry. This is especially true in my role as a mom. I can't remember the last time I went a whole day without screaming at my kids. After I explode, I see their terrified faces in my mind and I feel so much shame and guilt, but I feel it is beyond me to change.*

*I have been in bondage to food for years. I struggle with it every day.* I constantly feel that it is beyond me to change and that I will never be victorious. *I might do well for a while, but the lies creep back in and destroy me.*

Remember that what we believe determines the way we live. If *we believe* we are going to sin, then *we will.* If *we believe* we have to live under the dominion of sin, then *we will.* If *we believe* we can't live victorious lives, *we won't.*

The second and third women above are absolutely right in their sense that "it is beyond me to change." And strange as it may seem, that realization is actually a major step toward experiencing victory over sin.

The Truth is, you and I are powerless to change ourselves, for "Apart from me," Jesus said, "you can do nothing" (John 15:5).

So what are we to do? How can we be set free from habitual sin?

It's the Truth that sets us free. And the Truth is that through Christ's finished work on the cross, we can live in victory over sin; Satan is no longer our master, and we are no longer slaves to sin.

That means (fasten your seat belt) *you don't have to sin anymore!*

Now, before you think I've gone off the deep end . . . that doesn't mean you *won't* sin anymore. As long as you are on this earth, you will be subject to temptation from the devil, the world, and the residue of sin in your flesh. But if you are in Christ,

- you are a new creation

- you are under new management

- you are under no obligation to yield to temptation

- you have been set free to love, follow, and obey your new Master

If you are in Christ, the Truth is:

Having been freed from sin, you became slaves of righteousness. . . .
For the law of the Spirit of life in Christ Jesus
has made me free from the law of sin and of death.

—Romans 6:18; 8:2 NKJV

## GOOD NEWS FOR SINNERS

As we have seen, Satan promised Eve that if she would eat the forbidden fruit, her eyes would be opened, she would be like God, and she would know good and evil. But the moment she ate,

- she became spiritually blind, unable to see the Truth

- the image of God in her was marred, and she took on a sinful nature, as unlike God as darkness is unlike light

- she did gain the knowledge of evil (something God never in-tended), but fellowship with God was broken, and she became incapable of being righteous

Likewise, every man, woman, and child who has ever lived since that day has been born into that same fallen condition: spiritually blind, a sinner, separated from God, and incapable of doing anything to please Him. Because of our sin, we are all under the righteous judgment of God.

The good news—the gospel—is that Jesus came to this earth and took upon Himself the penalty for all of Eve's sin and ours, so the devastating consequences of that sin could be reversed. Through His sinless life, His death on Calvary as the sinner's substitute, and His victorious resurrection, we can be fully forgiven for all our sin, we can be reconciled to the God we have offended, and we can have the power to live holy lives.

We do not receive this forgiveness and this right standing before a holy God by being born into a Christian home, growing up in the church, being baptized or confirmed, doing good works, responding to an altar call, having an emotional experience, reciting a prayer, or being active in church. We are not saved from sin by anything we have done or could ever do. The only means of eternal salvation is through placing our trust in what Jesus did for us on the cross when He died in our place.

I have known women who are plagued with doubts about their salvation. There can be a variety of reasons for such doubts. But in some cases I believe people lack assurance and peace because they have never truly repented of their sin and placed their faith in Christ alone to save them. They may be religious, they may know all the right answers, but they have never been made righteous.

What about you, my friend? The Enemy wants to keep you enslaved to fear, doubt, and guilt. God wants you to walk in freedom, faith, and assurance of forgiveness. No matter how "good" you may be, the only way you can ever be made right with God is through faith in Christ. And no matter how great a sinner you may have been, His grace is sufficient for you. Through the death of Christ, God has made the only acceptable provision for your sin.

If you have never dealt with the issue of your sin in this way, if you do not know that you are a child of God, I want to appeal to you to stop and get it settled before moving on to the next chapter. Don't let the Enemy blind you or hold you hostage any longer. Your eternal destiny is at stake.

Acknowledge to God that you have sinned against His law and that you cannot save yourself. Thank Him for sending Jesus to take the penalty that you deserve by dying for your sin. By faith, believe on Christ to save you and receive His free gift of life. Tell God that you want to turn away from your sin, to place all your trust in Christ alone, and to let Him be the Lord of your life. Then thank Him for forgiving your sin; thank Him for the gift of His Spirit, who has come to live in you and who will enable you to walk in victory over sin as you yield to Him.

Whether you have just become a child of God or you have been in His family for many years, in light of where God found us and what He has done for us, this timeless Puritan prayer should be the cry of our hearts until the day we see Jesus face-to-face:

> Grant me never to lose sight of
> the exceeding sinfulness of sin,
> the exceeding righteousness of salvation,
> the exceeding glory of Christ,
> the exceeding beauty of holiness,
> the exceeding wonder of grace.[5]

| THE LIE | 13. I can sin and get away with it. |
|---|---|
| THE TRUTH | • The choices I make today will have consequences. I will reap what I sow.<br>Genesis 3:4–5; Galatians 6:7–8<br>• Sin's pleasures only last for a season.<br>Hebrews 11:25<br>• Sin exacts a devastating toll. There are no exceptions.<br>Psalm 10:6, 11, 13<br>• If I play with fire, I will get burned. I will not escape the consequences of my sin.<br>Psalm 32:1–5; Ecclesiastes 8:12; 12:13–14; James 1:13–15 |

| THE LIE | 14. My sin isn't really that bad. |
|---|---|
| THE TRUTH | • Every act of sin is an act of rebellion against God.<br>Romans 5:6–7, 10; 1 John 1:5–10<br>• No sin is small.<br>Proverbs 5:21; 20:27; Habakkuk 1:13; Romans 6:23; Galatians 5:19–21; James 5:19–20 |

| THE LIE | 15. God can't forgive what I've done. |
|---|---|
| THE TRUTH | • The blood of Jesus is sufficient to cover any and every sin I have committed.<br>1 John 1:7<br>• There is no sin too great for God to forgive.<br>Psalms 85:10; 130:3–4<br>• God's grace is greater than the greatest sin anyone could ever commit.<br>Romans 3:24–25; 6:11–14 |

| THE LIE | 16. It's not my fault! |
| --- | --- |
| THE TRUTH | • God does not hold me accountable for the actions of others.<br>Genesis 3:11–13; Ezekiel 18:19–22<br><br>• I am responsible for my own choices.<br>Psalm 51:1–10; Philippians 4:8–9; Colossians 3:1–17 |

| THE LIE | 17. I can't live in consistent victory over sin. |
| --- | --- |
| THE TRUTH | • If I am a child of God, I don't have to sin.<br>Romans 6:14<br><br>• I am not a slave to sin. Through Christ I have been set free from sin.<br>John 8:31–32, 36; 14:6; Romans 6:6–7; Galatians 5:1; Hebrews 10:10<br><br>• By God's grace and through the finished work of Christ on the cross, I can experience victory over sin.<br>John 15:5; 1 Corinthians 6:9–11; Galatians 2:20; 5:22–25 |

# CHAPTER FIVE

# LIES WOMEN BELIEVE...
## ABOUT *Priorities*

*Whew! Life these days is a whirlwind. It's been months since I've had a chance to sit down and put my thoughts on paper. We hardly have time to breathe these days. The boys are so active; I feel like I spend all my time chasing them around and picking up after them. It's amazing how fast they can make a mess! They are growing up so quickly—they'll be gone before we know it. I don't want to miss out on the opportunity, while they are still young, to play together, to enjoy being together, and to teach them the things that really matter in life.*

*It's harvest time, which is always the busiest time of year for Adam. We don't get to see a lot of each other these days. I wish we had more time to just sit and talk—about us, about the children, about our future.*

*With all the activity around here, I haven't had much time to take walks and to talk with God like I used to do. Things were a lot simpler before we had kids. There just aren't enough hours in each day. I fall into bed exhausted at night, then get up and go through the same old routine the next day . . . and the next . . . and the next . . .*

We have looked at what I believe are the three most fundamental and universal areas of deception that trip women up: what we believe about God, what we believe about ourselves, and what we believe about sin. To a large measure, these determine what we believe about everything else. If we have been deceived in these areas, there is a far greater chance of our being deceived in other matters.

In the next several chapters, we want to examine a number of practical areas where we are vulnerable to deception, beginning with the matter of our priorities. Maybe you've seen this meme:

I am woman.
I am invincible.
I am tired.

A throwback to Helen Reddy's Grammy-winning song of the early 1970s, this expression was undoubtedly intended to evoke a smile. But it also captures something of the struggle in every woman's life to juggle the many demands and responsibilities that come with each season of life.

Most of the women I know do not feel invincible. But they *are* tired. Whatever their age, marital status, or season of life, they feel stressed and stretched from trying to manage the many hats they wear and balance the various responsibilities they carry.

Those frustrations are fueled by a number of lies the Enemy has planted in our collective and personal thinking. Lies such as . . .

## 18. *" I don't have time to do everything I'm supposed to do."*

This belief is something I battle perpetually. And by a long shot, this was the number-one lie the women we surveyed identified with.

I wasn't surprised. After all, if you ask a woman, "How are you doing?" chances are the response will be a sigh or a groan, followed by something like:

- "I'm so busy!"
- "We've got so much going on in our family!"
- "I just can't keep up with everything I've got to do!"
- "I'm exhausted!"

We often feel overwhelmed by how much we have to do and how little time we have to do it. As a result, many of us live breathless, frazzled, discouraged lives. Social media fuels this lie. After scrolling through your Facebook feed, you might feel you should foster children, remodel your kitchen, do daily crafts with your children, cook up a storm, eat all organic produce, vacation regularly, parent differently, and make sure your kids are involved in every possible event so they won't miss out on their life calling!

Years ago, I read that the average woman today has the equivalent of *fifty* full-time servants in the form of modern time-saving devices and equipment. We certainly have many conveniences available to us that were unknown to women of past generations. Imagine going back to the days when there were no dishwashers, microwaves, washing machines, dryers, or online shopping and free shipping—or even further back to a time when people had never heard of indoor plumbing or electricity.

I remember as a child going through a World's Fair exhibit that attempted to envision "the lifestyle of the future." High-tech and electronic gadgets performed all kinds of household chores and daily tasks, leaving people free to sit back and relax or to use their time for more "important" things. Well, that future is here. We have devices and gadgets that even the most imaginative minds never dreamed of when I was a little girl. So why are our lives more harried and hurried than ever? Why are we so stressed out?

There are probably a number of explanations. However, one reason is that we've accepted the lie that we don't have time to do everything we are supposed to do.

The fact is, each of us has no more or less time than any other human being who has ever lived. No one, regardless of his or her position or responsibilities, has ever had more than 24 hours in a day (okay, it happened once . . . see Joshua 10:13), 168 hours in a week, 52 weeks in a year.

In fact, the Lord Jesus Himself was given only a few short years on earth to accomplish the entire plan of redemption. Talk about a long to-do list! Yet at the end of His life, Jesus was able to lift His eyes to His

Father and say, "I glorified You on earth. I have *finished* the work which You have given Me to do" (John 17:4 NKJV).

I find that truly amazing. Rarely can I say at the end of the day that I have completed the work I set out to do that day. To the contrary, I frequently drop into bed at night with a long mental list of the unfinished tasks I had hoped to take care of that day.

How was it possible for Jesus to complete His life's work—especially in such a short period of time? We find a clue in His own words—a powerful Truth that can set us free from the burden of hurry and frustration about all we have to do. Notice what work Jesus completed in the thirty-three years He was here on the earth: "I have finished the work *which You have given Me to do*" (John 17:4 NKJV).

And that's the secret. Jesus didn't finish everything His disciples wanted Him to do. (Some of them were hoping He would overthrow the Roman government!) He didn't finish everything the multitudes wanted Him to do. (There were still people who were sick and lonely and dying.) But He did finish the work *God* gave Him to do.

## MY TO-DO LIST OR HIS?

There is virtually never enough time in a twenty-four-hour day for me to do everything that's on my to-do list. And there is never time to do everything that's on everyone *else's* list for my life. I cannot meet with every person who wants to grab coffee; counsel with every person who has a need; tackle every project people think I would be good at; respond to every "urgent" text, email, and call; read all the books people think I need to read; stay in regular contact with all my friends and family members; keep up with who's saying what on social media; keep every room in my house presentable for guests who may show up; and host large groups for dinner. It's just not physically possible.

And what a relief to realize *I don't have to do all those things*!

The Truth is that all I have to do is the work God assigns to me. What freedom there is when I accept that *there is time for me to do everything that is on God's to-do list for my day, for my week, and for my life*!

The frustration comes when I attempt to take on responsibilities that are not on His agenda for me. When I establish my own agenda or let others determine the priorities for my life rather than taking time to discern what God wants me to do, I end up buried under piles of half-finished, poorly done, or never-attempted projects and tasks. I live with guilt, frustration, and haste rather than enjoying the peace-filled, God-ordered life that He intends.

Now, if you're scrambling to keep up with young children, managing the care of two sets of elderly parents, or perhaps juggling multiple part-time jobs to make ends meet, a peaceful, well-ordered life may feel completely out of reach. I get that. And I'm not saying everything will always look tidy and organized behind your front door. What I am saying is that no matter what your circumstances, there is time for you to accomplish God's assignment for you each day.

It's important to keep in mind that God's to-do list for your life is not the same as His list for everyone else's life. Jesus said, "I have finished the work which You have given *Me* to do"—not "the work which you gave Peter or John or My mother to do." The work God has for me to do is not the same as what He has for you or for your friends or coworkers. And what God has called you to do as a mother with three toddlers will not be the same as the "job description" He has for your husband, for a young single woman, or for an empty nester.

Further, God's assignments for me today as a sixty-something woman are not the same as what He gave me to do in my twenties or what He will have for me down the road as an elderly woman. There are seasons in our lives, and God's to-do list will vary according to the season He has placed us in.

## EMBRACING LIMITATIONS

There's another, related lie that many of us buy into. In a sense, it's the opposite of the lie that we don't have enough time to do everything we're "supposed" to do. It's the belief that *"I can do it all."*

Perhaps you've felt the pressure to be an ideal wife and mom, keep your house clean and organized, prepare healthy meals for your family, be active in your kids' school and in your church and community, stay physically fit, maintain your social media profile, keep up on current events, and have a full-time job. And it's not just wives and moms who deal with this issue. I was single until the age of fifty-seven. And I frequently struggled to stay on top of never-ending ministry responsibilities, maintain relationships with family and friends, keep up my home, extend hospitality, eat right and exercise regularly, and have any space to breathe.

Women who subconsciously believe they are supposed to be able to "do it all" flawlessly—to meet everyone's demands and expectations—are likely to end up exhausted and overwhelmed by all the demands on their time. The truth is, no woman can wear all those hats effectively. Sooner or later, something (or someone) is going to suffer.

Frustration is the by-product of attempting to fulfill responsibilities God does not intend for us to carry. Freedom, joy, and fruitfulness come from seeking to determine God's priorities for each season of life and then setting out to fulfill those priorities in the power of His Spirit, realizing that He has provided the necessary time and ability to do everything *He* has called us to do.

The following testimonies illustrate how lies we believe about priorities and time put us in bondage and how the Truth has the power to set us free:

> *I have not been meeting my responsibilities adequately, and I have experienced a desperate, hopeless feeling because my home is always messy and my children are behaving poorly.*
>
> *Once I realized that I have enough time to do what God has given me to do, I had to admit that I was attempting to do things He has not assigned to me. I am starting the process of removing things from my life as I discover what doesn't belong and finding things I can delegate. I am also learning to communicate with my husband so he can release me from things he doesn't care about and be clear about what he does care about. This is not an easy process, but I have simplified a few things so far, and I hope to*

*gain momentum as I continue, until my life is under control and I
am free to do what God has given me.*

⤸

*I believed it was my duty to serve whenever the church needed
me. If I saw something that needed to be done, I had to do it. As
a result, I was overextended—doing something at church almost
every day of the week. I felt I was the only one who could do all
the things I did.*

*After I finally burned out, my pastor was able to help me see
that I did not have to do everything—only the things the Father
gave me to do. I continue to do some activities, but only those I
know are what God wants me to do. I have learned to say no when
I know it is not something God is calling me to do. God set me
free from the bondage of busyness to allow me to truly be
His servant.*

## 19. *"I can thrive without consistent time in the Word and prayer."*

Unlike the lie we've just considered, few of us would actually make this statement aloud. Yet half of the women I interviewed for this book admitted to living as if this is what they believed.

The essence of this lie is that we can live our lives independently of God. The Enemy doesn't care if we believe in God, if we have memorized lots of Scripture, or if we fill our schedules with a lot of spiritual activities as long as he can get us to run on our own steam rather than living in conscious dependence upon the power of the Holy Spirit.

If he can get us to try to live the Christian life without cultivating an intimate relationship with Jesus, he knows we will be spiritually anemic and defeated. If he can get us to do a great many things "for God" without seeking the will of God through His Word and prayer, we may stir up a lot of religious dust, but we won't do Satan's kingdom any real damage.

If he can get us to operate on our own thoughts and ideas rather than seeking the wisdom that comes from God, he knows we will eventually get sucked into the world's destructive way of thinking.

When our lives are not anchored to Christ and His Word, we become more vulnerable to deception in every area of our lives. "Yvette" shared the practical impact this lie has had in her life:

> When I spend time in the Word and prayer, my daily life seems to flow along smoothly—even with three children under the age of five. But then I get complacent and think what a wonder woman I am and stop making it a priority. Before I know it, my life is in chaos. I am screaming at my kids and on the verge of child abuse, trying to figure out how I ended up like this. And what can I do to fix it? Unfortunately, it takes me a while to realize I can't—I need God! The lies of Satan creep in so subtly, and if I'm not in the Word I start believing them.

King David in the Old Testament is a prime example of the necessity of seeking the Lord. Six times in the Old Testament we're told that David "inquired of the LORD" (1 Sam. 23:2, 4; 30:8; 2 Sam. 2:1; 5:19, 23). He knew he couldn't make it without God. In fact, the first thing he did every morning—before turning to the business of the day—was to turn his heart toward the Lord in prayer:

> O LORD, in the morning you hear my voice;
> in the morning I prepare a sacrifice for you and watch.
>
> I rise before dawn and cry for help;
> I hope in your words.
> —Psalms 5:3; 119:147

In another psalm, David went so far as to say that of all the many responsibilities, relationships, and opportunities that were his as the king of Israel, the *one thing* that mattered more to him than anything and everything else was seeking and knowing God:

> *One thing* I have desired of the LORD,
> That will I seek:
> That I may dwell in the house of the LORD
> All the days of my life,
> To behold the beauty of the LORD,
> And to inquire in His temple.
>
> —Psalm 27:4 NKJV

I know all too well what it is for the tasks of each day to crowd out this "one thing" David desired above all else. Some days, from early in the day till late at night, there just doesn't seem to be any margin. Frances Ridley Havergal, the nineteenth-century British hymn writer, recognized that there is a spiritual battle involved here: "The devil is very fond of persuading us that we have no leisure so much as to eat when it is a question of Bible study. He never says that if we have a novel or a clever magazine on hand!"[1]

Had Frances lived today, she might have included social media and Netflix in the things we manage to find time for when we find it hard to squeeze in time to read and meditate on the Scripture. Her words remind us that if we miss out on the latter, we are missing out on the very delight and fullness we are seeking in earthly pursuits and pleasures that can never truly satisfy our souls.

Psalm 132 records the determination and intentionality with which David set out to build a temple for the Lord:

> I will not give sleep to my eyes
> or slumber to my eyelids,
> until I find a place for the LORD,
> a dwelling place for the Mighty One of Jacob.
>
> —Psalm 132:4–5

What a wonderful challenge can be found in this passage, to make sure that each day, before we pillow our heads, we have taken time to "find a place for the Lord" in our hearts.

I know the value and importance of spending time alone with God in His Word and prayer each day—the first book I ever wrote was on this subject![2] Both my dad and my husband have been incredible examples of seeking the Lord first thing in the day. (Robert often says: "The Throne before the phone.") But I'll confess that too often I find myself turning my attention to the details and tasks of the day without first taking time to "inquire of the Lord." When I do that, what I'm really saying (though I'd never actually speak the words) is that I can handle that day on my own—apart from the presence, wisdom, and grace of God. I am saying I can do my work, keep my home, handle my relationships, and deal with my circumstances without Him.

That self-sufficient spirit is an expression of pride. And Scripture teaches that "God opposes the proud" (James 4:6). If I walk in pride, I must be prepared for God to oppose me and my efforts.

Sometimes I get the sense that God may be saying to me, "You want to handle this day by yourself? Go ahead." At best, the result is a fruitless day lived by and for myself. At worst, what a mess I end up making of things!

On the other hand, James 4:6 says that God "gives grace to the humble." When I start the day by humbling myself and acknowledging that I can't make it on my own—that I *need* Him—I can count on His divine enabling to carry me through the day.

*Apart from abiding in Christ*—living in conscious union with and dependence on Him—*we cannot do anything of spiritual or eternal value.* Oh, we can create a lot of activity, we can make a lot of decisions, but we'll end up having nothing of real value to show for our lives.

The Truth is, *it's impossible for you and me to be the women He created us to be apart from spending consistent time cultivating a relationship with Him in the Word and prayer.*

## 20. *"My work at home is not as significant as the work or other activities I do outside the home."*

*A*dam and Eve had a perfect home in Eden and a unified marriage before the fall. But their "home sweet home" didn't make it to "happily ever after." As a consequence of their sin, they were exiled from the place God had lovingly created for them. And ever since, in an attempt to mar God's good and loving plan, Satan has sought to rob us of the blessings of family and home.

We've heard it said that home is where the heart is. But, sadly, too often our hearts are being pulled everywhere but home.

> *For me the whole family idea is kind of overrated. It is not about families and having kids anymore. Women are expected to have careers too.* (Fifteen-year-old girl in a focus group for *Lies Young Women Believe*)

> *I love my husband. I love my children. But at the end of the day, I just have nothing left to give them. By the time I work all day, take dinner to my aging parents, and shuttle the kids to soccer/band/ piano practice, I'm spent. Night after night we end up grabbing dinner at the drive-through and eating it on the couch while we watch mindless TV. I want to invest more in my family, I just don't know how!*

The pace of modern life has created homes that are often little more than physical structures where people park their bodies at night, take their showers in the morning, and then disperse in a hundred different directions as they start their day.[3] Instead of being the epicenter for the cultivation of family life, relationships, productivity, and fruitful service, home has become the place where the equipment (cleats, lunch boxes, backpacks, electronic devices) is stored for the many activities that happen *outside* the walls of our homes. But as we've been seeking to identify lies and replace them with God's Truth, we've seen that the *norm* is not necessarily what's *best* for us as women or for those we love.

One of my favorite passages in God's Word is found in Titus 2. Practical and timeless, it is a call to Christ followers of every era and culture.

Paul wrote these words to Titus, the young pastor of a fledgling church plant on the island of Crete. False teachers were popping up in the church, promoting teachings contrary to God's Word. The same Enemy who lied to Adam and Eve in the garden was lying to believers in this new fellowship of believers. To handle this situation, Titus needed a game plan. And here's what Paul had to say to him, under the inspiration of the Holy Spirit:

> But as for you, teach what accords with sound doctrine. . . .
>
> Older women . . . are to be reverent in behavior,
> not slanderers or slaves to much wine.
> They are to teach what is good, and so train the young women
> to love their husbands and children, to be self-controlled, pure,
> working at home, kind, and submissive to their own husbands,
> that the word of God may not be reviled.
>
> —Titus 2:1–5

Paul's blueprint for Titus gives us the tools to combat lies in our lives and churches. We need sound teaching. We need godly role models—intentional and intergenerational discipleship. And we need homes where the gospel is put on display.

Now, your home may not seem all that strategic to you. In fact, it may seem more messy than missional. Maybe your home is a literal mess, full to the brim with evidence that you're in the "little" years—diapers, jumpers, ExerSaucers, toys, high chairs, and car seats. If you have a house full of teenagers, you may look around and see a "mess" of sports equipment, homework in progress, or snacks left out on the kitchen counter. Or maybe your house looks like it could pass for a Pinterest pin, but truth be told, it's a home with relationships in disarray, characterized by hurt, neglect, or even open hostility.

Titus 2 speaks into this messy reality, reminding us that home is not an optional add-on to our "spiritual" life. As Paul describes how Christian women should live in light of the gospel and God's Truth (aka "sound doctrine") he reminds them that their faith must be evident in their *homes*.

We may know God's Word from front to back. We may never miss our weekly Bible study or small group. We may be the first to volunteer for every need at church. But if we're not demonstrating *self-control* at home, if our children or husbands (or roommates or neighbors or guests) wouldn't describe us as *kind*, if the way we unwind is to read erotic literature (not exactly *pure* entertainment!), then something is off. Daily life behind the four walls of our homes reveals the fruit of lies as nothing else will.

Love, self-control, purity, kindness, submission—Titus 2 says Christian women should excel in these qualities, not least of all in their homes. Which brings up one more quality Paul includes in this passage: *"Working at home"* (v. 5). So what are we to make of that? Is this something, as some have suggested, that God meant just for first-century women that He doesn't expect us to apply in our day and age? Was Paul a hopeless chauvinist, as others are convinced?

I've addressed this concept of "working at home" more extensively in my book on Titus 2 (*Adorned: Living Out the Beauty of the Gospel Together*). To summarize briefly, examining this instruction in light of the whole of Scripture, here are some things I think Paul does *not* mean:

- He's not saying that women should *only* work at home or that our homes demand our round-the-clock care and attention.

- He is not suggesting that we are solely responsible to do all of the work that needs to be done in the home. Adam was commanded to "work and keep" the first couple's garden home with his wife (Gen. 2:15). It is appropriate for husbands, children, and others to help with care of the home.

- He is not prohibiting us from doing work outside the home. When Paul addressed the widows in 1 Timothy 5:9–10, he placed emphasis on a widow's good deeds to those outside her family.

- He is not forbidding us from being compensated financially for such work. Lydia was a "seller of purple goods" and a "worshiper of God" (Acts 16:14). Priscilla ran a tent making operation alongside her husband, Aquila (Acts 18:1–3), and was a huge blessing to Paul and his ministry.

- He is not implying that women have no place in the public arena or that we should not contribute to our church, community, or culture.

So what *does* this term mean? For starters, it's a reminder that our homes matter. We cannot separate our home life from our Christian life. Christian homes are vital to glorifying God and advancing His mission in the world.

Now, our homes don't matter *supremely*. They're not museums or collector's items to be shown off to the public, and they're absolutely not idols to be worshiped. But the work that women (particularly "young women" in their childbearing years) do in relation to their homes is an important way they serve and bless others and advance the kingdom of Christ.

The work we do at home has eternal value. The Holy Spirit, through the apostle Paul, is urging us not to neglect our homes, not to miss the opportunity to use them as a means to point others to the beauty of Christ and the gospel.

When we buy into the lie that being a curator of the home is somehow a "less than" calling, when we value and prioritize our hobbies or friends or our work outside the home at the expense of our work and relationships at home, when we fail to recognize the vital roles of homemaker, wife, and mother, we miss out on a key component of our calling as women.

This heart for honoring Christ in and through our homes may express itself in different ways and may require more or less time and effort, depending on our season of life. But whether young or old, married or single, whether we own or rent our home or share an apartment or dorm room, the place we call "home" provides an opportunity to magnify Christ and bless others.

The pendulum of what the culture values is constantly swinging. It should not determine our priorities. What happens inside our front doors, not just outside of them, is an indicator of our spiritual health. Our marriages, our children, and our interactions with guests and neighbors are all to tell the gospel story.

Even if the culture does not validate the significance of our work within our homes, God values it. He is the "God of seeing" (Gen. 16:13). He doesn't miss a single kind word spoken, boo-boo kissed, dish washed, dinner cooked, or relationship restored. He is weaving even the "small" things we do at home into the larger narrative for His glory.

And even though we may not be rewarded tangibly for it, God will reward our labors. The work we do in our homes has eternal value. So Paul is being strategic for the gospel when he says to women, in effect, "Don't fumble what matters in eternity."

## INSIGHTS FROM A REFRIGERATOR

My refrigerator serves as a backdrop for photographs of my friends and their families. Mounted in acrylic frames with magnets on the back, the pictures cover almost every square inch of available space. The nearly ninety families represented have a total of some three hundred children, not to mention scores of grandchildren.

Recently I spent a couple of hours in an annual ritual of replacing old photos with new ones that had been sent to me during the Christmas season. When all the new photos were in place, I sat back to survey the "big picture." I reminisced over some of the highlights these families had experienced over the past year—births of children and grandchildren, weddings, moves, job changes . . .

Nearly all the faces in these photos were smiling. But behind some of the near-perfect poses, I knew there was more—health issues, financial struggles, heartbreaking loss of loved ones, unresolved relational conflicts, and, tragically, divorce.

As I pondered the scene before me, I was struck with the wonder and significance of family—for better or worse. Family is at the heart of the gospel—intended to reflect our Father, who has chosen us to be adopted into His forever family.

If things aren't well at home, every other area of life is affected. I looked at those scores of women sitting like mother hens surrounded by their broods of young ones, and I felt an enormous sense of gratitude for the heart those women show for their homes . . .

- with every meal they prepare and every load of clothes they wash

- with every trip they make to the grocery store, to school, to the dentist, to piano lessons, or to soccer practice

- with every scraped knee they bandage and every encouraging word they speak

- with every dispute they arbitrate and every night hour they spend rocking a sick or scared child

- with every moment they spend building with Legos, coloring, helping with math problems, reading a Bible story, or listening to a husband or child describe his or her day

- with every moment they spend interceding for the spiritual growth and protection of their family and the family of God

Day in and day out, these women are building their homes. They are bearing and nurturing life. They are laying a foundation and building a memorial that will outlive them for generations to come. And in the process, they are honoring their Creator in profound ways.

| THE LIE | 18. I don't have time to do everything I'm supposed to do. |
|---|---|
| THE TRUTH | • There is time in every day to do everything that God wants me to do.<br>Psalm 90:10–12; Luke 10:38–42; John 17:4; Acts 20:24; Ephesians 2:10 |
| THE LIE | 19. I can thrive without consistent time in the Word and prayer. |
| THE TRUTH | • It is impossible for me to be the woman God wants me to be apart from spending consistent time cultivating a relationship with Him in the Word and prayer.<br>Job 23:12; Psalms 5:3; 27:4; 119:147; Proverbs 2:1–6; 3:5–6; Matthew 6:25–34; 14:23 |
| THE LIE | 20. My work at home is not as significant as the work or other activities I do outside the home. |
| THE TRUTH | • Keeping our homes is an important way we glorify God and advance the work of His kingdom.<br>1 Timothy 5:9–10<br><br>• The work we do in our homes is strategic for the gospel.<br>Titus 2:4–5 |

# CHAPTER SIX

# LIES WOMEN BELIEVE...
## ABOUT *Sexuality*

*I think this fur makes me look fat. There are times when I just long to be naked and free like we were in Eden. I never felt self-conscious about my body then, and I don't think it's just because I'm a few years older now. It's more than that. I used to so enjoy being alone with Adam for hours on end. We would just talk and talk—but not anymore. And sometimes when he touches me, I feel so . . . oh, what are the words?*

*He's pretty frustrated. He says the way I think about my body is affecting our intimacy. But it's not just me! He doesn't look at me the same way he used to. It's like he's embarrassed or something. Just about the time I get the desire to be alone with him again, I see that distant look in his eye. Even when he's moving toward me and drawing me close into his arms, his eyes seem so far away. When he slips my clothes off, I just feel so . . . ashamed. That's the word! I feel naked and ashamed.*

*And there's no one I can talk about it with. Not anyone. Not Adam. Not even God.*

The original edition of *Lies Women Believe* did not include a chapter on sexuality, but I felt it was important to add one to this new edition. This is an area where deception impacts women's lives as deeply as any other. And the lies about sex being promoted in our world have only become more widely accepted since *Lies* was first released. In reversing God's plan and order, the Enemy has managed to pervert the beauty of sex and steal this good gift from many.

Dannah Gresh, my longtime friend (and coauthor of *Lies Young Women Believe*), has devoted much of her life to helping women understand their sexuality from a biblical perspective and encouraging them to embrace God's amazing plan for sex.

Dannah graciously offered to help me write this chapter, and it is written in her voice. You can learn more about Dannah's ministry and books at PureFreedom.org.

*—Nancy*

We've come a long way in past decades, but many women still feel that the topic of sexuality is off-limits in the Christian world. Telling a mature Christian woman that you need advice on post-abortion depression, same-sex attraction, or porn is not easy. Many opt to suffer silently with private pain and defeat.

Some Christian mothers admit that they delay sex education at home because of the shame they feel from their own past. Our discomfort in talking to those meant to disciple us and those we're meant to disciple only puts a megaphone to the confused and confusing conversation our culture is having about this subject. Nancy's and my good friend Mary Kassian wrote this in her excellent book *Girls Gone Wise*:

> Given the modern-day obsession with sex, I'm going to say something that may sound radical: We don't make as much of sex as we should. . . . The problem is not that we value sex too much— but that we don't value it enough.[1]

I think you'll agree as we dive into these lies about sex and God's Truth about sex that sets us free. This chapter is your permission slip to study, discuss, and (if you are married) enjoy God's beautiful gift of sex.

## 21. *"I can't tell anyone."*

*I*f you've believed the lie that no one needs to know about your sexual issues, you're not alone. It's probably the most universal lie the Enemy tells women about sex, whether they are compulsive addicts, sexually repressed, or are suffering the consequences of someone else's sexual sin.

"I can't tell anyone that my husband is addicted to Internet porn."

"I can't tell anyone that *I'm* looking at porn."

"I can't tell anyone that I had an abortion when I was seventeen."

"I can't tell anyone that I haven't had sex with my husband in months."

"I can't tell anyone that I'm hooking up with my boyfriend."

"I can't tell anyone that I don't really like sex and avoid it at all costs."

"I can't tell anyone that my stepfather forced himself on me sexually at least once a week from the time I was five until I was eleven."

"I can't tell anyone that I overeat to avoid a relationship because I hate my body so much."

I don't know how this lie is customized for you, but I do know that underneath the lie is a deep root of shame. And that's a problem because it strikes at the very heart of God's design for your sexuality.

Satan seeks to shroud our sexual sins, challenges, shortcomings, and fears in shame. But as we see in the very first marriage, there is no shame in healthy, God-honoring sex and sexuality:

> And the man and his wife were both naked
> and were not ashamed.
>
> —Genesis 2:25

Maybe you're thinking: "But I've sinned. I *should* feel shame." When we sin, guilt in the conscience is a gift from God, intended to drive us back to His best for us. But God doesn't want us to be paralyzed by shame. Guilt and shame are often used interchangeably, but they are not the same thing.

*Guilt* says, "You did something bad." This message is meant to bring you to the cross, to a place of repentance, restoration, and right living. It is a healthy part of the sanctification process, which calls you to press into the belief that your relationship with Christ—not your sin—defines you. It is free of undue condemnation (1 John 2:1; Rom. 8:1).

But *shame* sends a different message. It says, "You *are* something bad." This message causes you to feel victimized, hide, and go further into your pain. It is Satan's tool to drive you away from God. It fuels hopelessness and makes you even more vulnerable to sinful addictions and strongholds. You begin to believe that your sexual past and current temptations define you.

When you embrace shame, you look a lot like Adam and Eve hiding from God in the garden (Gen. 3:10). But God doesn't want you living like that. He wants you to be free, and He's already given you what you need to find that freedom. *If you have asked God's forgiveness and begun to live as a redeemed woman in obedience to His Word, your sexual past and current temptations do not define you.*

In 1 Corinthians 6:9-10, Paul writes to church members living in a sexually broken culture, many of whom were bound up in shame. The apostle appeals to them to stop allowing their sexual past and their current temptations to define them. He identifies sexual sin in general as well as adultery and homosexuality. And he encourages them to let go of those labels and embrace their identity as saints who have been washed in the blood of Christ.

If you have repented of your sin, you are not the sex addict anymore. You are not the lesbian anymore. You are not the woman who had an affair. You are washed. You are sanctified. You are justified in the name of your Lord Jesus Christ. You are beloved, of infinite value to the One who knows exactly who you are, what you need most, and who you can become.

## DEFINED BY THE SAVIOR

While traveling in the region of Samaria, Jesus met a woman at a well. (You can find this story in John 4.) This woman felt she was defined by her sexual sin—both past and present. She had already been through five husbands and was currently living with a man she was not married to. I'd imagine that each relationship had left her more ashamed than the last. Maybe that's why she walked to the well in the heat of the day, alone. She was a woman with a past, and she couldn't seem to break free from it.

In striking up a conversation with this Samaritan woman, Jesus broke the social conventions of the day. But He was more concerned about rescuing her than about what others would think. Through a series of direct questions, He probed the most intimate parts of her heart and her past and led her to confess things she couldn't imagine telling anyone. Then He offered her what her heart was truly thirsting for—the "living water" of Truth. As long as she sought satisfaction and validation in sexual relationships, she would feel shame and remain unsatisfied. But in acknowledging the truth to Jesus and opening her heart to what He offered, she would find satisfaction for her deepest unfulfilled longings and desires. More important, she would find a new identity.

As this woman ran through the town after her encounter with Jesus, she called out, "Come, see the man *who told me everything I ever did.* Could this be the Messiah?" (John 4:29 CSB). She was no longer covered in shame over "everything she ever did." In fact, she was so overcome by how her encounter with Christ had redefined her life that she was *unashamed* to bring into the light what she had done in the past. (Trust me. Those who heard her testimony knew what she was referring to, and it wasn't washing the dinner dishes.)

She was no longer defined by her sin, but by her Savior. But for that to happen, she had to come out of hiding. If shame over your sexual issues is keeping you bound, you need to come out of hiding too.

Of course, Jesus isn't going to walk up to you while you're filling up your water bottle at your kitchen sink and audibly talk to you about your past. But He has instituted the church, His body here on earth, to provide a context for confession and healing today.

Have you confessed your sin to another person—to an older, wiser, stronger believer? That's what Scripture instructs. James 5:16 says, "Confess your sins to one another and pray for one another, that you may be healed." Only God can forgive sin. But He has designed the church to be the place where healing from our shame can take place.

Tell someone. Be wise and choose someone discrete and dependable, but don't sit on your secrets and your shameful feelings. Revealing your sexual sins and struggles to someone can be one of the most frightening things you'll ever do, but it's an important step in the journey to freedom.

The lie that whispers, "I can't tell anyone" often comes with companion lies like "It won't happen again" or "I can handle it on my own." Sometimes we think God can't forgive what we've done *until we stop doing it.* Such lies set us up to be our own savior, something none of us is capable of doing. If that kind of thinking is haunting you, see Lie #15, "God can't forgive what I've done" on page 100.

But maybe you *have* told someone—and you still feel trapped in shame. Maybe you're still in pain over something that happened many years before. Or maybe you've confessed again and again, but you're still in the clutches of some sinful sexual pattern. You may even feel paralyzed by the lie: "I'll never overcome this—ever!" If this is true for you, see Lie #17, "I can't live in consistent victory over sin" on page 104.

Breaking free of entrenched patterns of sexual sin and shame is seldom easy. It rarely happens overnight. But God is faithful, and He gives supernatural grace to those who humble themselves and cast themselves on His mercy. If you keep turning to Him and seeking wise counsel instead of giving in to your instinct to hide, you can move out of the lies and into the light. In that light you will experience growing freedom and the fullness of your identity as Christ's beloved.

## FROM SHAME TO FREEDOM

Of course, not all sexual shame comes from our own sin. It can also come from sins committed against us. Perhaps you've been abused as a child or date-raped, or maybe as a child an older sibling exposed you to pornography. For many women who have been abused, "I can't tell anyone" is accompanied by another twisted lie: "It was my fault." This toxic combination creates shame that's painfully difficult to overcome, so let me share with you the beautiful story of one who has walked through that kind of shame to freedom.

Author Nicole Braddock Bromley knows what it's like to live locked in the silence of childhood sexual abuse. Her stepfather did terrible things to her while warning her repeatedly, "Don't tell anyone." (How believable lies are when they are told to us by people entrusted with our protection.)

When Nicole was fourteen, she finally had the courage to break the silence by telling her mother, who responded with grace and courage. Her stepfather's response was to commit suicide one week later. This pushed Nicole back into a place of secrecy and shame. She didn't want people to know it was her "fault" that her stepfather was dead.

But God didn't give up on Nicole, and eventually she broke the silence and shame so powerfully in her own life that she's become a strong voice encouraging others to "break the silence." Nicole's books, such as *Hush: Moving from Silence to Healing after Childhood Sexual Abuse*,[2] have helped set many women free. She is also the founder of a ministry dedicated to stopping child sex trafficking around the world.[3] Her freedom is so big! Yours can be too.

## FINDING HIS BEST

Finally, maybe it's not sin that causes secrecy and shame, but sexual dissatisfaction or dysfunction in your marriage. Maybe the lie is accompanied by a subtle sense of resignation that has convinced you, "This is just how it is." That's the lie a missionary confessed to me in quiet whispers. The woman shared that she and her husband just weren't enjoying each other and she didn't feel like there was anyone she could tell. She'd just decided she'd have to live with things the way they were.

That all changed when a message on the true purpose of sex (which we'll explore in the next section) opened her heart to the truth that she should never settle for less than God's best in her marriage. She resolved to be intentional about romancing her husband and training her body to respond, and asked a close friend to help hold her accountable. In so doing, she found the healing she needed to enjoy the expression of God's gift within her marriage bed.

If you struggle with this kind of dissatisfaction, I'm asking you to be brave and to tell someone—ideally, a wise, godly woman who can help you walk into the light. Secrecy only intensifies the power of temptation and shame. Whether you're feeling shame over sexual sin (past or present), quietly suffering in the shadows from sexual abuse, or settling for less than your marriage could be, God has something so much better for you.

## 22. *"My sexuality is separate from my spirituality."*

One secular writer perpetuated a common myth when she wrote, "Christian and Jewish texts and teachings contain no mention of . . . sex. In fact these two religions make little or no connection between sex and worship at all."[4]

That's simply not true. For example, the Song of Solomon in the Old Testament stands out among religious books as an unapologetic celebration of marriage and sexuality. And from Genesis to Revelation, the Bible frequently uses language related to marriage and sexual intimacy to inspire our understanding of God's *design* for sex, and to instruct us as we *define* Christian sexual behavior. Both are important for Christians to explore and understand.

Sadly, many Christian discussions about sex put all the emphasis on the definition of sexual behavior—what we should do and especially what we should *not* do. The result is often a list of rules without an understanding about *why* we have them. Such an approach tends to give rise to the Pharisee in all of us. We pridefully believe we're getting our sexuality right, when in fact we may be getting it wrong. And we get it very, very wrong when we believe the lie that "my sexuality is separate from my spirituality."

Some women use this lie to defend sexual choices that are contrary to God's Word. Others use it to justify how they have shut down their minds and bodies to their marriage bed. To confront the heart of this lie, we have to consider the often-overlooked design of sex and understand *why* God puts protective boundaries on sex.

## GOD'S DESIGN OF SEX

The design of sex begins with God's good creation of humans as *male* and *female*:

> Then God said,
> "Let us make man in our image, after our likeness. . . ."
> So God created man in his own image,
> in the image of God he created him;
> male and female he created them.
>
> —Genesis 1:26–27

God created mankind in His image. And He highlights one particular trait that reflects that image: biological sex. Maleness. Femaleness. God created the two sexes to display something important about God.

What's that?

We'll never fully understand this side of heaven why He created two biological sexes, but we can begin with the realization that God is a relational being. This nature is seen in the Trinity. God the Father, God the Son, and God the Holy Spirit are three distinct persons, and yet they are one God, one in essence. The Hebrew word *echad* is used to describe this unity in Deuteronomy 6:4, a prayer familiar to any Old Testament Jew: "Hear, O Israel: the LORD our God, the LORD is one [*echad*]."

This magnificent diversity and unity of the Godhead is glimpsed when the male and female become one in marriage.

Let's unpack that thought. What happens when the first man and woman meet each other? They are married—right there in the beautiful Garden of Eden. There may never have been a more romantic destination wedding, perhaps with butterflies fluttering like confetti as the bride and groom stood before one another. And no sooner had the wedding bells sounded than the Lord of creation established this marriage as the prototype for every subsequent marriage:

> Therefore a man shall leave his father and his mother
> and hold fast to his wife,
> and they shall become one [*echad*] flesh.
>
> —Genesis 2:24

The male and female are two distinct, independent humans, but when they come together they are *echad*. One.

As we wrap the full counsel of God's Word around this Genesis account, we learn that this oneness points toward an even greater wonder. This is stated most succinctly in Paul's letter to the Ephesians, beginning with a restatement of God's original declaration about marriage:

> "Therefore a man shall leave his father and mother
> and hold fast to his wife,
> and the two will become one flesh."
> This mystery is profound,
> and I am saying that it refers to Christ and the church.
>
> —Ephesians 5:31–32

The mystery and ultimate meaning of that sacred union is revealed in Christ. The joining together of one man and one woman is a picture of our heavenly Groom who loves His bride and who, by means of an indissoluble covenant of grace, is eternally united with her. From the very beginning, God intended human sexuality and marriage to be a picture of the gospel.

Is it any surprise, then, that Satan would be motivated to lie to us about its value and meaning and use?

Leonardo da Vinci's *Mona Lisa* is one of the most famous paintings in the world. The mystery of the subject's expression and other subtleties of the painting have been the subject of centuries of study and discussion. After five hundred years, we still yearn to understand it completely. Marriage and sexuality are like that.

Abuses and misuses of marriage and sexuality today—pornography, erotica, adultery, hooking up, same-sex marriage, and other forms of sexual sin—are akin to defacing the beautiful *Mona Lisa* with a can of graffiti paint.

But the masterpiece of marriage faces another, less obvious, threat.

In 1911, the *Mona Lisa* was stolen from a wall of the Louvre Museum in Paris. A handyman pulled off the heist early one morning, when the museum was closed to the public. Few guards were on duty that day, and the handyman was able to escape with the painting without attracting attention, leaving just the four iron pegs that had held the masterpiece on the wall.

Surprisingly, some twenty-four hours would pass before the missing painting raised any concern. It was not unusual for pieces of art to be temporarily moved to another part of the building to be cleaned or photographed. So when the greatest painting in the world went missing, those entrusted with protecting it were oblivious and did *nothing*.[5]

That's how we treat God's masterpiece of marriage and sexuality when we believe the lie that sex and spirituality are unrelated—that we can be a godly woman and at the same time have sex outside of marriage or not be interested in having sex with our husband. When we who have been entrusted with protecting and preserving God's precious gift of sex allow that picture to be stolen, observers can no longer see and marvel at the wondrous gospel it is intended to portray.

## PAINTING THE PICTURE

When I shared this truth with the married missionary friend who had a boring sex life, she was inspired to pay attention to her marriage relationship until it was rekindled with fresh passion. She wanted her marriage to showcase the mystery of the love of Christ. And it's the same truth that ignited in "Jenna's" heart a fresh love for the Lord and for the man who would become her husband.

Jenna was a young professional who was living with her boyfriend. In her mind they were deeply compatible sexually and in many other ways. She did feel a spiritual disconnect between them because she was a Christian and he was not. This bothered her a little, but not enough to change what she was doing.

Can you see that she believed the lie that her sexuality and her spiritual life were unrelated? She believed she could have sex and live with a man she was not married to, in disobedience to the clear direction of God's Word, while at the same time having a vibrant spiritual life.

One Sunday Jenna talked her boyfriend into coming to church with her. And she was pleasantly surprised after several weeks when "Tanner" responded to the pastor's invitation to follow Christ. Now, she thought, their relationship would be everything she wanted it to be. But a few days later, Tanner explained that they couldn't live together any longer. His heart had been stirred and awakened by the love of Christ, and now he wanted to live his life to please Him. And the Holy Spirit had been speaking to his heart through the pages of his new Bible, which he had been devouring.

Tanner's resolve almost led to a breakup. Jenna insisted that their sex life was separate from their spiritual lives. But Tanner was resolute. In the end, Jenna came to heartfelt repentance and turned from her sinful way of thinking and living. She integrated her sexuality with her spirituality by moving out and pressing in to obey God's Word. The couple went through counseling and were married a year later. Today they are painting a beautiful picture of the gospel, reflecting the image of God and portraying the story of Christ's faithful love for His bride, the church.

## 23. *"This is who I am."*

*M*y husband, Bob, and I (Dannah) certainly have not always been poster children for sexual purity. I gave away the gift of my virginity when I was fifteen. Bob has struggled with pornography. As a result of my past sin and his battle with temptation, there have been times in our marriage when we have had to fight together to restore the picture of the gospel in our marriage.

This made Nancy's request for me to help write this chapter a great honor. She's seen firsthand the way Bob and I have worked to overcome the lies of the Enemy and replace them with God's healing truth. In addition, friends who love us both encouraged me during the process, saying, "You're the right person to do this." How big God's grace is in my life! I know firsthand that we are not defined by our past sins, but by the redeeming work of Christ in our lives.

I also know firsthand the heartache that sexual brokenness can produce. I remember feeling emotionally paralyzed for the first decade of my adult life. In my mind I was so tightly bound to my past sexual sin that I felt like it wasn't just something I did, but it was who I was.

"This is who I am," was a lie that left me feeling hopeless day after day. Shame became my identity for years, even though I'd long since turned my heart to God and was walking in sexual purity. Perhaps you feel that way or have felt that way in the past.

But belief in this lie isn't always rooted in shame. For some it reflects an unwillingness to accept who God has created them to be—a form of pride. Today's gender revolution screams, "Be true to yourself" and "You were born this way." Individuals are applauded when they "come out" as transgendered, gay, lesbian, bisexual, queer, or asexual. Maybe you've thought: "I've always felt this way. I've tried everything to change the way I feel, but this is who I *am*."

This helps us understand why sexual sin can be so difficult to overcome. It is often a crisis of identity.

## WHEN FEELINGS LIE

Whether it is shame or the prideful rejection of who God created them to be that binds people to this lie, the common denominator is that their sense of identity is fueled by how they *feel*. And here's the problem with that: feelings aren't facts. In fact, the Bible reveals that our hearts—apart from being indwelled and transformed by Christ—are deceitful and wicked (Jer. 17:9). The most important thing about your sexuality is not how you feel, but what God says is true.

What does God say about your sexuality and your identity? He says that you are His image bearer and that your femaleness is part of this image (Gen. 1:26–27). Before the earth was even formed, He knew you and chose for you to be a woman, and that fact is an indispensable component of how you reflect Him. You are a female image bearer of God. But note that *female* is still just an adjective describing what kind of image bearer you are for God. Your womanhood matters, in other words, but not more than your identity as an image bearer of God. Image bearer is what you are.

Rosaria Butterfield, a former lesbian professor, is now a mother in a traditional marriage and an author and speaker on the subject of same-sex attraction and sexual identity. She has faced this lie and knows how personal and real the struggle can be for those who feel their identity is rooted in their sexuality. Rosaria makes this observation:

> Sexual orientation as a category was invented by Freud. . . . No one had ever talked before about a person who *was* a homosexual—or a person who *was* a heterosexual. Prior to the nineteenth century, sexuality was understood as something that was a verb. It was something you did, not something that you were.
>
> One of the reasons that this is important for Christians to realize is that God has already given us an identity, that we are born male or female with souls that will last forever. And so our identity is exclusively as a male or female image bearer of a holy God. And that is true for all of humanity. . . .

That's the heart of my rejection of this concept of gay Christianity. It's not that I reject the idea that people struggle with same-
sex attraction. . . . The problem is that when it becomes a term
of identity, it actually separates you from your image-bearing
responsibilities and also from the joys that are inherent in that.[6]

## OUR TRUE IDENTITY

The heart of homosexual and transgender sin is not as much specific sinful *actions* as it is *what people believe about who they are*. Ultimately, they are
rejecting their true identity as image bearers. The first chapter in the book
of Romans explains that disregarding God's definitions for manhood and
womanhood and His design for sexuality is ultimately a refusal to glorify
our Creator. This rebellion is often at the root of sexual sin, whether rejecting God-given gender or engaging in homosexual or heterosexual sin.

You may have had homosexual sex or had sex with a boy when you
were in high school. You may have struggled with porn or even a full-
fledged sexual addiction. But if you are in Christ, that is not who you *are*.
It is something you have *done*.

Rosaria Butterfield went on to say something that ministers grace to
every believer's heart, no matter what category of sin we may battle:

In Christ . . . you can struggle with any manner of sin this side of
heaven, but you do it with the Lord's kind company. You do it as
a *son* or a *daughter* who stands in robes of righteousness, not
someone who [is hopelessly enslaved to] a category of the flesh
that will have absolutely no place in the New Jerusalem.[7]

Even though my (Dannah's) sexual sin was different from Rosaria's,
we each had to choose to look at ourselves as daughters of Christ who
stand in robes of righteousness presented to us by our Savior. We had
to embrace our true identity to find healing and to change our feelings. Today we each enjoy a rich ministry of passing on comfort to
those who've struggled as we did and providing a biblically reasoned
approach to difficult subjects of sexuality.

Our lives testify to the redeeming power of Christ the same way the lives of those broken by sexual sin in the church of Corinth did. In chapter 6 of his first letter to that church, Paul lists many of the believers' past sins, including various kinds of sexual immorality. Perhaps they were facing an identity crisis, because he reminds them of their true identity in verse 11:

> And that is what some of you were.
> But you were washed, you were sanctified,
> you were justified in the name of the Lord Jesus Christ
> and by the Spirit of our God. (NIV)

No matter what kind of sexual (or other) sin you may have struggled with, the cross is where we may each find mercy, cleansing, and redemption. But in His presence, we must submit to God's truth about our sexuality rather than succumb to the whims of our feelings.

Every sexual choice is also a spiritual choice. By faith, you can choose to deny any feelings that don't line up with the Truth, reject every lie about your identity, and accept your new identity as the image bearer you were created to be.

Be washed, my dear friend. Be sanctified. Be justified in the name of the Lord Jesus Christ and accept your identity as a beloved child of God. That is who you are.

## 24. *"God's standards for sex are out of date."*

The Bible is amazingly candid when it comes to sexual activity and sin; it doesn't gloss over the faults and flaws of key figures. The Scripture is also straightforward in defining the proper way to handle the gift of sex. And the Designer of sex gets to define our sexual ethic.

Put another way: if God truly is the Lord of our lives, He gets to be the Lord of our sexuality.

Today it is a common but false belief that biblical standards of sexuality and morality are outdated simply because the majority of people in our modern era have rejected them. But in truth, what God's Word teaches us about sexual behavior was never *in* style.

In fact, horrific sexual sin was not uncommon in the culture of the Old Testament era: homosexuality, bestiality, incest, polygamy, and cult prostitution tied to pagan temple worship were all openly practiced in certain quarters (see Gen. 38:22; Lev. 18; Judg. 19:22; 1 Kings 11:1–8). And New Testament believers practiced their faith against the backdrop of a Greek and Roman culture rife with sexual sin. Promiscuity, adultery, pedophilia, homosexuality, and open prostitution were widely accepted. In fact, Paul wrote that some in the church of Corinth used to practice such things before they were washed in Christ's blood (1 Cor. 6:9).

Our world today is not all that different from the world in which Old and New Testament believers found themselves. God's precepts for sexuality were in stark contrast to the prevailing culture then, just as they are for us today. Our spiritual forebears had to trust that God's ways were good and right, and they had to choose to swim upstream against their culture, just as we can and must do through the power of the Holy Spirit.

## SEXUAL ETHICS FOR THE CHRISTIAN WOMAN

If we agree that our sexuality and our spirituality are not separate, then we must embrace what Christian author Dr. Juli Slattery calls *sexual integrity*. She defines it this way:

> Your sexual choices are a consistent expression of your relational and spiritual commitments.[8]

It should be no surprise that today's college women have on average 7.2 sexual partners during their university years, that "friends with benefits" is commonly accepted as a way to satisfy an urge, or that women are embracing erotic books and porn as normal and acceptable. This is just the lost acting like the lost. It is consistent with their relational and spiritual commitments.

But what about those of us who are Christ followers? What does it mean for us to act with sexual integrity?

The sexual ethics of a Christian woman should in no way resemble the sexual ethics of this world. We are called to display the gospel by conforming our behavior and relationships to God's Word. In her Bible study, *Sex and the Single Girl*, Juli breaks a biblical sexual ethic down into two core commitments:[9]

## COMMITMENT #1:

"I don't engage in sex outside of marriage."

Author and teacher Joseph Dillow has compiled a list of sexual acts that God expressly forbids in the Scripture:[10]

- **Fornication.** A broad term used to refer to intercourse outside of marriage (1 Cor. 7:2; 1 Thess. 4:3), sleeping with a stepparent (1 Cor. 5:1), sex with a prostitute (1 Cor. 6:15), and adultery (Matt. 5:32).

- **Adultery.** Sex with someone who is not your spouse. Jesus expanded adultery to mean not just physical acts but emotional acts of the mind and heart, which could include pornography and erotica (Matt. 5:28).

- **Homosexual relations.** For a man to have sex with a man or for a woman to have sex with a woman (Lev. 18:22; 20:30; Rom. 1:26–27; 1 Cor. 6:9).

- **Impurity.** The Greek word *moluno* can mean to lose one's virginity or to become defiled due to living out a secular or pagan lifestyle (Rev. 14:4). The Greek word *rupose* often refers to moral uncleanness in general (Rev. 22:11).

- **Prostitution.** Paying or being paid for sex (Lev. 19:29; Deut. 23:17; Prov. 7:4–27).

- **Lustful passions.** Unrestrained, indiscriminate sexual desire for men or women other than the person's marriage partner (Col. 3:5; 1 Thess. 4:4–5).

- **Sodomy.** In the Old Testament, sodomy refers to men having anal sex with other men.

- **Obscenity and coarse jokes.** Sexual humor (Eph. 5:3–4).

- **Incest.** Sex with family members or relatives (Lev. 18:7–18; 20:11–21).

Basically, the list can be summarized this way: *sex is created by God to be experienced only within a covenant marriage between one man and one woman.* So a biblical sexual ethic for every Christian woman at any age is "I don't engage in sex outside of marriage."

## COMMITMENT #2:

### "Sex within my marriage is mutually pleasing and happens on a regular basis."

We fall short of aligning our sexual and spiritual lives if we only focus our sexual ethic on what we should *not* do. God's rules about sex are not one big "thou shalt not!" A biblical sexual ethic also takes care to observe what God instructs we *should* do, and Scripture speaks to mutually satisfying and frequent sexual pleasure between a husband and wife. Passages like Proverbs 5:18–19 and the entire Song of Solomon celebrate the gift of marital sexual pleasure—and so should we! First Corinthians 7:3–5 (CSB) is one such passage in the New Testament:

> A husband should fulfill his marital duty to his wife,
> and likewise a wife to her husband. . . .
> Do not deprive one another—except when you agree for a time,
> to devote yourselves to prayer.
> Then come together again;
> otherwise, Satan may tempt you
> because of your lack of self-control.

Married men and women are to be committed to mutually pleasing sex on a regular basis. While what is "pleasing" or "regular" will differ from couple to couple, the husband and the wife should both eagerly approach their marriage bed and have a mutual sense of satisfaction. The one exception to this pattern is when they agree together that they need to abstain from sex for a time of focused prayer.

Before I step on some of my Christian sisters' toes, let me point out that this Scripture first instructs men to please their wives. But we're not writing this book for men. It's for us women. So let me be direct.

There are many reasons why women may not want to have sex. Some of these are legitimate and even serious. You may be exhausted from child care or other duties, or perhaps you aren't finding sex to be all you'd hoped. You could be in a season of deep grief or depression or you may have physical challenges. Perhaps your husband has struggled with pornography and you're in a season of healing from that sense of betrayal.

Any of these could be legitimate reasons to abstain on occasion or for a season, but if those times do not include intentional prayer, how can you hope to receive the wisdom and grace you need to deal with whatever issues you're facing? Without the element of prayer, withholding sex from your husband is contrary to God's best for your life and marriage.

And God's best for you in this area far surpasses whatever this world may consider good or right.

## 25. *"I have to have an outlet for my sexual desire."*

I (Dannah) get a lot of letters from single women who claim to want to live lives of purity but also want to know, "How can I satisfy my sexual desires if I'm destined to be single my whole life?" Married women whose husbands are physically disabled or disinterested or whose bedrooms have become boring also write, seeking ways to be sexually alive.

Earlier in the book, Nancy reminded us that we will always have unfulfilled longings this side of heaven (Rom. 8:23). I love what she wrote for my own heart, and I'd like to build upon it a little to help you recognize what you *can* do with your "sexual" longings.

First, let me reiterate that your longing, in and of itself, is not sinful. In fact, our "sexual" longings point to a legitimate need. You may have noticed that I keep putting the word *sexual* in quotation marks in this section. If you did, you're on to something—because whether you are married or single, you are looking for more than sex. Your body, mind, and spirit were created to desire true intimacy with another. That's part of how you reflect the image of God. But be careful not to confuse a legitimate longing for intimacy with a physical desire for sex.

Let me unpack this a little so we can be on the same page as we differentiate between sex and intimacy.

The first time the act of sex is referenced in the pages of the Scripture: "Now the man had relations with his wife Eve . . ." (Gen. 4:1 NASB) or, as the CSB puts it: "The man was intimate with his wife." The Hebrew verb used here means "to know, to be known."[11] Transcending the physical act, it speaks of a deep emotional, intimate knowing.

The physical act of sex was never intended to be separated from its relational and divine meaning—a man and woman, united in the covenant of marriage, knowing each other deeply. But our culture tends to hyperfocus on the physical aspect while largely overlooking the importance and beauty of emotional and spiritual intimacy. And sex without intimacy is a cheap counterfeit. It's why we're seeing so much addiction to things like porn, erotica, and hooking up.

Sexual activity apart from the way God designed it to be experienced—in a covenant commitment to know and be known—is an empty substitute for true intimacy and will never satisfy. It leads to the craving for more, which can result in addictions and strongholds that are difficult to break.

## BREAKING FREE, FINDING SATISFACTION

"Charla" was a middle-aged Christian homeschooling mom that Dr. Juli Slattery and I interviewed when working on a project to address the erotica that many Christian women use as an outlet for their sexual desire or to "spice up their bedroom." (Erotica is a form of porn that uses words and storylines rather than photos to arouse.) Charla had left a promising career in banking to focus on her family. Her husband had maintained his busy life as a business leader in the local chamber of commerce and was also an elder in their church.

After a few years, Charla started to feel ignored romantically and sexually. Her sex life, which was infrequent, had begun to bore her, and her husband didn't understand. She believed she needed some sort of outlet for her sexual desires, and a friend gave her some erotica. She loved it because it gave her the release she needed. Soon erotica wasn't just something she enjoyed now and then; it had become a time-consuming addiction. She no longer wanted to have sex with her husband, and she started having sexual conversations on the Internet—first with men, then with other women—to "meet her needs."

Within two years of reading her first erotic novel, Charla found herself packing her bags to meet a woman she'd found online. Just as she was about to walk out the door, she realized that none of this had actually satisfied her. Her unfulfilled sexual longings had only escalated, leading her to justify more and more sinful behavior.

Scripture warns us against becoming enslaved to things that can never satisfy:

> Stand fast therefore in the liberty
> by which Christ has made us free,
> and do not be entangled again with a yoke of bondage.
>
> —Galatians 5:1 NKJV

This verse offers a vivid picture of how we lose our freedom. The Greek word translated "entangled" is a word commonly used for being trapped as if by a snare.[12] Now, you may not be into hunting, but there's an important lesson to be learned here.

## TRAPPED!

A snare isn't your typical steel foothold trap, which looks painful and nasty with its iron teeth. A snare is far more subtle. A simple piece of cable that forms a loop, it appears nonthreatening—if it is even noticed at all. When an animal walks through a snare, it walks calmly. It just keeps walking through, feeling nothing. Soon it may feel a little tension, but it just plods on. As the animal feels greater tension, it pulls harder and presses forward, causing the loop to tighten. Soon its own force of movement has enslaved the animal to the snare. If it had backed out earlier, it might have gotten away. But by the time it recognizes that it's stuck, it's too late. The capture is subtle and is *empowered by the animal's own actions.*

That's a vivid and frightening picture of what happened to Charla. And it all started with the lie, "I have to have an outlet for my sexual desire." Sin doesn't just happen. We empower it with our own actions. And often those actions are fueled by a belief that's simply not true. Charla had incorrectly assumed that what she needed was sex, when in fact she'd reached a place where she was relationally and spiritually isolated and lonely. Little by little, she had been caught in the snare.

When Charla came to her senses, she reached out to two mature women in her church and asked for help in repairing her broken marriage. And the first thing her older, wiser friends helped her understand was that her longing was not for sex, but for intimacy. Her greatest need wasn't to work on techniques in the bedroom, but to tend to her friendship with her husband (who gladly agreed to attend to her heart). Together, they pressed into their friendship and intimacy not only with each other, but with Jesus.

Yes, that's right. Fixing Charla's sex life had a lot to do with fixing her relationship with Jesus.

## CREATED FOR INTIMACY

When Jesus met the woman at the well, she'd had five husbands, and the man she was living with currently wasn't even her husband. Jesus didn't focus on her unfulfilled sexual longings or give her a three-step process to stop those cravings. He pointed her to the only thing that would satisfy her thirst: Himself. He called her into a deep, intimate relationship with Himself.

If marriage is a picture of our relationship with Christ, we must know the love of Christ in order to paint it. You can't paint a picture of something you've never seen, right? We often make the mistake of focusing on finding emotional and sexual intimacy in marriage, but intimacy with Christ must come first. His love is faithful and unfailing in a way that love from a man never can be. That's why marriage is a picture of Christ's love and not a replacement for it.

God created us with a capacity and need for relational intimacy (a reflection of the relational oneness within the Trinity). Whether you are married or single, stuffing your longings for intimacy and love or pretending they don't exist doesn't make them go away, but attempting to feed them with sex won't work either. If need be, you can live without an outlet for your sexual desires. And physical sexual activity in and of itself cannot fulfill your longings for intimacy. Jesus desires to fulfill that need first and foremost with Himself, and through the gift of appropriate, pure human friendships.

If you're a single woman, let me share with you this encouragement from author Carolyn McCulley, a close single friend of Nancy's and mine:

> As a volunteer for a local crisis pregnancy center, I was asked on several occasions how I could handle living without sex. These clients didn't ask me flippantly. They were really concerned they couldn't do the same, as if maybe they would explode from all the built-up pressure. I would assure them God's grace was sufficient, but they remained doubtful.
>
> It's the same with a number of my friends who knew me as an unbeliever. The seriousness of my conversion was quickly established when they discovered now I actually was going to wait until marriage. That commitment then became the litmus test—more so than other aspects of my faith. When an unbelieving client asked me out shortly after my conversion, my colleagues insisted I declare myself and my standards to him. "You have to tell him you're not normal," they said.
>
> *"You're not normal."* You're a Christian single woman called by

Scripture to sexual purity and abstinence until marriage, living and working in a sex-saturated society during the week. On the weekends, you fellowship with families in your church, where marriage and family are generally held in high regard. But you don't feel that you fit in either place. After a while you may start to think it's true; maybe you're really *not* normal.

It's true. You're not normal. But this is good news. If you've repented of your sins and put your trust in the finished work of Jesus Christ and his substitutionary death on the cross for the punishment of your sins, then you're definitely not "normal." Your identity has been reclaimed and reordered by the Lord.[13]

My dear sister, normal is overrated. It doesn't satisfy. Saturate yourself in the extraordinary living water that Jesus gives. His is the only love that will ever truly fulfill the deepest longings of your heart.

| THE LIE | 21. I can't tell anyone. |
|---|---|
| THE TRUTH | • Healthy sex and sexuality is free of shame.<br>Genesis 2:25<br>• Guilt is God's tool to bring you back to Him and is free of undue condemnation.<br>1 John 2:1; Romans 8:1<br>• Shame is Satan's tool designed to drive you away from God.<br>Genesis 3:10<br>• God designed the Church to help bring healing to those struggling with sin and shame.<br>James 5:16<br>• Your sexual past and current temptations do not define you. The cross does.<br>1 Corinthians 6:9–12 |
| THE LIE | 22. My sexuality is separate from my spirituality. |
| THE TRUTH | • God created the biological sexes of male and female to reflect something about His image.<br>Genesis 1:26–27<br>• When one man and one woman join together in marriage and sexual intimacy, they reflect the oneness of God the Father, God the Son, and God the Holy Spirit.<br>Genesis 2:24<br>• Marriage and sex are a picture of the gospel.<br>Ephesians 5:31–32 |

| | |
|---|---|
| **THE LIE** | **23. This is who I am.** |
| **THE TRUTH** | • Feelings are not facts. The heart—my feelings—can be deceptive and wicked.<br>Jeremiah 17:9<br><br>• The most important thing about my sexuality is not how I feel, but what God says is true.<br>I John 3:20<br><br>• My identity is as an image bearer of God.<br>Genesis 1:26–27<br><br>• Claiming that my identity is in my sexuality denies my purpose to glorify God.<br>Romans 1:20–23 |
| **THE LIE** | **24. God's standards for sex are out of date.** |
| **THE TRUTH** | • God's standards were never "in style."<br>Genesis 19:5; 38:22; Leviticus 18; Judges 19:22;<br>1 Kings 11:1–8; 1 Corinthians 6:9<br><br>• Sexual integrity is when my sexual choices are a consistent expression of my relational and spiritual commitments.<br>Ephesians 5:3; 1 Thessalonians 4:3–5;<br>1 Corinthians 6:13–20<br><br>• God does not want me to engage in any form of sex outside of marriage.<br>Leviticus 18:22; 19:29; 20:10; Proverbs 7:4–27; Matthew 5:28; Mark 7:21–22; Romans 1:27; 1 Corinthians 6:9; 7:2; Ephesians 4:19; 5:3–4; 1 Thessalonians 4:3<br><br>• If I am married, God wants me to engage in regular and mutually pleasing sex with my husband—except when we agree together to abstain for a time of focused prayer.<br>1 Corinthians 7:1–5 |

| THE LIE | 25. I have to have an outlet for my sexual desire. |
|---------|---------------------------------------------------|
| THE TRUTH | • My longing for intimacy is legitimate. The physical act of sex is an expression of the deeper work of intimacy a person longs to experience. Genesis 4:1 |
| | • My longing for sexual expression can be a snare. Pursuing it apart from God's plan and order will lead to enslavement, not fulfillment. Galatians 5:1 |
| | • I can live without a sexual outlet, but I cannot live without the unfailing love of God. Proverbs 19:22 NIV |

# CHAPTER SEVEN

# LIES WOMEN BELIEVE...
## ABOUT *Marriage*

*Things are pretty quiet around the house at the moment—mostly because Adam and I aren't exactly on speaking terms. We had a big fight last night. I should've seen it coming.*

*The day got off to a rough start. He had been up all night helping one of the cows give birth. Then he had to leave before breakfast to get the rest of the hay stored. When he finally got home, he was hot and sweaty, exhausted, and not in the greatest mood.*

*I had been cooped up in the house all day with two sick kids, and when he asked why dinner wasn't ready, I suggested that if he wanted dinner, maybe he'd better fix it himself. I don't know why I chose that moment to remind him that I wished he'd clear out the path in front of the house. (It looks like a jungle with all the weeds.)*

*One thing led to another, and soon we were arguing about the children. Adam had told Abel he could go on a special hunting trip with him next week. I feel Abel's too young, and besides, I don't think he should take Abel and leave Cain behind.*

*Adam wouldn't back down, and things got pretty tense. We both said a lot of things we probably shouldn't have said. I went to bed early and pretended I was asleep when he came in.*

*You'd think after all these years together we would have this marriage thing down. Funny thing is, for the most part, I think Adam would say our marriage is doing fine. But sometimes I feel like we're total strangers—even though we've known each other all our lives. He always thinks he's right about everything. When I ask him to try and see things from my point of view, he says that nothing will make me happy.*

*I just wish he would be more sensitive to my feelings.*

*M*arriage was designed by God to reflect the gospel and the story of redemption. What took place in the Garden of Eden thousands of years ago was an attack on that important picture. In undermining that sacred institution, Satan struck a forceful blow against God's eternal plan and His very character.

It's no coincidence that Satan launched his sinister plan by approaching a married woman. He lied to her about God, about His character and His Word, and about sin and its consequences. She believed and acted on his lie, then turned to her husband and drew him into sin with her.

The implications in their marriage were profound. Shame replaced freedom. Pretense and hiding replaced transparency and fellowship. The oneness Eve and her husband had experienced in their original state now turned to enmity and animosity—not only toward God, but toward each other.

Instead of providing loving leadership for his wife, the man was now prone to extremes ranging from domineering control to passive detachment. The protection the woman had been granted under her spiritual "head" was removed, and the independent spirit she had exerted toward God now displayed itself toward her husband, leaving her vulnerable to greater deception and sin. The relationship between a man, a woman, and their God that was intended to be selfless and joyful now became self-protective and toxic.

And so it has been ever since in marriages that attempt to function independently of their Creator.

As with other areas of our lives, Satan uses deception to achieve his destructive purposes for marriage. If he can get husbands and wives to believe and act on his lies, he can succeed in stealing their joy and destroying their intimacy. His lies are legion, lies such as . . .

## 26. "I have to have a husband to be happy."

*L*ike many other lies, this lie is actually a subtle distortion of the Truth. The Truth is that marriage is a good gift. It is God's plan for most people, and there can (and ought to) be great joy and blessing in a Christ-centered marriage. But Satan twists the Truth about marriage by suggesting to women that marriage is their sole ticket to personal happiness and fulfillment and that they can't be truly happy without a husband to love them and meet their needs.

Once they have a husband, many women start to believe variations of this lie: "I have to have this or that kind of husband to be happy" or "My husband is supposed to make me happy." Only after years of heartache did "Myrna" recognize the folly of this way of thinking:

> After ten years together, my husband and I split up. I had believed
> that it was his responsibility to make me happy. It never was, and
> it never worked. Not only was I in bondage, but he was also.

The Truth is that the highest and ultimate purpose of marriage is not to make us happy, but to glorify God. Women who get married for the sole purpose of finding happiness are setting themselves up for almost certain disappointment; they seldom find what they are looking for. And women who believe they have to have a husband in order to be happy often settle for less than what God intended to give them.

"Joan" shared with me how believing this lie led to unanticipated consequences:

> During my college years, having a boyfriend, a fiancé, and then a
> husband who was a good man but not necessarily committed to
> Christ was more important to me than waiting upon God and ask-
> ing Him to bring a strong believer into my life to marry. As a result,
> we have not been able to grow in Christ together. After twenty-
> eight years of marriage, we do not do many things together. My
> friends are Christians; his friends are not Christians. My priority is
> my children; his priority is his work.

This woman believed she had to have a husband to be happy. She acted on that belief by marrying a man who was not a believer, contrary to the clear teaching of Scripture. She got what she thought she wanted—a man—but ended up with spiritual leanness in her soul (Ps. 106:15).

Only by recognizing and embracing the Truth can true freedom be found—with or without a husband, as the following true stories illustrate:

*I lost my father when I was fourteen and got married at age sixteen. I see now that I let my husband become my security and my reason to live. As our children grew up and we had struggles in our marriage, I was in bondage to the feeling that I couldn't live without my husband. My husband could not tolerate the suffocation I was causing and started thinking he needed to get out to breathe.*

*God used some friends to show me that I needed to turn loose of "Carl" and take hold of Him. Once I did so, I was free. My husband grew through all this and never did leave. We praise God all the time for bringing us through to celebrate thirty-six years of marriage.*

*I have struggled with the lie that without marriage I have no value, that perhaps something is wrong with me that I'm still single. Believing this lie has robbed me of the joy of serving God and others (because I have been so absorbed with my own goals).*

*It has taken me many years to trust that God is sovereign and that He has a plan for me. My focus now (at age forty) is to spend my remaining years taking advantage of the many opportunities to serve Him and allowing Him to change me into the most Christlike woman I can be. This life is so short. He has helped me have an eternal perspective so the sorrows and disappointments of this world can be happily endured.*

I love the final sentence of that last testimony. In this fallen world, no one, married or single, is exempt from "sorrows and disappointments."

There simply is no such thing as cloudless happiness this side of heaven. However, as this unmarried woman has learned, we can "happily endure" whatever circumstances we may face here on earth by looking beyond this life and gaining an eternal perspective.

Between here and heaven, neither our marital status nor, for those of us who are married, the status of our marriage can provide or deprive us of ultimate happiness.

I have known both single and married women who were chronically unhappy. I have also known both single and married women who were truly happy in spite of facing "sorrows and disappointments." They had found a source of joy that is not dependent on their marital status.

I have been on both sides of the marital divide myself. Until my late fifties I was single. Those years included periods of loneliness and longing for companionship. But throughout that lengthy season, which I was sure would be for the rest of my life, the Lord kindly allowed me to experience His friendship and His all-sufficiency and gave me the privilege of serving Him and others "without distraction" (1 Cor. 7:35 CSB). By God's grace I received those years as a gift and was blessed with contentment and joy in that calling.

Then the Lord surprised me (to say the least) by bringing a wonderful man into my life. I love Robert dearly and am deeply grateful to be loved and cherished by this tender, humble, godly man. But Robert Wolgemuth is no substitute for God, and as much as he might want to, he cannot meet the deepest needs of my heart. And this new season of marriage, sweet as it is, has brought new challenges as well as new opportunities.

Still, I am receiving these years as a gift and finding contentment and joy in this calling. And if God, in His wisdom and providence, ordains for one or both of us to be incapacitated or for me to be widowed at some point, I know that the spring of joy that Christ has been to me all these years will remain unchanged and will sustain me through those seasons of loss and grief.

In all this, I am relying on the same Truth that has sustained me through the years:

- The source of deepest happiness is not found in (or out of) any particular marital status. It is not found in any human relationship. True, lasting joy cannot be found in anything or anyone other than Christ Himself.

- Happiness is not found in having everything we think we want, but in choosing to be satisfied with what God has already provided.

- Those who insist on having their own way often end up with unnecessary heartache, while those who wait on the Lord, while not immune from heartache, always get His best.

- God has promised to give us everything we need and to conform us to the image of His Son. If He knows a husband (or a changed husband) would make it possible for a woman to be more like Jesus or to bring greater glory to Him, then He will provide what is needed, in His perfect way and time.

### 27. "It's my job to change my mate (or children or friends or . . .)."

*M*any of us women are born "fixers." If something is wrong, we've got to fix it. If some*one* is wrong, we've got to fix him or her. The instinct seems almost irresistible, especially when it comes to those who live under our own roof. But the mindset that it is our responsibility to change others invariably leads to disappointment and discord.

In the context of marriage, this thinking places a wife's focus on someone else's failures and needs—which she can do very little, if anything, about. Further, it takes her focus off of her own needs and her own walk with the Lord—which she *can* do something about.

As I've often heard my husband say, "You can't change your mate [or your office mate or your roommate]! The only person you can change is *you*!"

Years ago a friend shared with me something she was learning in her marriage—a Truth I have found important to remember in my own marriage: "I am not my husband's mother," she said, "and I am not his Holy Spirit." Simple enough to say, isn't it? But so easy to forget!

So does that mean that when we see sin or blind spots in our mate's life we are to say and do nothing? Not at all. Your husband needs your timely, respectful, kind input (as you need his). But when we're obsessed with trying to change our husband or correct what we perceive to be his faults and flaws, we're likely to end up frustrated and resentful toward him and perhaps even toward God. We may also limit God from doing what He wants to do in our spouse. I sometimes wonder how God might move in our mates' lives if we were willing to let Him take over the process.

What many women may not realize is that we have two powerful tools available to us that are far more effective than lecturing, nagging, or whining. The first is *a godly life*, which God often uses to create irresistible conviction and spiritual hunger in others (see 1 Peter 3:1–4).

The second tool is *prayer*. When we continually and critically point out the things we wish our husbands would change, they are likely to become defensive and resistant. But when we take our concerns to the Lord, we are appealing to a far higher power—to Someone who is far more effective than we are at helping him see his needs and motivating and enabling him to make needed changes.

Mike Neises has served with me on the *Revive Our Hearts* team for over twenty years. I've often heard him share the sweet story of how he and his wife came to know Jesus. They had been married for several years and had two children when Chris, sensing her need for spiritual guidance, turned to a Christian neighbor for help. This neighbor offered to do a couple's Bible study with Mike and Chris in their home. Mike acquiesced, knowing this was important to his wife but assuming he was immune to anything "religious."

It wasn't long before Chris became a follower of Christ. Mike quickly realized something was different in her life; he was intrigued, but something held him back from following her. At the time, he remembers,

Alcohol was my besetting sin. I worked hard to keep it separate from my family, but it was bankrupting me morally, emotionally, and physically.

Over the next several months, however, Chris quietly prayed for the Spirit to work in her husband's heart. Mike recalls:

Chris remained respectful of me and never pressed me. She never tried to be the Holy Spirit in my life. I know I would have resisted if she had started preaching at me. What struck me the most was the incredible patience and restraint she showed when it could have been easy for her to lecture, scold, or prod.

Finally, one evening "it all came crashing down." After playing racquetball, Mike stopped at a bar with a friend for "just one drink." Five hours later the bartender called his name to let him know he had a phone call. It was Chris. The Lord used her calm response in the midst of that crisis to open Mike's eyes and heart to the gospel.

I was ashamed and remorseful, and after I sobered up it was the wake-up call I needed, showing me that I had no control over this and that Christ was my only hope.

Immediately following that episode, the Lord completely took away Mike's desire for alcohol—he walked away from that lifestyle and never looked back. And within the next couple of months, he trusted in Christ and received assurance of his salvation.

As Mike and Chris have walked through many different seasons, Chris has continued to be a quiet, praying woman of God, trusting Him to lead and to work in both of their lives.

## WHEN GOD STEPS IN

Of course, the answer to prayer doesn't always come as quickly as it did in Chris' case. Some time ago a woman I didn't recognize approached me at a wedding reception and said, "You saved my marriage!" When I asked her to refresh my memory, she reminded me that we had met seventeen years earlier at a ministry event. At the time, she had shared with me her burden in relation to her husband's spiritual condition. "You told me back then," she said, "'It's not your responsibility to change your husband; that's God's responsibility. Tell your husband what's on your heart and then back off and let God do the rest.'" She continued, "For all these years, I have practiced that advice and have shared it with many other wives."

She went on to tell me what it had meant for her to wait on the Lord to change her husband. For sixteen long years she had prayed and waited, without seeing any evidence that God was hearing or answering her prayers. Though her husband professed to be a Christian, the lack of spiritual hunger or fruit in his life had made her question whether he had a relationship with the Lord at all.

Then, "unexplainably," after all those years, the Spirit turned on the light and brought about a dramatic change in that woman's husband. It was as though he had come out of a coma. All of a sudden he couldn't get enough of the Word. He even started keeping a notepad with him to record what God was saying to him through his study. She said, "Before this change I could hardly get him out of bed for breakfast. Now, he's going to a men's prayer meeting at six thirty every morning!" Recently, he had even talked about the possibility of selling his business so they could spend more time in some form of ministry. There is no human explanation for what happened to change this husband—except a faithful God and a faithful wife who persevered in prayer for her husband.

I love the example of Mary, the mother of Jesus, in this regard. An angel appeared and told her she was going to be the mother of the Messiah—an incredible experience. But you had to be there! When she told Joseph what had happened, initially he apparently did not believe her explanation. He hadn't seen any angel. Reason led him to conclude that she had been unfaithful to him.

There's no indication that Mary pressured Joseph to believe what she knew God had told her. Instead, she waited on God and gave Him the opportunity to communicate directly to her husband—which is exactly what happened. Once the angel appeared to Joseph, Joseph was quick to respond and believe. Mary knew how to keep things in her heart and ponder them (see Luke 2:19). She could afford to wait quietly because she knew the power of God and trusted Him to fulfill His plans for her life and her family.

To be clear, your godly life and prayers, no matter how faithful and earnest, do not guarantee that your husband will turn to the Lord or that he will repent of sinful choices and habits. But as you pray and trust the Lord for your marriage, I can guarantee that *something* will change. You will grow stronger and wiser. Your example may influence others and inspire them to trust God too. And you can experience supernatural peace as you steadfastly entrust yourself, your mate, and your marriage to Christ to do what only He can do.

## 28. *"My husband is supposed to serve me."*

*M*en don't do their fair share of the dirty work," some feminists complain. And statistics indicate that despite more than fifty years of feminism, married mothers still do more than three times as much cooking, cleaning, and laundry than married fathers do.[1]

Sheryl Sandberg, Facebook's second-highest ranking executive behind CEO Mark Zuckerberg, is determined to change all that. In 2015, Sandberg's Lean In organization enlisted NBA stars LeBron James, Stephen Curry, and some of the basketball league's other top players to convince men to do more work around the house. The players delivered the message in public service announcements aired during NBA games on major TV networks. Sandberg hoped to persuade men that they would be better off financially and emotionally if they took more responsibility for housework and child care while also backing equal rights for women at work. Her efforts were supported by some of America's largest corporations and banks.[2]

The commercials didn't mention the fact that men typically perform a multitude of other chores around the home, from taking out the trash to yard work, renovations, and general repairs. Nor did they explain that men work longer hours[3] and often contribute the major share of the family income. The NBA spots simply lectured men to take more responsibility for housework and child care—suggesting that it isn't fair for this responsibility to fall on the woman's shoulders more than it falls on the man's.

In Sandberg's socially engineered utopia, men and women should split work, financial, home, and child-care responsibilities equally—fifty-fifty. When it comes to roles and responsibilities, there ought to be no difference between the sexes.

Christian women are not unaffected by this blaring cultural message. The Christian community rightly challenges men to love their wives and children and to express that love through sacrifice and service. However, in the midst of this emphasis, we need to be careful that we don't swallow culture's ideas about gender and lose sight of the gender-specific roles God has given us to fulfill.

In Genesis 2:18 we find an important clue to our God-given purpose:

> Then the LORD God said, "It is not good that
> the man should be alone;
> I will make him a helper fit for him."

God created Eve to be a helper suited to Adam. The Hebrew phrase literally means "a helper matching him,"[4] or "a helper corresponding to him."[5]

Now, at first glance, God creating woman as a helper "for the man" might be taken to mean that the help the woman provides is all about making the man's life easier. She picks up his socks so he doesn't have to bother. She cooks his dinner and washes his clothes so he is free to do other things. She helps him like a plumber's assistant helps a plumber—by doing all the trivial and dirty work the plumber doesn't want to do.

But this idea is not indicated by the text. The word used for helper in this passage is *ezer*. An *ezer* is so much more than someone who folds the laundry and brews the coffee. Rather, it suggests someone who is an "indispensable partner."[6] It means "support" in the broadest sense possible. While it's a word used here to describe Eve's relationship to Adam, it's most often used in reference to the Lord's relationship to us. In passages like Psalms 33:20 and 72:12, God is our helper (*ezer*). We can't make it without Him!

In every season of life, whether married, single, or widowed, with or without biological children, we uniquely bear the image of God by offering indispensable help to others. How can it be an inferior calling for our husbands, children, friends, neighbors, and fellow believers to look at us and say, "I couldn't have done it without you"?

It's also important to understand what it is that woman was created to "help" man do. She was not made merely to help the man do whatever he wants to do. God created woman to cooperate and partner with man in making God known and bringing Him glory. The Lord said, "Bring my sons from afar and my daughters from the end of the earth . . . whom I created for my glory" (Isa. 43:6–7).

The idea that woman exists to make man's life easier by being his personal cook and maid simply isn't supported by Scripture. However, the Bible does teach that God created women with a distinct responsibility regarding the home. Scripture encourages young women to "manage their households" (1 Tim. 5:14). It praises the woman who "looks well to the ways [affairs] of her household" (Prov. 31:27). It casts in a negative light those women whose hearts are inclined away from the home—those whose "feet" are always running elsewhere (Prov. 7:11). And "working at home" is on the Bible's top-ten list of important things that older women need to teach the younger ones (Titus 2:4–5).

This does not imply that husbands and other members of the household cannot or should not contribute to caring for the home. But it does indicate that God wired women to be connected to home and relationships in a way men are not. (Just as the Lord wired men to be connected to work, financial provision, and protection in a way women are not.)[7]

One of the things that strikes me most about the "virtuous woman" of

Proverbs 31 is the fact that she is so utterly selfless, starting with her care for those in her own home. She nurtures her children, helps her husband, and makes sure their home is running smoothly and that everyone's needs are cared for. She notably also has interests outside of the home. She runs a successful small business and is involved in charitable work. She is a busy woman, to be sure! But those efforts are not in competition with or detached from her heart for her family and home. She does not neglect that calling in order to pursue another or to advance her own independent agenda in life. She serves the Lord by serving her family and others, in order that God might be glorified.

And lest you think this woman is on the losing end of the deal, take a fresh look at what the Bible says about her:

- She is well dressed (v. 22).

- She and her family have food to eat and enough to share with others (vv. 15, 20).

- She lives a well-ordered life; she is emotionally stable and free from fear about the future (vv. 21, 25).

- Her husband is crazy about her—he is faithful to her, he feels she is "one in a million" and tells her so, and he brags about her to his friends (vv. 11, 28–29, 31).

- Her children honor and praise her (v. 28).

How did she get all those "benefits"? Not by insisting that her husband roll up his sleeves and help with the household chores (although there's certainly nothing wrong with men doing so), but by choosing the path of servanthood.

## A JOYFUL SERVANT

Speaking of children honoring their moms . . . My desire to be a helper suitable to my husband has been greatly influenced by the example of my mother. Nancy DeMoss (the first—I am named after her) is an exceptionally gifted woman. She put every one of those gifts to good use in the unique partnership she and my dad shared for twenty-two years, growing a large family and building a successful business and a fruitful ministry together. She gave up a promising career as a vocalist when she married my dad and they started a family. But she never thought of this as a sacrifice.

Amid the climate of the 1960s, when women were encouraged to pursue independence, careers, and self-realization, my mother modeled a different kind of thinking—in which a woman's heart and calling and the heart and calling of her husband were knit together as one for the purpose of serving and glorifying Christ. She loved being her husband's *ezer*—his "indispensable partner." She masterfully managed the domestic affairs of an active household and extended endless hospitality. She offered wisdom and added creativity and beauty to every undertaking they embarked on.

This "helper" role was not something my dad demanded of my mother. She truly adored him and found delight in being his partner and encourager. And like the virtuous wife in Proverbs 31, my mother was far from downtrodden. To the contrary, my father cherished and esteemed her as a full partner; he cheered as her God-given abilities were utilized in the service of Christ and His kingdom.

What it looks like for a woman to be an *ezer* to her husband will vary from couple to couple. It does not look exactly the same in my marriage as it did in my parents' marriage. There will also be differences from season to season. But this reality doesn't take away from the beauty and importance of the helper role as the Bible has established it or the spiritual Truth that undergirds it—the call to loving service in all we do.

The Truth is: we are never more like Jesus than when we are serving. In the kingdom of God, true greatness is demonstrated by a person's willingness to set aside his or her personal interests, put others first, and serve (Mark 9:33–35).

Without question, men are called to love their wives as Christ loved the church, which is expressed in the willingness to serve and to lay down their lives for their wives, even as Christ did for His bride. My precious husband sets a mighty high bar when it comes to serving me and helping out around our home in practical ways. I consider myself greatly blessed and could not be more grateful! The fact is, we each make it our goal to "outserve" the other.

But if you and I focus on what we "deserve," on our "rights," or on what our spouses "ought" to do for us, we will become vulnerable to hurt and resentment when our expectations are not met. Blessing and joy are the fruit of seeking to be a giver rather than a taker, of looking for ways to fulfill our God-given responsibility to come alongside our husbands and to bless and serve them, our families, and others.

Unlike Sandberg's model, the Bible doesn't present marriage as a fifty-fifty, you-do-your-fair-share-and-I'll-do-mine proposition. The pattern God has given us is radical. He expects that husband and wife will *both* be 100 percent all-in to do what He asks of them. So yes, the Bible calls husbands to serve their wives selflessly and wholeheartedly. But no, it's not our responsibility to demand that they do. Our responsibility, before God, is to emulate Jesus and joyfully *be* a servant.

One hundred percent.

All in.

## 29. *"If I submit to my husband, I'll be miserable."*

*S*ome time ago, a major Protestant denomination ignited a firestorm in the evangelical world when it adopted a statement of biblical beliefs regarding marriage and family that included this sentence:

> A wife is to submit herself graciously to the servant leadership of her husband even as the church willingly submits to the headship of Christ.[8]

When I first started ministering to women four decades ago, this statement would not have been likely to set off alarms in your average women's Bible study or conference. But today such thinking, no matter how carefully worded, is distasteful, if not downright repugnant, to many in the church. Promoting submission in marriage is considered tantamount to advocating for slavery or domestic abuse. An increasing number of Christian bloggers and authors argue that this teaching is not biblically defensible and that it sanctions and fuels the abuse of women. (It doesn't help that there are men claiming to be Christians who twist the Scripture and use it to justify treating their wives, daughters, and other women in cruel, sinful ways.)

The concept of submission, particularly in marriage, does not go over well in our day. But this struggle is not a new one. In fact, submission was the essence of the issue Eve faced in the Garden of Eden. At the heart of the Serpent's approach to Eve was this challenge: Does God have the right to rule over you? You can run your own life; you don't have to submit to anyone else's authority.

The Serpent convinced Eve that if she submitted to God's direction, she would be miserable and would miss out on something good or necessary. From that day to this, Satan has done a masterful job of taking a beautiful, holy, and powerful Truth and making it look ugly, frightening, and undesirable.

At the core of fallen human nature is a problem with authority. We simply don't want anyone telling us what to do. We want to run our own lives and make our own decisions. And we assume that being subject to authority will automatically make us miserable.

When it comes to a wife's submission to her husband, I believe much of the resistance is due to some basic misconceptions about what is actually meant or implied by submission.

## LIES ABOUT SUBMISSION

1. *"The wife is inferior to her husband."* There are those who insist that submission inherently implies inferiority. But the Scripture affirms just the opposite—that both the man and the woman are created in the image of God, both have equal value before God, and both are privileged to be subjects of His redeeming grace through repentance and faith (Gen. 1:27; Gal. 3:28; 1 Peter 3:7).

**2.** *"The principle of submission gives husbands the right to be harsh or dictatorial with their wives."* To the contrary, husbands are commanded to love their wives as they love themselves, in the same selfless, sacrificing, serving way that the Lord Jesus loved His bride—the church—and laid down His life for her (Eph. 5:25–29).

**3.** *"A submissive wife can't provide input or express her opinions to her husband."* God created the woman to be a "helper suitable" to her husband. That means he *needs* her help. He needs the wisdom and insight she is able to bring to various situations. However, once a wife has graciously expressed her view on a matter, once she has shared her concern and appealed to her husband to reconsider a particular direction, at the end of the day, she must be willing to back off, accept her husband's decision (assuming it does not require her to sin), and trust God with the consequences.

**4.** *"The husband is always right."* The apostle Peter specifically addresses women whose husbands "do not believe the word." The husband may be unsaved or he may be disobedient to God in some area(s) of his life. According to 1 Peter 3:1–2, the most effective means of influencing such a husband is not through tearful pleading, irresistible logic, or persistent reminders, but through the power of a submissive and holy life.

## TELLING THE GOSPEL STORY

Submission doesn't come naturally to me. (News alert: it doesn't come naturally to anyone.) I am a strong woman with strong views about, well, pretty much everything. And for fifty-seven years of my life, I was pretty much responsible for myself.

Sure, as a child, I had been under the authority of my parents. As a college student I had learned an important lesson about submission when I got pulled over (twice) for speeding on the Pasadena Freeway. As an adult, I had learned to respect and submit to bosses. And of course I had long been under the authority of God. But submission to other people wasn't something I had a lot of practice in from day to day.

On November 14, 2015, however, at the College Church in Wheaton,

Illinois, I looked up into the eyes of a man I had been dating for just nine months and spoke these words:

*In the presence of God and these witnesses . . . I promise to respect you, to reverence you, and to submit to you in everything as my earthly head.*

Here I was, (voluntarily) entering into a permanent, covenant relationship with a man, vowing before God to respect, reverence, and submit to him in everything!

What was I thinking?

Did I think we would agree on everything? That Robert's judgment and decisions would always be right? Not at all.

In making that vow, was I asking to be relegated to an inferior position or agreeing to a life sentence in a marital penitentiary? Not by a long shot.

You see, my vows were a response to the promises Robert had made to me just moments earlier:

*I, Robert, take you, Nancy, to be my wife. . . . I promise to love you and to shepherd you, as Christ loves and shepherds His church; to give myself for you, as He has laid down His life for us.*

Beginning six months earlier, when Robert knelt at a sofa in my living room, told me he loved me, and asked me to marry him, and then as we exchanged our vows at the altar, he was displaying one part of the mystery we read about in Ephesians 5.

Marriage between a husband and a wife, says Paul, tells a story: "It refers to Christ and the church" (v. 32). When a man initiates a covenant relationship with a woman, when he loves and sacrifices himself for her, he is painting a picture of the way Christ initiates a relationship with His bride and loves and lays down His life for her.

But that is just one part of the mystery that Christian marriage reveals. When a woman gratefully says yes to her suitor's initiative, when she respects, reverences, and submits herself to him, she is telling the story of the way the church is to respond to her heavenly Bridegroom.

On our wedding day, when I vowed to respect, reverence, and submit to Robert "in everything as my earthly head," I continued, *"as the church respects, reverences, and submits to Christ, her eternal Head."*

In loving and leading me well, Robert shows one part of this mystery.

In being responsive to his initiative and leadership, I get to display the other part.

And together, we showcase the great redemptive story.

## If You Are Being Abused

The following is a short segment from a fuller treatment of submission in my book *Adorned:*[9]

A wife's submission never gives license to her husband to abuse her. Never. Whenever women are instructed in Scripture to submit to their husbands, there is a corresponding command for husbands to love and cherish their wives. There is no possible justification for a husband to abuse his wife, whether in overtly physical or verbal ways or in more "respectable" types of manipulation and intimidation—what one pastor calls "polite abuses."[10]

If you are being abused (or suspect you are being abused), you must get help. There is nothing in the biblical teaching on submission that permits such treatment. If you (or your children) are being physically harmed or threatened, you should get to a safe place and contact both civil and spiritual authorities for protection.

Wherever people abuse the order God has established for any sphere, the problem does not stem from flaws in God's plan, but from humanity's sinful distortions of it. Therefore, the solution to problems that arise when this principle is applied in marriage is not to throw submission out with the bathwater, but rather to align our understanding and practice with what Scripture really says. Because when the system is working according to God's design, blessings flow to us from heaven, revealing to us, in us, and through us the beauty of His character and ways.

## THE LIBERATING TRUTH ABOUT SUBMISSION

I have discovered that the fundamental issue in relation to submission really comes down to our willingness to trust God and place ourselves under *His* authority. When we are willing to submit to Him, it will generally not be nearly so difficult or threatening to submit to the human authorities He has placed in our lives.

Proverbs 21:1 assures us that "The king's heart is a stream of water in the hand of the LORD; he turns it wherever he will." Our willingness to place ourselves under God-ordained authority is an evidence of how big we believe God really is.

The Truth is that a higher authority controls every human authority. So biblical submission places us in a position of being covered and protected by our wise, loving, all-powerful heavenly Father, who controls the "heart of the king."

The question is, do we really believe God is bigger than any human authority? Do we believe He is big enough to change that authority's heart if necessary? Do we believe He knows what is best for us, and are we willing to trust Him to fulfill His perfect, eternal purposes for our lives?

According to 1 Peter 3:1–2, a wife's submission to her husband makes room for God to work in his heart and to bring him to obedience. Peter goes on to say that a submissive heart attitude produces in a woman the most radiant and lasting kind of beauty:

> Let your adorning be the hidden person of the heart
> with the imperishable beauty of a gentle and quiet spirit,
> which in God's sight is very precious.
> For this is how the holy women who hoped in God used to adorn
> themselves, by submitting to their own husbands, as Sarah obeyed
> Abraham, calling him lord. And you are her children, if you do
> good and do not fear anything that is frightening.
>
> —1 Peter 3:4–6

That last line may seem hard to imagine. You'd think that a woman who submits to her husband could feel fearful and vulnerable. But Peter says she does not have to "fear anything that is frightening." That's because her hope is not in her husband, but in God. She has entrusted herself to the One who has ultimate control of her husband and of her situation and is always looking out for her best interests.

In her book *The True Woman,* my friend Susan Hunt sums up the heart behind submission:

> I cannot give logical arguments for submission. It defies logic that Jesus would release all the glories of heaven so He could give *us* the glory of heaven. Submission is not about logic; it is about love.
>
> Jesus loved us so much that He voluntarily submitted to death on a cross. His command is that wives are to submit to their husbands. It is a gift that we voluntarily give to the man we have vowed to love in obedience to the Savior we love. . . .
>
> God said that man needs a helper. The true woman celebrates this calling and becomes affirming rather than adversarial, compassionate rather than controlling, a partner rather than a protagonist. She becomes substantively rather than superficially submissive.
>
> The true woman is not afraid to place herself in a position of submission. She does not have to grasp; she does not have to control. Her fear dissolves in the light of God's covenant promise to be her God and to live within her. Submission is simply a demonstration of her confidence in the sovereign power of the Lord God. Submission is a reflection of her redemption.[11]

## 30. *"If my husband is passive, I've got to take the initiative, or nothing will get done."*

When I asked women which of the lies in this book they had believed, this lie ranked number three. I know of few subjects that are a greater source of frustration to women than passive men.

Once again, this is not a new struggle. As is true of so many issues, it all goes back to the Garden of Eden:

> When the woman saw that the tree was good for food . . .
> she took of its fruit and ate,
> and she also gave some to her husband who was with her,
> and he ate.
>
> —Genesis 3:6

This passage evokes a troubling picture in my mind. The couple is together in the garden. The Serpent approaches them, ignores the man, and strikes up a conversation with the woman. "Did God actually say, 'You shall not eat of any tree in the garden'?" (Gen. 3:1), he says.

At this point, notice what the woman does not do. She does not acknowledge her husband, "who was with her" (v. 6). She does not say to the Serpent, "I'd like for you to meet my husband." She does not turn to her husband and ask, "Honey, how do you think we should respond?" or "Adam, why don't you tell him what God said to you." She carries on the entire conversation with the Serpent as if her husband weren't there.

As far as we know, she doesn't consult with her husband on the matter; she doesn't ask his input or direction. She simply acts: "She took of its fruit and ate" (v. 6).

And what is Adam doing this whole time? He is doing what some women tell me their husbands do much of the time: *nothing*. He doesn't get involved—except to eat some fruit himself when his wife gives it to him. And so we have the first role reversal.

God created the man first and gave him the responsibility to *lead and feed* those under his care. The woman, created from the man, was made to be a receiver, to respond to the initiative of her husband. Even the physiological differences between men and women reflect these basic distinctions.

But who is leading and feeding in this account? Not the man, but the woman. And who is responding? Not the woman, but the man. And that reversal of their created roles became the pattern for the way fallen men and women often relate to each other.

On the one hand, we as women may be tempted to take the reins.[12] However, we also want our men to lead—to take action—and we can become resentful when they fail to do so.

As was true with Adam and Eve in the garden, it's reflexive to blame the other party for this problem. We're quick to fault men for being passive and to insist that if they weren't so inactive—if they would just do something—we wouldn't feel compelled to take over.

Over the years, I've heard women express frustration over how their husbands' passivity has "forced" them to take charge in a variety of realms—from major financial matters or parenting decisions to more mundane, daily issues.

Being something of an activist myself, I know what it is to be frustrated by apparent passivity on the part of some men. I have sat in numerous meetings over the years, biting my tongue to keep from jumping in and taking charge when I didn't feel the men in the room were being decisive enough, fast enough. I've been in prayer meetings when it seemed as if the men were content to leave all the praying to the women.

But I can't help but wonder to what extent we may have demotivated and emasculated the men around us by our quickness to take the reins rather than giving space and time for the Lord to move them to action. We may accomplish our desired goal in the moment, while in the process stripping men of the motivation and courage to provide godly, wise leadership.

I've seen this in a more personal way as a wife. My DH (*dear husband*) is far from passive. But he tends to do life at a more measured (and, I might add, more sustainable) pace than I do. I am learning the value of being "quick to hear" and "slow to speak" (James 1:19) in our relationship. Robert welcomes my ideas and input on just about everything (possible exception: his tools and the garage décor). But if I'm always quick to the draw, hasty to speak and to act, without giving him a chance to step up or speak up, I can wear him out and leave him in my wake.

Further, when men do take action, instead of giving them encouragement and affirmation, we may find ourselves telling them how they could have done it differently or better. Again, I can testify to this in my own marriage. I am a born editor. Much of my work requires me to have an eagle eye for the tiniest mistakes. My husband greatly admires my aptitude in this regard. But let's just say that skill doesn't bless him when I apply it to him! Robert needs to know that I'm cheering for him (as he does for me) and that I notice and appreciate his efforts to please me rather than pointing out the one thing he may have forgotten or that didn't get done exactly the way I thought it should.

I remember hearing one husband talk about how when he and his wife were first married, he led her in a time of prayer. When they were finished, she began to criticize the way he had prayed. Not surprisingly, this husband said years later, "I decided that was the last time I would pray with her." He couldn't handle the rejection. Not until years into their marriage, when God did a fresh work of grace in his heart, did he get the courage to risk stepping out again to lead his wife.

The fact is, more often than not, if the woman is going to take charge, the man is going to stand by and let her. We simply can't have our cake and eat it too. We can't insist on running the show and then expect men to be proactive, take initiative, and be "spiritual leaders."

At times I have asked women who are discouraged by the inactivity of their husbands, "What's the worst that could happen if you didn't quickly jump in to handle the situation?" Yes, some things might fall through the cracks. There might be some inconvenience or discomfort involved. But is it possible that the fallout may be what it takes to motivate your husband to step up to the plate? Do you trust the Lord enough to be willing to let your husband fail in some way, if necessary, and to leave the consequences in the hands of our unfailingly loving and sovereign God?

## WAITING FOR HIM TO ACT

Sarah is lifted up in the Bible as an example of a woman who reverenced and obeyed her husband. However, on at least one occasion, when God did not act as quickly as she felt He should, she fell into the trap of trying to handle matters on her own. Ten years earlier, God had promised her husband, Abraham, that he would have many descendants and that they would become a great nation. Now she was seventy-six years old and still childless. Impatient with waiting, she decided someone had to do something, so she put pressure on her husband to take action:

> She had a female Egyptian servant whose name was Hagar.
> And Sarai said to Abram [later called Sarah and Abraham],
> "Behold now, the LORD has prevented me from bearing children.
> Go in to my servant; it may be that I shall obtain children by her."
> And Abram listened to the voice of Sarai.
>
> —Genesis 16:1–2

What Sarah convinced Abraham to do was a common practice of the day. It was widely accepted that barren women could get a child by using a servant as a kind of substitute womb. And at first, Sarah's plan seemed to work splendidly—Hagar quickly conceived and bore a child. But it didn't take long for the situation to turn sour. The relationship between the childless wife and the expectant servant grew increasingly troubled, leading Sarah to go back to Abraham and say, "*You* are responsible for the wrong I am suffering" (Gen. 16:5 NIV).

Thirteen years later, when Sarah was ninety years old, God supernaturally intervened to give Abraham and his wife a child of their own. Isaac would bring great blessing to the elderly couple and to every future generation yet to be born. But Ishmael, the son born of Abraham and Hagar's union, became a lifelong source of conflict and grief. How many times must Sarah have looked back in regret and said to herself, "Why did I have to take control of the situation? Why didn't I wait on the Lord?"

So many women I know can relate to Sarah's experience. We may be able to achieve some immediate results by taking matters into our own hands. But we may also end up with a bitter taste in our mouth, even resenting and blaming those we feel pushed us into taking action.

Here's some advice from the psalms that I find myself turning to again and again when I'm feeling agitated about the behavior (or lack of initiative) of others:

> Fret not yourself...
> Trust in the LORD, and do good....
> Commit your way to the LORD;
> trust in him, and he will act....
> Be still before the LORD and wait patiently for him....
> The meek shall inherit the land
> and delight themselves in abundant peace.
>
> —Psalm 37:1–11

No, it's not easy to sit on your hands and bite your tongue when you see that something needs doing and no one, including your husband, seems to notice or be willing to step up to the plate. But the words of the psalmist here can relieve frustration in the moment and prevent regret down the road.

Don't fret—choose not to become agitated, hot, or angry. Trust in the Lord—who is always trustworthy. While you're waiting, look for opportunities to do good. Commit your way to God—who is always working and who alone knows what needs to happen.

And above all, be still. Wait patiently for God to act.

At the proper time, in His perfect way, He will.

## 31. *"There's no hope for my marriage."*

Over the years, I've walked with many women through some terribly difficult seasons in their marriage. The details and the contributing factors vary, but the pain has felt unbearable at times for each of these women. Many have come to a place where it seemed there was no hope for reconciliation or restoration.

You (or someone you love) may be at that point today.

When Robert and I were dating, it seemed that people were forever giving us a knowing look and saying (as if warning or consoling us or both), "Marriage is hard!" This really bothered me. On more than one occasion, I said to Robert, "Why all this counsel of despair? Why aren't people telling us how wonderful a godly marriage is?"

As this book is being released, we've been married for two and a half years. God could not have chosen a more perfect man for me, and no man could treat his wife more tenderly and thoughtfully than Robert treats me. But I now find myself telling couples considering marriage, "Marriage (between two people who love Christ and each other) is wonderful. And . . . marriage is a lot of work." Hard work. If both spouses don't work hard at it, the marriage may well become just plain hard.

Every married couple is "incompatible"—if for no other reason than that men and women are vastly different, not to mention that every marriage involves two people who are naturally inclined to look out for themselves. Any two people living under the same roof are going to be insensitive at times. They are going to hurt each other. There is going to be miscommunication and misunderstanding. They are going to fail to meet each other's needs. The only place where people get married and "live happily ever after" is in fairy tales. Never, since Genesis 3, has there been such a thing as an easy or pain-free marriage.

The Enemy knows this, of course, and actively seeks to exploit it. No sooner does a couple say "I do" than the Serpent rears its ugly head. Before the rice has been cleaned up from the send-off, the Enemy is looking for opportunities to plant seeds of division in the hearts of the newlyweds. He knows that every time he succeeds in tearing apart a Christian marriage, this earthly picture of divine redemption is tarnished, and the world is given a distorted view of the character of God. No marriage is immune to this attempt to sabotage a good and holy gift. Not yours. Not mine.

And how does the Enemy do his evil, divisive work? You know the answer by now. He lies! Deception is one of his most effective tools. But this deception doesn't usually start with full-blown falsehoods. Most of those would be quickly rejected. It starts subtly, with partial truths mixed with partial deception, with thoughts that *seem* to be true and emotions that *feel* true.

It can start with a simple offense or misunderstanding. Say your brand-new husband

- forgets the two-year anniversary of the day you first met

- shows up an hour late for a date and forgets to call

- agrees for the two of you to work in the preschool department at church without talking with you first

- tells his parents you'll be there for Christmas when you were hoping to spend Christmas with *your* parents

- or commits any one of a thousand other offenses. (Remind me sometime to tell you about Robert and me shopping for Christmas lights at Pier One a few weeks into our married life.)

And how do you respond? To nurse the offense rather than assuming the best, communicating honestly and graciously, and choosing to forgive and let it go is to become vulnerable to believing things that aren't true, things that lodge themselves in your mind and heart. Over time these can intensify and escalate, until you're thinking:

- He's always inconsiderate.

- He doesn't care that he hurt me.

- He'll never be any different.

- _____ (some other man at work or at church) is so much more thoughtful and considerate; he doesn't treat his wife that way.

- I'd be happier if I were married to _____ (the other man).

- Sometimes two people just can't make a marriage work—apparently, we weren't meant for each other.

- I'd be better off getting a divorce than staying in this miserable marriage.

- I don't have any alternative. There's just no way I can stay married to him.

It doesn't happen all at once, of course. But years of compounded hurt and falling prey to deception can so easily lead to hardness of heart and giving up—which causes still more hurt and deception. It's a vicious cycle that can lead someone like "Keisha" to conclude:

*I have a right to be happy. My life is at least half over, and I deserve to spend the rest of it in wedded bliss with someone who will love and cherish me—obviously not my husband.*

Humanly speaking, that response is totally understandable. No doubt a ton of hurts have piled up in the heart of a woman who has come to this point. She feels hopeless and has lost the will to continue working toward the restoration of her marriage. But she is also deceived. Chances are the Enemy's lies, aided by her only human selfishness, have become deeply entrenched in her thinking. She desperately needs Truth to stabilize and anchor her heart.

How does she access that Truth? It can begin by questioning her own assumptions. Here are some questions it might be helpful for her to ask—and answer honestly—in the midst of her frustration and pain:

- Have I come to believe that the problems in my marriage are totally (or mostly) my husband's fault?

- Am I being honest and humble about how my responses or spirit could have contributed to the breach in our relationship?

- Do I see myself as a sinner, as much in need of God's grace as my husband is?

- Does my focus revolve mostly around myself—my happiness and my hurts?

- Am I more interested in getting our problems solved and my needs met than in the process of restoration and sanctification—in my life, my husband's life, and our marriage?

- Am I willing for God to use me as an instrument of grace in my husband's life?

- Have I left God out of the picture? Do I believe He has good and holy purposes for me, for my husband, and for our marriage?

- Do I believe that the difficulties in our marriage (including my husband's flaws) could contribute toward those purposes?

- Do I believe that God is able to transform this mess into something of beauty and worth, as a testimony of His power?

- In wanting out of this marriage, am I elevating my personal happiness above what God has to say about the permanence of marriage vows and the seriousness of breaking those vows?

The next step after asking questions is to look for answers—the right answers. The cycle of pain and deception will remain unbroken unless someone in the marriage has the courage to counter Satan's lies about marriage with the Truth as God has revealed it in His Word:

- There is no marriage God cannot heal. There is no person God cannot change.

- The ultimate purpose of marriage is to glorify God and reflect His redeeming, covenant love.

- Our mate's weaknesses can become a tool in God's hand to help conform us to the image of Christ.

- True love—God's love—is unconditional and never fails. We cannot love a sinful human being that way on our own, but God can love anyone through us if we are willing to let Him. Love is not a feeling; it is a commitment to act in the best interests of another. By God's grace we can choose to love anyone, even if we do not have warm feelings toward that person.

- God is a covenant-keeping God. He kept His promises to the nation of Israel even when they were spiritually adulterous and pursued other lovers (see Jer. 11:10; Ezek. 20:16; Hosea 2:13). Jesus is faithful to His bride—the church—even when we are unfaithful to Him. Marriage is intended to be a picture of the covenant-keeping love of God and the redemptive relationship between Christ and His people.

- As Christ's suffering was the means by which we were healed (1 Peter 2:24–25), so your faithfulness and willingness to extend sacrificial love to your mate may be the means of his restoration (1 Cor. 7:12–14).

- God's grace is sufficient to enable you to be faithful to your mate and to love and forgive without limit.

- Regardless of what you may go through in your marriage or what your mate may do to you, God will never forsake you. He will always be with you.

- The rewards of faithfulness in this life may not be fully experienced until eternity. But every moment of faithfulness will be rewarded, and it will be worth the wait!

Years ago, a woman handed me a piece of paper after hearing me speak at a conference. The handwriting at the top read:

Forgiveness is the only way to receive God's best!

There followed a series of simple sentences that outlined the touching story of this woman's journey from deception to the truth that set her free:

- Many years ago, my husband wronged me.
- I filed for divorce.
- I received a note from a friend whose wife had died. His note said simply, "Humble yourself."
- I did so—unhappily, unwillingly, at first.

- The more I humbled myself and sought to love my husband, the more he became a wonderful man of God.

- I became proud to be his wife. I actually enjoyed it! (A lot.)

- One Christmas Eve, we held each other in amazement. God had restored all aspects of our marriage beyond what we ever dreamed.

- On December 26 we prayed together and embraced. I kissed him goodbye. One hour later he was dead.

- As hard as it is to live without him, God gave me a gift of no regret.

- I would say to a married woman: humble yourself. Give your husband room and time to be God's man. It takes time and sacrifice, but the blessing is amazing!

The Enemy does his best to make a mess out of marriage. He aims to wound hearts, turn husbands and wives against each other, convince them their situation is impossible, and leave them feeling hopelessly trapped. His lies have resulted in countless fractured lives and homes. But Christ came to bring hope, to give beauty for ashes (Isa. 61:3 NIV), and to reconcile all things to Himself. His Truth has power to redeem, restore, and renew your heart, regardless of what choices your mate may make. As you embrace the Truth, even in the midst of hardship, you will be sustained by His covenant-keeping love, and your life will reflect His faithfulness in a world of broken relationships and promises.

| THE LIE | 26. I have to have a husband to be happy. |
|---|---|
| THE TRUTH | • Being married (or not married) does not guarantee happiness.<br>James 1:16–17<br><br>• There is no person who can meet my deepest needs. No one and nothing can make me truly happy apart from God.<br>Psalms 62:5; 118:8–9; Jeremiah 17:5–7<br><br>• God has promised to provide everything I need. If He will receive more glory by my being married, then He will provide a husband for me.<br>1 Chronicles 29:11–12; Job 42:1–2; Proverbs 16:9; 1 Corinthians 7:25–38<br><br>• Those who wait on the Lord always get His best. Those who insist on getting what they want often end up with heartache.<br>Psalms 37:4; 106:15; Jeremiah 17:5–8 |

| THE LIE | 27. It's my job to change my mate. |
|---|---|
| THE TRUTH | • A godly life and prayer are a wife's two greatest means of influencing her husband's life.<br>James 5:16; 1 Peter 3:1–4 |

| THE LIE | 28. My husband is supposed to serve me. |
|---|---|
| THE TRUTH | • If I expect to be served, I will often be disappointed. If I seek to serve others without expecting anything in return, I will never be disappointed.<br>Proverbs 31:10–31; Mark 10:42–45<br><br>• A wife has a distinctive calling to be a "helper"—an "indispensable partner"—to her husband.<br>Genesis 2:18<br><br>• We are never more like Jesus than when we are serving others.<br>John 13:5 |
| THE LIE | 29. If I submit to my husband, I'll be miserable. |
| THE TRUTH | • Through submission, a wife has the privilege of painting a picture of the church's submission to Christ.<br>Ephesians 5:21–22<br><br>• Through submission, a wife entrusts herself to the One who has ultimate control of her husband and of her situation and is always looking out for her best interests.<br>Proverbs 21:1<br><br>• A wife's respectful, submissive spirit can be a powerful means of influencing a husband who is disobedient to God.<br>1 Peter 3:3–6 |

| | |
|---|---|
| **THE LIE** | **30. If my husband is passive, I've got to take the initiative, or nothing will get done.** |
| **THE TRUTH** | • If a woman jumps in to take the reins, rather than waiting on God to move her husband, her husband is likely to be less motivated to fulfill his God-given responsibility.<br>Genesis 16:1–2; Psalm 27:14 |
| **THE LIE** | **31. There's no hope for my marriage.** |
| **THE TRUTH** | • Marriage is a lifelong covenant that is intended to reflect the covenant-keeping heart of God.<br>Genesis 2:18–24; Ecclesiastes 5:4–6; Malachi 2:13–16; Mark 10:2-12<br><br>• There is no marriage God cannot heal. There is no person God cannot change.<br>Matthew 5:44; 18:21–22; Mark 11:25<br><br>• God uses the rough edges of each partner in a marriage to conform the other to the image of Christ.<br>Ephesians 5:24-27<br><br>• God's grace is sufficient to enable a woman to be faithful to her husband and to persevere in extending Christlike love and forgiveness.<br>2 Corinthians 12:9 |

# CHAPTER EIGHT

# LIES WOMEN BELIEVE...
## ABOUT *Children*

*Adam has been talking about having another child. I'm not so sure about the idea. I love our sons more than anything else in the world. But being a mother is hard work! I can't imagine how Adam thinks we could handle another one.*

*There's been a lot of tension between the boys recently. Cain never seems to feel that he measures up to his younger brother. It's like he's got something to prove. His attitude has gone from bad to worse. He has been unusually withdrawn and at times becomes sullen and depressed. He just won't communicate. I keep trying to affirm him, but nothing I say seems to help. He used to be so close to God, but now he says he's not sure he even believes in God.*

*His dad gets pretty frustrated with him at times. They just don't seem to be able to relate. Sometimes I think Adam is too hard on him. I remind him that there was a time when we experienced some of these kinds of struggles ourselves.*

*I wonder how all this will affect Abel. I feel so helpless as a mother. I've never had anyone to show me how this is done. I keep wondering what more I could/ should be doing to do to make sure my boys turn out all right. Would things be different if I were a better mom?*

My longtime friend **Mary Kassian** was a great help in researching and revising this chapter—including writing the content for Lies #35 and #36. I think you'll be encouraged by her perspective as someone who has been there as a mom. Mary has coauthored two books with me: *True Woman 101: Divine Design* and *True Woman 201: Interior Design*.[1] You can find out more about Mary and her ministry at GirlsGoneWise.com.

—*Nancy*

Because the mother-child relationship is the most sensitive and tender of human relationships, many women find themselves particularly vulnerable to deception in this sphere. As in every other area, Satan has a vast arsenal of lies that he uses to deceive a woman in relation to her reproductive capacity, her children, and her role as a mother.

Satan's intent in promoting these lies is not only to place mothers in bondage, but also to pass his deception down to the next generation, so they will never know the Truth or experience its liberating power.

In this chapter, I've chosen to focus on several subtle lies and half-truths that have become widely accepted in our contemporary Christian culture. These faulty ways of thinking have created costly consequences in our Christian homes—consequences that will be even further magnified in future generations if we do not recognize and reject the lies and replace them with the Truth.

### 32. *"I have the right to control my reproductive choices."*

When would you like to have a child?" asks a woman's doctor. "What would you like to do between now and then? How often do you want to have your period?" Based on her answers, the doctor recommends contraceptive methods that will produce her desired result.

Prior to the 1900s, the idea that a woman of childbearing age could have sexual intercourse with little to no chance of becoming pregnant was unfathomable. In the early part of that century, though, the invention of latex rubber provided a moderately reliable means to prevent pregnancy—latex condoms.

Then a woman named Margaret Sanger (1879–1966) appeared on the scene.

When I was in my late teens, I happened onto a made-for-TV movie about this woman who was the founder of the American reproductive rights movement. I've searched and not been able to locate it since. But it made an indelible impression on my mind and led me to do further research.

In 1914, Sanger published the first issue of her feminist publication, *The Woman Rebel*—a monthly newsletter with the byline, "No Gods, No Masters." She also distributed one hundred thousand copies of her pamphlet "Family Limitation." Two years later she opened the first birth-control clinic in the U.S.

Sanger's writings spelled out her core beliefs—among them:

> No woman can call herself free who does not own and control her body. No woman can call herself free until she can choose consciously whether she will or will not be a mother.[2]

She advocated using a combination of birth control (a term she coined), forced sterilization, and segregation to "improve" society by keeping "unfit" people from reproducing. Her definition of "unfit" included people who were disabled, poor, sick, or "feeble-minded" (people with a low IQ).

In 1950, Sanger's Planned Parenthood Federation (originally called the American Birth Control League) started funding research into the development of oral contraceptives. Her desire was to develop a highly reliable method of birth control that would put an end to "the wickedness of creating large families"—particularly by the less desirable segments of society.[3]

Ten years later, the FDA approved the use of the first birth control pill. Planned Parenthood lauded the freedom it gave women. For the first time in the history of mankind, sex could be separated from its reproductive consequences. It comes as no surprise that the Pill precipitated the sexual revolution and the "women's lib"/feminist movement that went with it.

It would be hard to overstate the far-reaching, lasting effects of Margaret Sanger's life and influence. Our culture has embraced wholesale the idea promoted by Sanger and Planned Parenthood—that controlling our fertility is a basic human right. It tells women:

- You have the right to control your body.

- You have the right to decide when or whether to have a child.

- Every child should be wanted and loved. [Unwanted/unloved children shouldn't be born.]

- You are entitled to sexual pleasure and fulfillment [without the necessity of marriage or the fear of pregnancy].[4]

Christian women are not unaffected by these popular ideas. They've seeped into our minds like an IV drip into the vein of an unconscious patient. That's why it's important for us to go to the Word of God. And what does the Bible teach about children and reproduction?

- Children are a blessing from God and a fulfillment of His command to multiply and fill the earth (Gen. 1:28).

- Children are God's gift to us—"a heritage from the LORD, the fruit of the womb a reward" (Ps. 127:3).

- Children give purpose, meaning, and joy to our lives (Ps. 127:4–5; Prov. 23:24).

- Children come from the Lord (Heb. 2:13; Isa. 8:18).

- God expects Christian parents to raise children in the discipline and instruction of the Lord (Gen. 18:19; Eph. 6:4).

What's more, childbearing is an earthly picture of a heavenly reality. As the physical union of a husband and wife produces physical children, so the spiritual union of Christ and the church produces spiritual children (John 1:12; Gal. 4:19).

The Bible indicates that it is the Lord who opens and shuts the womb (Gen. 20:18; 29:31; 30:22). There are times when God, for reasons unknown, deliberately keeps someone from having a child, no matter how desperately she wants one. Hannah longed for a child, but the Lord "closed her womb" until such time as He saw fit for her to conceive Samuel (1 Sam. 1:1–2:21). Sarah, too, was forced to wait many years (until she was ninety!) before God blessed her with Isaac (Gen. 21:1–7; Heb. 11:11). From these and many other examples, we can see that God has far more to do with human fertility than we often give Him credit for.

So what does all this mean for Christian women and couples seeking God's will for their family?

One popular position, taken by many Bible teachers, Christian leaders, and other believers today, is summarized on this Christian website:

> Since modern birth control and fertility options were not available during biblical times, the Bible is silent on the matter of using these methods to prevent or encourage pregnancy. Preventing pregnancy for family planning purposes, either temporarily or permanently, is a neutral act and not considered sinful.[5]

It's not possible in these few pages to thoroughly unpack the biblical principles and societal implications related to this subject. But as you consider what you believe about childbearing and contraception (whether for yourself or as you interact with other women), rather than mindlessly accepting the prevailing worldview, I would encourage you to prayerfully seek God's perspective in His Word and to take seriously His view that children are a blessing to be welcomed.

After all, if God were to open the windows of heaven and pour out some other sort of blessing, say, hundred dollar bills, how many of us would protest, "Stop! Please, no more blessings!"

My friend Holly Elliff and her husband, Bill, found their hearts and their thinking changing as they began to bring this area of their lives before the Lord. They had practiced contraception off and on for the first dozen years of their marriage, suspending it whenever they felt they were ready to have another child. It wasn't until they were expecting their fourth child that they began to rethink their position on birth control. A friend they asked for advice encouraged them to study what the Scripture had to say about childbearing. Here's how Holly describes that journey:

### HOLLY'S STORY

It was frightening for me to think of taking my hands off that area of my life. One of my worst nightmares was of wearing maternity clothes for the rest of my life. I had a vision of mothers of large families that was not flattering, and I did not want to be one.

But I was troubled about this issue. And so, for six months I searched the Scriptures for every reference to children and child-bearing. To be honest, I was looking for a way to avoid releasing control of that area of my life. But what I found, over and over, was that children are a blessing and that God is the one who opens and closes the womb.

I remember one night sitting down at my kitchen table and making a list. At the top I wrote, "Reasons I don't want to have a million children." I began to record my objections to what I was seeing in God's Word. There were a lot of fears on that list, things like:

- What would this do to my physical body?

- Will I be pregnant every nine months for the rest of my life?

- Can we afford more children?

- Can we love a larger number of children?

- What will other people think?

As I put down the pencil and read back through what I had written, I realized that most of the things on my list were rooted in selfishness. It became clear to me that this was a heart issue. It was a matter of my choosing to let God be the Lord in this area of our family, as I wanted Him to be in every other aspect of my life.

Bill and I prayed about what to do with our money, where to serve in ministry, and what car to buy, but in this area it was as if we had said, "This is ours to determine." For the first time, I was confronted with the fact that I had never said to the Lord, "What is *Your* will for our family's size?"[6]

That night was a turning point in Holly's heart as she surrendered this area of her life to Christ. Even so, it was not without some apprehension that she and Bill determined to simply enjoy normal sexual relations, trusting Him to determine the number of children He wanted to entrust to them. As she shared with me, "I really thought at that point, 'If I let God be in control of this, I'm going to have twenty-five children!'"

As it turned out, God gave Bill and Holly six more children, two of whom are in heaven. Now, as a grandmother of fifteen under twelve years of age, she says: "Looking back, we don't have a single regret about our decision, and we can't imagine what we would have missed without these six children in our lives!"

## WRESTLING WITH THE ISSUES

Many women I talk with have the same fears Holly did when she first started thinking through the implications of surrendering her childbearing to the Lord. Holly and Bill ended up having eight children on earth. You may know other women, as I do, who've had more. But I also know other couples who used no form of birth control and only had two or three—or none. At the end of the day, the God who opens and closes the womb determines how many children a woman will have. The question is whether He can be trusted to be God and to do what is good and wise for all involved.

You may not land where Holly did on this subject, or where someone else does. I know godly couples who have sought the Lord with a surrendered heart and a sincere desire to follow His leading and felt that He gave them the freedom to prayerfully plan the number and timing of their children and to use nonabortive methods of birth control.

If this is an issue you are facing, whether for yourself or with a family member or friend, my appeal is simply this: Dig into the Scripture. Don't just blindly follow the crowd or the culture. See if your attitude toward children, fertility, and God's role in it all lines up with what the Bible says. Seek wise, godly counsel. Pray and ask the Spirit to guide you. And be sure to do your research about the different kinds of birth control!

Natural methods and barrier methods prevent conception from taking place. But some birth control measures abort a fertilized egg, bringing an end to a life that has already begun. Clearly this is not something God approves of.

I would also encourage you to study the facts if you are on or are considering going on the birth control pill. Some physicians and medical professionals contend that at least some forms of the Pill have the potential of acting in an abortive manner rather than merely preventing ovulation. In an article called "Can Christians Use Birth Control?," Albert Mohler acknowledges that possibility and stresses, "Christian couples must exercise due care in choosing a form of birth control that is unquestionably contraceptive rather than abortifacient."[7]

Infertility is another difficult issue many couples face. According to the Centers for Disease Control and Prevention (CDC), some 7.3 million Americans, or 12 percent of the population in their reproductive years, are infertile,[8] resulting in no small heartache for those affected. In response to this reality, a number of "assisted reproductive technologies" (ART) have been developed. Advances in this field have increased women's options in relation to childbearing and have been helpful to many infertile couples.

However, for the Christian, some of these technologies raise another whole realm of ethical and moral issues. For example, what about the unused embryos resulting from in-vitro fertilization (IVF) that are frozen and stored?[9] And at what point do some of these options move beyond impacting the likelihood of pregnancy into the realm of playing God? If God has shut your womb, to what extent do you go to try to force it open? What does it mean to trust God to give you children in His timing, if at all?

In all these matters, wisdom, prayer for discernment, and a desire to honor the Lord are vital. Again, not all women who love Christ come to the same conclusion about contraception and other reproductive decisions. But how we address these questions can say a lot about our attitudes toward life, children, God's providence, God's sovereignty, and more.

### The Legacy of Motherhood

*Being a mom presses every button I have and tests everything I think I know about spiritual growth and trusting God to provide. Mothering is a life choice that stretches me, consumes me, squeezes me, and shapes me.*

*Being a mom means I will live my life in a matrix that is never-ending and paradoxical. One in which great love and great pain often go hand in hand. One in which the tiniest of moments produces incredible joy. One in which my fatigue or frustration or fear or lack of wisdom become doorways to the throne of grace.*

*And there I find a Father who welcomes me, lifts the weight of the task from my weary shoulders, and reminds me of what I know to be true: Generations from now, Lord willing, my descendants will be scattered across His earth, standing against the tide of whatever ungodly culture exists in their day. They will have the potential to proclaim the simple truth of the gospel that changes the hearts of men.*[10]

*—Holly Elliff*

## 33. "We can't afford (more) children."

Diapers. Baby food. Sports teams. Braces. The U.S. Department of Agriculture (USDA) projects that raising a child from cradle to high school graduation will cost you a quarter of a million dollars—$245,340, to be precise, or $304,480 when adjusted for projected inflation. And that's before you pay for his or her college education![11]

If you were to do an Internet search on "How much does it cost to raise a child?" you'd find this staggering sum quoted by every media outlet from *CNN Money* to *Huffington Post* to *Today's Parent*, not to mention innumerable parenting and mommy blogs. The message that young women are hearing—loud and clear—is that raising kids is prohibitively expensive, that a large family is a luxury that few can afford.

Unfortunately, the process by which most couples—even believers—determine the size of their family is often driven by the assumption that they simply don't have the financial, emotional, physical, or time resources to add another child (or any children at all) to their lives:

- "How will we ever provide for more children? We're barely making ends meet as it is. What about college tuition?"

- "We wouldn't be able to provide the kind of lifestyle we want our kids to have. They couldn't be on sports teams and take music lessons. We'd limit their potential."

- "I can't physically handle more children. I'm exhausted trying to take care of the two I already have."

- "I'm not cut out to have kids. I just don't have the patience."

- "If we have more children, we won't have enough time for us as a couple."

- "My friends [or parents] will think we're crazy if we have more kids. They already think we have too many."

- "I'm happy not having kids."

Not long ago, *Time* magazine featured a cover story entitled "The Childfree Life: When Having It All Means Not Having Children." The photo that graced the cover pretty much summed up the argument: a young, fit couple lounged contentedly on a beach and gazed up at the camera with blissful smiles—with no children anywhere in sight.[12] Journalist Lauren Sandler, the author, lauded the growing demographic of women who are child-free by choice. One of them is Jenna Johnson, a New Yorker, who explained why the child-free life is a great option:

> I get to do all sorts of things: buy an unnecessary beautiful object, plan trips with our aging parents, sleep in, spend a day without speaking to a single person, send care packages to nieces and nephews, enroll in language classes, go out for drinks with a friend on the spur of the moment. . . . I know all of this would be possible with kids, but it would certainly be more complicated. My plans—professionally, daily, long-term, even just for vacation—are free from all the contingencies that come with children.[13]

Christians are not immune to the cultural message about the undesirability of children. Take Amy Becker, for example. She and her husband were both on staff with a Christian organization. They thought they would remain child-free "for the sake of the gospel"—that is, until Amy realized what was really motivating their decision:

> For a long time after marrying, my husband and I considered never having kids. We could justify our desires according to our Christian beliefs. We worked with students as full-time Christian ministers. For us, having a family seemed to detract from our ability to spread the Good News. It may well be the case that there are Christian missionaries called to limit their family size for the sake of the gospel. But in our case, those arguments were a facade, covering up the fear and ambivalence we had about limiting our lives by the presence of children. It took the gentle questions and witness of other Christians to convince us that we were using Christian-sounding arguments to cover up a selfish and fearful motive.[14]

One of the important purposes of marriage is to produce children who fear and follow the Lord (Mal. 2:15). The apostle Paul exhorts younger widows to "marry, to *have children*, to manage their homes and to give the enemy no opportunity for slander" (1 Tim. 5:14 NIV). He also states that "women will be saved through childbearing—if they continue in faith, love and holiness with propriety" (2:15 NIV).

Of course, Paul is not suggesting that a woman's eternal salvation is obtained through becoming a mother and raising children. Rather, in the context,[15] he is saying that a woman's willingness to embrace her God-given calling as a bearer and nurturer of life is a fruit that will accompany genuine salvation. It is proof that she belongs to Him and follows His ways.

## WELCOMING CHILDREN

I still remember the morning a friend in another state told me she was expecting her fourth child. Though she and her husband were elated by the news, they were quickly discovering that not everyone else shared their enthusiasm. "In fact," she told me, "some of the most critical comments we've heard are from people in our church."

Sadly, I've had many similar conversations with expectant moms over the years—reflecting a mindset that children are something other than a blessing. The Lord Jesus modeled a vastly different value system when He welcomed children into His life, took time for them, and urged His followers to do the same (Matt. 19:13–15). And when His disciples wanted to know how to be big in God's kingdom, He turned to a little one:

And calling to him a child, he put him in the midst of them
and said, "Truly, I say to you, unless you turn and become like children,
you will never enter the kingdom of heaven.
Whoever humbles himself like this child is the greatest
in the kingdom of heaven.
Whoever receives one such child in my name receives me."

—Matthew 18:3–5

All this is not to say that women ought to have as many children as they possibly can. Nor is it to say that all women are called by God to marry and bear children. But God's Word does make clear that motherhood is a gift from the Giver of life and vital to the furthering of His kingdom in our generation and beyond.

Mary of Nazareth is a beautiful example of a woman who demonstrated faith by her willingness to bear a child, even when doing so was neither economically or culturally advisable and when it intruded on her personal plans, dreams, and convenience. We can only imagine some of the objections that might have gone through the heart of this teenage girl when the angelic visitor announced that she was to give birth to a son:

- "I'm too young! I'm not ready to have a child."
- "I won't be able to spend time with Joseph and my friends if I get tied down with a baby."
- "I want to get settled in our new house first."
- "What will everyone say? No one will understand."
- "We can't afford a child yet. Joseph is just getting his business going."

But there is no indication of any such hesitation or reservation on Mary's part. Her response was simply, "I am the Lord's servant. . . . May it be done to me according to your word" (Luke 1:38 CSB). She said, in effect, "You are my Lord. I accept any inconvenience or hardship this will mean for me. All that matters to me is fulfilling the purpose for which You created me. I trust You. I am confident that You will take care of this and give me all I need."

How thankful I am for a mother who responded the same way to God's call in her life. When Nancy Sossomon, an accomplished classical musician, married Art DeMoss at the age of nineteen, they planned to wait at least five years before having children so she could continue her vocal career. However, the Lord had other plans. Within the first five years of their marriage, He gave them six children! At the same time, my mother was helping my dad start a business. Throughout those early years of marriage and childbearing, she welcomed each child God gave her—including a seventh child several years later. This calling was not without its challenges, but I have never heard my mother express anything other than gratitude for the blessing of having children and being a mother.

When it comes down to it, reproductive choices reflect the heart. If you find yourself hesitating to have children—or have more children—I want to gently urge you, as Amy Becker's friends did with her, to honestly evaluate your fears, attitudes, and motivations. Does your unwillingness to have more children stem from financial fears? From a desire to maintain a certain standard of living? From doubt that God can and will provide? From an unwillingness to be inconvenienced? From fear of what others will say? From selfishness or a lack of faith? From unwittingly buying in to the world's beliefs and standards?

I suspect that Mary, the mother of Jesus, also had some apprehension about motherhood. Raising children is not easy. Providing for them is not easy. Serving is not easy. Giving up or curtailing personal dreams is not easy. Motherhood is one of the most difficult things a woman can do.

But the Truth is that your weakness and need provide an opportunity for you to experience the limitless resources of God's grace—and that the indwelling Spirit of Christ will provide all you could ever need to do His will. He has promised to be with you, to sustain and uphold you, to guide you, to give you strength, and to supply your every need according to His riches in glory in Christ Jesus (Phil. 4:19).

If He sees fit to bless you with children, He will also bless you with all that you need to welcome them and raise them for His glory.

### 34. *"I can't control/can control the way my children turn out."*

Perhaps the most common type of prayer request women have shared with me over the years is for the spiritual condition of their children and grandchildren. I could fill a book with the pain and longing expressed by mothers like these:

*My sixteen-year-old ran away nine months ago and moved in with her boyfriend—the hurt is so deep.*

*My twenty-eight-year-old daughter has denied her faith in Christ and is involved in a gay relationship.*

*Pray that God would break my eighteen-year-old son's heart and deliver him from an addiction (from early childhood) to pornography.*

*I am struggling with disappointment with my teenage sons, who don't care about the things of the Lord—and with my failure to raise godly children.*

Since I've never had children of my own, I can only imagine the enormous heartache these women carry. But from my years of listening to hurting mothers, it seems to me that the Enemy uses two opposite lies to put such parents in bondage.

The first lie is that parents have no influence over how their children turn out—that children will inevitably experiment with sin and must just be allowed to find their own way. Believing this lie leads parents to deny any personal responsibility and to feel that they are helpless to influence the course of their children's lives.

The second lie is that parents are totally responsible for how their children turn out—that it is their fault if their children stray. They fail to recognize that, regardless of how well or poorly anyone is parented, each individual must ultimately assume responsibility for his or her own choices.

When children rebel, it seems that parents often veer from one of these lies to the other. They either sit back and just let sin take its course, or they become overwhelmed with shame and self-recrimination. Both lies are actually subtle distortions of the Truth and can leave parents with a sense of despair and hopelessness.

## LIKE PARENT, LIKE CHILD?

The Scripture includes accounts of godly parents who had ungodly children, as well as ungodly parents whose children had a heart for God. Seldom is an explanation given for why this is so. However, we are given some clues that provide insight for parents who long for their children to become true followers of Christ.

The story of Abraham's nephew, Lot, illustrates the influence of a parent's example and values. After traveling for years with his godly uncle, Lot eventually opted for a lifestyle of ease and affluence. His worldly values led him to settle his family in Sodom, a city characterized by arrogance, immorality, and perversion. We also know that later Lot's wife struggled to leave behind the godless city where she and Lot had taken up residence (Gen. 19:17, 26; Luke 17:32).

Is it any wonder, then, that their daughters married men who disdained Lot's spiritual beliefs and rejected his pleas to escape the coming judgment? Should it surprise us that after fleeing Sodom, Lot's daughters schemed to get their father drunk and then took turns sleeping with him so they would not be childless (see Genesis 19)?

The New Testament tells us that Lot was a "righteous man." He did not personally participate in the outright wickedness of Sodom; in fact, he was "tormented in his righteous soul by the lawless deeds he saw and heard" (2 Peter 2:8). But though he had an affinity with God, he also had an appetite for the things of this world. And by his example, he led his family into the natural consequences of such an appetite.

The price Lot and his wife paid for their temporal values seems high, but the law of sowing and reaping means that the seed sown will invariably yield a multiplied harvest. As more than one person has pointed out: "What parents tolerate in moderation, their children will likely excuse in excess."

The account of the high priest Eli's family demonstrates the necessity of parents establishing godly standards for their children's behavior and then exercising the necessary discipline to enforce those parameters. Eli was priest over Israel during the dark period of the judges, a devoted servant of the Lord. His two sons, Hophni and Phinehas, were a different story. Though they had grown up in an extremely religious setting and even became priests themselves, they were "scoundrels" who "had no regard for the LORD" (1 Sam. 2:12 NIV). They corrupted their sacred calling, extorted offerings that belonged to the Lord, and went so far as to engage in sexual relations with the women who served at the tabernacle (1 Sam. 2:13–17, 22).

How did a dedicated man of God end up with two such sons? Undoubtedly, they were influenced by the decadent culture around them, but the Scripture tells us some things about their father that may have contributed to the outcome.

For instance, we know that at the time of his death, Eli was overweight (1 Sam. 4:18). Could there be a connection between his lack of physical discipline and his sons' practice of filling their own bellies with meat they had extorted from those who came to offer sacrifices? The words of a prophet sent by God to confront Eli hint at such a possibility:

> Why do you scorn my sacrifice and offering . . . ?
> Why do you honor your sons more than me
> by fattening yourselves on the choice parts
> of every offering made by my people Israel?
>
> —1 Samuel 2:29 NIV

The Scripture tells us that on at least one occasion, Eli heard what his sons were doing and confronted them about their wicked behavior (1 Sam. 2:22–25). However, by that time, he was "very old." One can only wonder why he waited so long and whether he had overlooked their behavior prior to that time. At any rate, "his sons . . . did not listen to their father's rebuke" (v. 25 NIV). And God clearly held Eli responsible for his permissive parenting, as became clear when He sent a message to Eli through Samuel, Eli's young protégé:

> I am about to punish his house forever,
> for the iniquity that he knew,
> because his sons were blaspheming God,
> and he did not restrain them.
>
> —1 Samuel 3:13

These examples do not suggest that there is always a direct cause-and-effect relationship between parents' spiritual condition and how their kids turn out. However, they do illustrate the significance of a parent's example and influence. Certainly peers, teachers, entertainment, church youth groups, and secular culture are influential as well. But God has entrusted to parents the sacred responsibility to oversee and tend to the flock God has given them to shepherd.

## THE IMPACT OF A GODLY PARENT

Okay, I'm going to step way out on a limb here (as if I'm not already out there). I've never been in your shoes as a mom, but I've loved and walked closely with a lot of families through difficult and challenging seasons. Could I share an observation with you?

Every parent has to prayerfully determine what kinds of parameters to establish for their own children. Those boundaries will vary from family to family and child to child, and they will certainly change as children get older.

But I confess to being mystified and concerned when I see some of the choices well-meaning Christian parents allow their children to make—as if they (the parents) had no say in the matter. Choices such as permitting their kids to use social media without clear guidelines and accountability, to have unsupervised close friendships with peers who don't have a heart for God, to date non-Christians, to talk disrespectfully, to dress inappropriately, and to be entertained by music, television, and movies that promote the values of this world. Then they end up shaking their heads and wondering why their children have more of a heart for the world than for Christ.

As I'm writing this chapter, there are about eight inches of snow on the ground, and it has been snowing steadily all day. No one would think of taking a tender, young seedling and planting it outside on a day like today. It would have no hope of surviving. That's what a greenhouse is for—to provide an optimum environment for young plants to grow. Later, when their roots have developed and they're strong enough to withstand the elements, they can be transplanted to the outdoors.

The apostle Paul cautions believers of every era and every culture, "Don't let the world around you squeeze you into its own mould" (Rom. 12:2 PHILLIPS). We are not to be shaped by the culture, but to be so filled with the Spirit and the Word of God that our lives will penetrate and impact that culture. That is the challenge Christian parents face—to raise up a generation of young people who are not conformed to the world but who are transformed from the inside out by the gospel and who will be used by God to transform the world.

Even children whose parents provide godly, wise direction sometimes reject that direction. But when seeds of rebellion surface, wise parents don't just shrug and say, "I guess all kids have to go through this." As needed, they deal with issues head-on, with love and firmness, seeking to preserve relationships, to maintain open lines of communication, and to keep pointing their children to Christ and the gospel.

The Scripture teaches that each generation is responsible to pass on to the next a heritage of godliness. This is both an awesome privilege and a weighty responsibility. The sobering fact is that we are responsible for the seeds we sow, and we must live with the harvest that results. We cannot plant seeds of undisciplined, half-hearted commitment to the Lord and then hope that the next generation won't also exhibit those same characteristics.

Of course, the balancing biblical Truth is that each generation is responsible for its own walk and obedience. Regardless of what their parents have or have not done, each individual will one day give account to God for his or her own choices (Deut. 24:16; Jer. 31:29–30).

## MARKS OF TRUE FAITH

Parents can also be deceived when it comes to the eternal condition of their children's souls. For example, they may believe that if they follow the right formula, and parent in the right way, their child's salvation will be guaranteed. The problem is that our children were born with the same inherent sinful bent that we were born with (Pss. 51:5; 58:3; Isa. 59:2–8). As is true with each of us, apart from a work of the Spirit drawing our children to Christ and giving them the gift of repentance and faith, they will never turn to Him and be saved.

Further, it's tempting to assume that a child who was raised in the church and made a childhood profession of faith is therefore a true Christian. However, the Scripture is clear that a person may know all about God, have all the right answers, and even have deeply religious experiences without ever being born again.

Only God knows anyone's heart. But He has given us some objective standards by which to examine a profession of faith—whether our own or someone else's. The first epistle of John identifies specific characteristics that distinguish between those who have been truly saved and those who may be religious but have no real basis for their profession of salvation:

> By this we know that we have come to know him,
> if we keep his commandments. . . .
>
> By this we may know that we are in him: whoever says he abides
> in him ought to walk in the same way in which he walked. . . .
>
> Whoever says he is in the light and hates his brother
> is still in darkness. . . .
>
> If anyone loves the world, the love of the Father is not in him. . . .
>
> Whoever does not practice righteousness is not of God,
> nor is the one who does not love his brother.
>
> —1 John 2:3, 5–6, 9, 15; 3:10

The essence of true salvation is not a matter of profession or performance, but of transformation: "If anyone is in Christ, he is a new creation. The old has passed away; behold, the new has come" (2 Cor. 5:17). The man or woman who has been truly converted has a new life, a new heart, a new nature, a new allegiance, and a new Master (Col. 1:13).

Included in the covenant God makes with those who belong to Him is the assurance that we will persevere in our faith. God promises: "I will put My fear in their hearts so that they will not depart from Me" (Jer. 32:40 NKJV). And the writer to the Hebrews indicates that perseverance to the end is a mark of true faith: "We have come to share in Christ, if indeed we hold our original confidence firm to the end" (Heb. 3:14).

It is certainly possible for those who have been truly converted to disobey God or to have a period of backsliding. But no true believer can sin willfully and habitually without experiencing the conviction of God's Spirit.

For parents to assume that their children have been born again when their lives give no such evidence can lull those children into a false sense of security about their eternal destiny. It can also keep parents from praying appropriately and waging spiritual battle on behalf of their children's souls.

Parents who know and love Christ long to see their children do the same. They want to live and parent in a way that makes their children hungry for God. But even the best parents are utterly dependent on the Holy Spirit to do a work in their children's hearts. That's why a mother's most powerful resource is prayer. Through prayer, you can fight for the hearts of your children—including those prodigals who have rejected the faith and are living in sin's grip.

What a great comfort it is to know that "the weapons of our warfare are not of the flesh but have divine power to destroy strongholds" (2 Cor. 10:4). The Bible assures us that "the prayer of a righteous person is powerful and effective" (James 5:16 NIV). The persevering prayers of a righteous mom or grandmom (or aunt or friend) can make a profound difference in a child's life.

The Enemy lies to parents in an effort to sabotage the relay of the gospel from one generation to the next. How we need parents who love the Truth and who will lead their children to love Christ, praying that the Spirit of God will capture these young hearts and that they will reflect His glory to the next generation.

## 35. *"My children are my number-one priority."*

You've probably heard the term "helicopter parent." It refers to parents who are overly focused on their children. They typically take too much responsibility for their children's experiences and, specifically, their successes or failures—so much so that they constantly hover over them like a helicopter.

In recent years I've noticed the rise (pardon the pun) of a religious sort of helicopter parent: these are well-intentioned mothers who make their worlds revolve around their children instead of engaging their children with them in a lifestyle that revolves around the gospel. There's a subtle, but important difference.

You see, if Satan can't get you to embrace the lie that your personal desires are more important than the needs of your children, then he'll try to convince you of the opposite lie: that your life is *all* about your children. If he can't persuade you to make an idol out of yourself or your career, then he'll tempt you to idolize your kids.

Satan never gives us the luxury of fighting error on only one front. Lies tend to come at us from both sides. We can see this two-sided pull in today's culture. On the one hand, children are devalued. Women are pressured to develop careers, put off marriage, delay having children, severely limit the size of their families (one and done), or choose a childfree lifestyle.

On the other hand, children are treated like demigods. Culture pressures parents to give kids all the latest-and-greatest gear and gizmos as well as designer clothing and toys; to enroll them in year-round sports activities, dance, music and art lessons; to pamper them, indulge them, cater to their feelings, and bow to their every whim.

No wonder parents get confused! But that's why we need the balanced guidance of Scripture.

The Bible teaches that it's human nature for us to idolize things (Col. 3:5). We can worship a person or relationship, sex, money, a career, possessions, an achievement, or an activity we love. Nancy Pearcey explains that an idol "is anything we want more than God, anything we rely on more than God, anything we look to for greater fulfillment than God."[16]

Do you think it's possible for a woman to want children more than she wants God? To rely on her family more than she relies on God? To look to motherhood for fulfillment more than she looks to God? Of course, it is!

Children are an incredible blessing from God. He places great value on them, and they can bring much satisfaction and joy to their parents. At the same time, mothers may be tempted to value their children above all.

Jesus challenged this way of thinking about the parent-child relationship in unmistakable terms:

> Whoever loves father or mother more than me
> is not worthy of me,
> and whoever loves son or daughter more than me
> is not worthy of me.
>
> —Matthew 10:37

Children ought to love their parents, and parents ought to love their children. The Bible is clear about that. But your love for your children should never outweigh your love for Jesus. Your highest priority is loving and following Him . . . and that means your children do not come first.

The net result of child-centered parenting is often a self-centered child. The child grows up thinking that the world revolves around him and that other people exist for the sole purpose of meeting his wants and needs. The Lord doesn't want us to be self-centered or child-centered . . . He wants us to be God-centered. He doesn't want your world to revolve around your children; He wants you to engage your children in a lifestyle that revolves around His kingdom.

Your daily walk speaks volumes about what holds first place in your heart. What are your actions saying? Are they teaching your child that she is at the center of the universe? Or are they showing that the *Lord* ought to be at the center of her world? Consider the message you are sending

- when you take your son to church instead of to football practice, knowing full well that consequently he might have to sit out the next game

- when you require your children to sit at the table and visit with guests instead of slipping away to play video games

- when you encourage your daughter to set aside a portion of her weekly allowance to give to the church

- when you require your preschooler to play quietly in her room for half an hour so you can spend time reading God's Word

- when you recruit your teen to peel potatoes for the meal you're cooking for the lady with cancer

- when you take your daughter to help you sort clothes at the local pregnancy center instead of enrolling her in yet another set of music or dance or cheer lessons

- when you invite a woman you're mentoring along for the ride to the out-of-town basketball tournament so you can speak Truth into her life

These are but a few ways your life and behavior might demonstrate that God is at the center of your universe, and communicate that He ought to be at the center of your child's universe too. As John Piper says,

> We were made to know and treasure the glory of God above all things; and when we trade that treasure for images [idols], everything is disordered. The sun of God's glory was made to shine at the center of the solar system of our soul. And when it does, all the planets of our life are held in their proper orbit. But when the sun is displaced,

everything flies apart. The healing of the soul begins by restoring the glory of God to its flaming, all-attracting place at the center.[17]

If you're not careful and prayerful, you can get swept up in the busy-ness of life and let your days pass by without determining to use them for God's purposes. You can lose focus. Life can become all about your kids. Resolve not to let this happen. And if it does, do what is necessary to put the Lord back in His rightful place at the center of your heart and your family life.

## 36. *"I'm not/she's not a good mother."*

"I suppose I could have stayed at home and baked cookies and had teas, but what I decided to do was fulfill my profession," Hillary Clinton famously quipped while on the campaign trail with her husband, Bill, in the early 1990s. Clinton's comment drew scorching responses from stay-at-home mothers (SAHMs) and cheers from fellow working-outside-of-the-home moms (WOHMs). The polarized public reaction led to a *Family Circle* magazine Presidential First Lady "Bake-off" between Clinton, wife of the Democratic contender for President, and Barbara Bush, the wife of Republican incumbent George H. W. Bush.

Clinton, a lawyer, worked full-time outside of the home. Bush was the quintessential stay-at-home mom and grandma. At root, the point of the contest was not to determine whether a Democrat could bake better cookies than a Republican. It was to provide a tongue-in-cheek answer to the question of who made a better mother—a SAHM or a WOHM. The home-baked cookies represented the heart of what it meant to be a warm, loving, nurturing mom.

Though most people thought Barbara Bush would bake better cookies, Clinton handily won the contest. Yet her victory didn't settle the question of what it takes to be a good mother. In the decades since her oatmeal chocolate chip (made with shortening) beat out Bush's more traditional chocolate chip (no oatmeal, and with butter), mommy wars have continued to rage.

Natural childbirth versus epidural. Vaccination versus antivaccination. Attachment parenting versus crying it out. Gentle parenting versus spanking. Breast fed versus bottle fed. Organic versus processed. Homeschooled versus private-schooled versus public-schooled. SAHM versus WOHM. These are but a few of the controversies that escalate the battles to meteoric levels—especially on the Internet, where everyone is an expert and the opinions of mommy bloggers and trolls are often reduced to vicious, inflammatory 280-character sound bites.

Mommy wars exist because of the sinful act of comparison. We weigh our performance against standards created by the media, mommy bloggers, child experts, friends, and countless others. We either torment ourselves for not meeting those standards, or we become self-assured that we've made the "right choice" and look down on women who have not.

Mommy wars erupted long before the Clinton-Bush Bake-off, of course. We can trace them back to the book of Genesis, which tells the story of Rachel and Leah, two sisters who were married to the same man, Jacob (see Gen. 30). These sisters constantly compared themselves with each other. Rachel viewed herself as a failure in the motherhood department, whereas Leah took pride in her motherhood success. In the marriage department, the situation was reversed. Leah felt the sting of envy because Jacob loved Rachel more than he loved her. The ongoing competition and comparison strained the relationship between the two sisters and led to quarrelling and division in the entire family.

Almost every mother wants to be a good mother. It should come as no surprise that Satan capitalizes on this deep desire and uses it as an opportunity to promote sin by encouraging moms to compare themselves with other moms. He'll tempt a mom to believe the lie, "I'm not a good mother," and to heap guilt, condemnation, and reproach on herself. Or he'll tempt her to believe the lie, "*She* is not a good mother" and to heap guilt, condemnation, and reproach on someone else. On the one side of the spectrum, the mom sees *herself* as falling short and is envious of others who she thinks are doing better. On the other side of the spectrum, she sees *others* as falling short and is prideful that she is doing better.

Throughout history, ancient writers and theologians have identified envy and pride as two of the deadliest and most destructive sins. The Bible warns:

> But if you have bitter jealousy and selfish ambition
> in your hearts, do not boast and be false to the truth.
> This is not the wisdom that comes down from above,
> but is earthly, unspiritual, demonic.
> For where jealousy and selfish ambition exist,
> there will be disorder and every vile practice.
>
> —James 3:14–16

No mother is certain she's doing a good job of parenting. All mothers, if they're being honest, secretly wonder at times: "Am I doing the right thing?" and "Are my choices going to negatively impact my children?" Our fears are heightened when our children are unruly and misbehaved, when we are snippy and irritable with them, when we use our TVs too often as babysitters, or when we forget to take the meat out of the freezer, prompting yet another trip to the drive-through for burgers and fries. We can go so far as to wonder how we can call ourselves Christians when we've had such an epic failure of a day as a mom.

Conversely, when our children appear to be doing well, we're tempted to credit ourselves and flaunt our smart parenting choices. It's hard to resist broadcasting our success on Facebook and acting like "Sanctimommies" who freely dispense advice, especially to those friends who obviously don't have their acts together like we do.

Most of the parenting decisions that are up for debate in the mommy wars are not a clear matter of right and wrong. Though some choices may be stronger than others, most are a matter of personal preference and individual circumstance. Each mom needs to prayerfully decide what's best for her and her family. And different women will make different choices.

The church was never meant to be a cozy club of cookie-cutter families who are identical in all respects. Variety in the family of God is a good thing, but it can also put strains on our relationships. How are we to coexist and get along?

Tensions between believers over differing preferences have existed since the beginning of the church. Romans 14 addresses how we are to live with others who love the Lord but who do not see eye to eye with us on the ideal way to live out the Christian faith:

> don't argue about disputed matters.
> One person believes he may eat anything,
> while one who is weak eats only vegetables.
> One who eats must not look down on one who does not eat,
> and one who does not eat must not judge one who does,
> because God has accepted him.
> Who are you to judge another's household servant?
> Before his own Lord he stands or falls.
> And he will stand, because the Lord is able to make him stand. . . .
>
> But you, why do you judge your brother or sister?
> Or you, why do you despise your brother or sister?
> For we will all stand before the judgment seat of God. . . .
>
> Each of us will give an account of himself to God.
> Therefore, let us no longer judge one another.
>
> —Romans 14:1–4, 10, 12–13 CSB

Scripture teaches that certain things are right and certain things are wrong. There are, however, other matters about which there may be legitimate differences of opinion.[18] The problem in Rome was that Christians were passing judgment on each other over these disputable issues. Paul argued that since each believer belongs to God, it is out of place to question the decisions of another believer in matters where God does not clearly specify the proper behavior.

Paul instructed the believers to stop arguing about personal opinions and to stop criticizing and looking down on those with differing opinions. As Christian moms, we would do well to heed this advice.

The Bible urges us to humbly and honestly hold up our own lives before the Lord for His scrutiny rather than comparing ourselves to others and expecting them to measure up to our standards.

> For if anyone considers himself to be something
> when he is nothing, he deceives himself.
> Let each person examine his own work,
> and then he can take pride in himself alone,
> and not compare himself with someone else.
>
> —Galatians 6:3–4 CSB

It's not the opinion of the experts or the opinion of the other moms at your church or the opinion of your mother or mother-in-law or friend that should dictate your parenting decisions.

The only opinion that truly matters is the Lord's. Let Him examine your heart.

- Is your personal identity based on your relationship with Jesus Christ, or on your success as a mom, or on being the perfect parent?

- Do you compare your husband, your children, your home and work situation, and your parenting choices to those of other moms?

- Do you feel guilty about failing to reach a self-imposed, culturally imposed, or community-imposed standard?

- Do you envy the freedom of other women to make choices that you can't make?

- Do you tell yourself that your inability to meet a certain standard means you're a failure as a mom?

- Do you look to other moms rather than the Lord for validation of your parenting choices?

- Do you feel that you are doing a better job and making better parenting decisions than others?

- Do you dispense parenting advice and take part in the mommy-war debates?

- Do you look down on moms who hold to a different position than you?

Resolve to be part of the solution rather than part of the problem. Be a grace giver. Stop arguing about parenting opinions, and stop criticizing and looking down on those with differing opinions.

Most of all, remember that true love is kind. It does not envy or boast; it is not arrogant or rude (1 Cor. 13:4–5). If we want to be loving, God-centered mothers, that's what we all should aspire to.

The wisdom from above is first pure, then peaceable, gentle,
open to reason, full of mercy and good fruits, impartial and sincere.
And a harvest of righteousness is sown in peace
by those who make peace.

—James 3:17–18

COUNTERING LIES WITH THE *Truth*

| THE LIE | 32. I have the right to control my reproductive choices. |
|---|---|
| THE TRUTH | • God is the Creator and Giver of life.<br>Genesis 1; 2:7<br><br>• God is ultimately in charge of a woman's body and her fertility. He is the One Who opens and shuts the womb.<br>Genesis 20:18; 29:31<br><br>• Life begins at conception. Abortive methods of contraception are the taking of a life.<br>Genesis 2:7; 9:6; Psalm 22:9-10; Job 31:15; Jeremiah 1:4-5 |
| THE LIE | 33. We can't afford (more) children. |
| THE TRUTH | • Children are a blessing from God and a fulfillment of the command of God to multiply and fill the earth. One of the purposes of marriage is to produce "godly offspring."<br>Genesis 1:28; Psalms 113:9; 127:3-5; Malachi 2:15<br><br>• The Lord will provide everything a woman needs to raise and provide for any children He gives her.<br>Luke 12:24; Matthew 6:31-32; Philippians 4:13, 19 |

| THE LIE | 34. I can't control/can control the way my children turn out. |
|---|---|

| THE TRUTH | • God promises a blessing to parents who keep His covenant and who teach their children to do the same.<br>Psalm 103:17–18; Acts 2:39<br><br>• Parents cannot force their children to walk with God, but they can model godliness and cultivate a climate in the home that creates an appetite for God and is conducive to the spiritual nurture and growth of their children.<br>Psalm 144:12, 15; Isaiah 54:13; Matthew 5:13–16<br><br>• Parents who assume their children know the Lord, regardless of their lifestyle, may give their children a false sense of security and may not be praying appropriately for their children.<br>Jeremiah 32:40; Hebrews 3:14 |
|---|---|

| THE LIE | 35. My children are my number-one priority. |
|---|---|

| THE TRUTH | • Loving and serving God is every believer's highest priority.<br>Deuteronomy 10:12; Luke 10:27; Matthew 12:50<br><br>• It is possible to sin by loving our children more than we love the Lord.<br>Matthew 10:37; Luke 14:26<br><br>• Children are taught to put God first by watching their parents put God first.<br>Deuteronomy 6:7; Proverbs 22:6; Ephesians 5:1<br><br>• Children need to be trained to be selfless rather than selfish.<br>Micah 6:8; Ephesians 6:4; Hebrews 12:9-10; Proverbs 22:15 |
|---|---|

| | |
|---|---|
| **THE LIE** | **36. I'm not/she's not a good mother.** |
| **THE TRUTH** | • The sin of comparison leads to pride and envy.<br>James 3:14-18; Proverbs 8:13; 1 Corinthians 3:3 |
| | • Ultimately, every mom is accountable to the Lord for her parenting choices.<br>Romans 14:1-14; Matthew 12:36; Romans 2:16;<br>1 Corinthians 4:5; Galatians 6:3-4 |
| | • Accepting people whose parenting opinions differ from our own brings glory to God.<br>Romans 15:7; James 3:12-18; Ephesians 4:2 |

# CHAPTER NINE

# LIES WOMEN BELIEVE...
## ABOUT *Emotions*

*It's been nearly two years since we lost Abel. I think about him all the time—it still hurts so much. We haven't heard anything from Cain for months. Sometimes I feel so angry toward him for what he did to us; other times I just want to hold him and sing to him like I did when he was a baby.*

*Adam won't talk about how he feels—sometimes I wonder if he feels anything at all. It seems to annoy him when I try to get him to understand how I feel.*

*I just can't seem to dig out of this empty, lonely hole. Some days I can hardly drag myself out of bed. I feel like the darkness is about to swallow me up. I don't know how much longer I can hang on. I can't remember what it was like not to hurt. Will I ever be happy again?*

*A*t a women's conference I attended some years ago, we were given a magnet with a list of words describing a variety of emotions words such as *confused, ecstatic, angry, frustrated, sad, confident, happy, lonely,* and *depressed*. Above each word was a humorous line drawing of a face depicting that particular feeling.

The list came with a smaller magnet in the shape of a frame that said, "Today I Feel . . ." This piece was designed to be placed over any one of the cartoon drawings to express "how I am feeling today."

If some of us changed the marker every time our emotions changed, we would be kept quite busy. In fact, some women feel most of those emotions at least once a month! As much as anything else, it's probably our female emotional makeup that sometimes causes men to throw up their hands and say, "I give up. I just can't figure you out!" In a sense, who can blame them?

When we wrestle with unpredictable or out-of-control emotions, it's easy to conclude that emotions are inherently sinful or wrong and should be suppressed. We need to remember that being created in the image of God means we have the capacity to experience and express a variety of emotions. God Himself exhibits a spectrum of pure emotions, including:

- joy (Neh. 8:10; John 15:11)
- delight (Num. 14:8)
- anger (Num. 22:22)
- jealousy (Ex. 20:5)
- sorrow (Isa. 53:3)

And He has designed us to be able to feel and express many different emotions in a way that reflects His heart and brings glory to Him.

The problem is not that we *have* emotions—they are a gift from God. The problem is that our emotions (unlike God's) are tainted by the fall. The challenge is to let the Spirit of God sanctify us in the realm of our emotions so that they can be expressed in godly ways.

Part of that process is to identify and correct the lies the Deceiver foists upon us concerning our feelings. Causing us to believe things about our emotions that just aren't true is one of his effective tools. And one of the best ways to fight him is to speak Truth in the face of lies like . . .

### 37. *"If I feel something, it must be true."*

The Enemy wants us to believe that if we feel unloved, we are unloved. If we feel we can't cope with the pressure, it must be true that we can't make it. If we feel God has deserted us or that He has acted unjustly in a matter that concerns us, then perhaps He has indeed let us down. If we feel our situation is hopeless, then there must be no hope. If we don't feel saved, then maybe we aren't. If we don't feel forgiven, then we must not be.

The Truth is that, due to our fallen condition, our feelings often have very little to do with reality. In many instances, feelings are simply not a reliable gauge of what is actually true. When we allow them to be tied to our circumstances—which are constantly changing—rather than to the unchangeable realities of God and His Truth, our emotions are prone to fluctuate wildly.

For many of us, it doesn't take much to put our emotions on an upswing—a clear, sunny day; a raise at work; a compliment from a friend; the successful completion of a big project; or losing five pounds.

Meanwhile, emotional lows can result from a variety of factors, including (but not limited to) a string of dreary days, a tough day at the office, a disappointing phone call, that time of the month, or a sleepless night.

And when you add in "big" things like the birth of a fourth child in five years, a major move, the loss of a job, the death of a mate or child, caring for a parent with Alzheimer's, going through menopause, or being diagnosed with cancer, those emotions can really go haywire.

If we want to walk in freedom, we must realize that our emotions are not necessarily trustworthy and be willing to reject any feelings that are not consistent with the Truth. In the midst of the roller-coaster ride our emotions sometimes take us on, we have to constantly bring our minds and thoughts back to the Truth:

- God is good, whether we feel like He is good or not. (Ps. 136:1)

- God loves us, whether we feel loved or not. (Jer. 31:3; John 3:16)

- Through faith in the shed blood of Jesus Christ on our behalf, we are forgiven, whether we feel forgiven or not. (Gal. 2:16)

- God will never leave us nor forsake us; He is with us all the time, even when we feel alone and forsaken. (Deut. 31:6)

"Connie" acknowledges having based her beliefs on what she felt, rather than on the Truth. Notice how her whole way of thinking changed once she realized she could let the Truth rule over her feelings:

*Although I was a child of God, I had believed throughout my life that certain aspects of the Truth applied to everyone except me. God was good to them, not to me. God loved them, not me. Others were of great worth to God, but not me. I knew the "facts"—that God is good, He loves me, and I am of great worth to Him—but there was a disconnect in my mind between the facts and how I felt. Surely if God loved me and I meant so much to Him, I would feel loved and valuable.*

*Through your seminar on "Lies Women Believe," God revealed that His Truth stands regardless of how I feel. Nothing can change God or the Truth of His Word and His character. He is good to me. He does love me. I can choose to cling to the Truth, or I can choose to buy into the lies of Satan. But God's Truth is unchangeable and irrefutable.*

In the last chapter of Philippians, the apostle Paul gives a prescription for preserving mental sanity and emotional stability even in the face of changing emotions:

Rejoice in the Lord always; . . .
Do not be anxious about anything,
but in everything by prayer and supplication with
thanksgiving let your requests be made known to God. . . .
Whatever is true . . . think about such things.

The result?

The peace of God, which surpasses all understanding,
will guard your hearts and your minds in Christ Jesus.

—Philippians 4:4, 6–8

## 38. *"I can't control my emotions."*

The Enemy uses this lie to make us believe we have no choice but to be controlled by our emotions. While there's a sense in which we can't help the way we feel, the Truth is that we don't have to let our feelings run our lives.

You may not be able to help feeling apprehensive about an upcoming medical exam, but that doesn't mean you can't stop fretting about the outcome. You may not be able to help feeling edgy or irritable at a certain time of the month, but that doesn't mean you can't refrain from speaking rudely to or acting unkindly toward whoever happens to get in your way on those days. You may not be able to help feeling vulnerable in a lonely season of your life when a married man takes an interest in you, but that doesn't mean you can't stop yourself from "falling in love" with him.

Another, related lie that feeds this one is that Christians should never feel sad, discouraged, angry, or lonely—that if we're really spiritual, we'll be happy all the time. Not true!

Like a warning light on the dashboard of our car, certain emotions can indeed be an indicator of a problem, and under certain circumstances they can lead to sin. But simply feeling a negative emotion is not sinful in and of itself. It's what we do with the emotion that matters.

"In your anger do not sin" (Eph. 4:26 NIV), Scripture tells us. When we feel anger rising up in our hearts, we can use it to justify a sinful response. Or we can let it press us closer to Christ.

We live in a culture that encourages us to avoid suffering at all costs. In response, we may try to numb negative emotions rather than surrendering them to God's authority or trusting Him with the circumstances that make us feel out of control.

Our collective addiction to social media and technology is just one way we try to escape the reality of living in a broken world. We may be tempted to avoid facing painful feelings or circumstances by spending hours staring at our screens. But can that ever really satisfy? Can it soothe anxiety, anger, boredom, or bitterness in any lasting sort of way? After hours of scrolling through pictures on your phone or social media posts on your laptop, does your heart truly feel at peace?

Does all that clicking lead you beside still waters? Does it restore your soul?

Technology is not a worthy substitute for opening God's Word, meditating on His goodness, and letting Him transform us with His Truth. No other substitute can ultimately satisfy either. No glass of wine, no late-night refrigerator run, no Netflix binge can make or keep this promise:

> You keep him in perfect peace
> whose mind is stayed on you,
> because he trusts in you.
>
> —Isaiah 26:3

Rather than simply escaping negative emotions, we have the God-given option to trade them for "perfect peace." But there's a catch. When we find ourselves suffering under the weight of negative emotions like anger, anxiety, bitterness, despair, hatred, or condemnation, we must learn to look toward God's Truth, keeping our minds stayed on *Him* rather than simply trying to escape or swap out negative emotions with a feel-good substitute. We must run, not walk, toward God's Truth for refuge.

The Scripture is filled with promises and commands that provide the means by which our emotions can be steadied in the midst of any storm:

- God's Word promises, "*I am with you always*" (Matt. 28:20). Therefore, we don't have to be overcome by loneliness.

- God's Word promises, "*My God will supply every need of yours*" (Phil. 4:19). Therefore, we don't have to stay awake at night worrying about how the mortgage will get paid.

- God's Word promises, "*The mountains may depart and the hills be removed, but my steadfast love shall not depart from you*" (Isa. 54:10). Therefore, we don't have to live in dread of an uncertain future.

- God's Word says, "*Let not your hearts be troubled, neither let them be afraid*" (John 14:27). That means we don't have to give in to fear, regardless of our circumstances.

- God's Word says, "*Do not be anxious about anything*" (Phil. 4:6). That means we don't have to be worried, even in the midst of stressful situations.

- God's Word says, "*Give thanks in all circumstances*" (1 Thess. 5:18). That means we can choose to be thankful, even when everything around us seems to be falling apart.

- God's Word says, "*Love your enemies*" (Matt. 5:44). That means that, by the power of the Spirit, we can choose to love any-one—no matter how greatly they have wronged us.

- God's Word says, "*Forgive, if you have anything against anyone*" (Mark 11:25). That means there is no one we cannot choose to forgive, no matter how deeply they may have hurt us or sinned against us.

Regardless of what emotions are whirling around inside, by God's grace, we can choose to fix our minds on Him and to "trust and obey." The Scripture invites us to do just that:

> If then you have been raised with Christ,
> seek the things that are above,
> where Christ is, seated at the right hand of God.
> Set your minds on things that are above,
> not on things that are on earth. . . .
> And let the peace of Christ rule in your hearts. . . .
>
> —Colossians 3:1–2, 15

> Take every thought captive to obey Christ.
>
> —2 Corinthians 10:5

When we fix our minds on Christ and bring every thought into subjection to the Truth, the Holy Spirit sanctifies our emotions and brings them under His control. He gives us His supernatural peace and the grace to be faithful, even though our circumstances may not change in the here and now.

### 39. *"I can't help how I respond when my hormones are out of whack."*

There are three primary symptoms many women experience as they go through menopause." I had just turned fifty and was sitting in my doctor's office, eager to get some answers for what was going on in my body.

"Are you having hot flashes?" the doctor asked.

"Yep."

"Difficulty sleeping at night?"

"Um-hum."

"Mood swings?" At this point, my eyes filled with tears, and all I could do was nod shakily.

Let's just say I'm really happy to have those couple of years behind me. At times I felt like I was twelve again. If you've been there, I don't have to tell you how hard it is to keep our emotions and responses in check during that season.

Speaking of being twelve . . . my recollection of that year is that I cried the whole year—for no apparent reason. As I look back on it, I understand better now than I did then some of the changes that were taking place in my body as I was becoming a grown woman. But I also understand better now than I did then that what was happening in my body was no excuse for the moodiness and mouthiness that were part of my pattern during that year.

If we're looking for an excuse to behave badly, it's always easy to find one—especially if we fall for the Enemy's lies. If we believe we can't control our emotions, we'll also believe we can't control how we act in response to them, especially when we're feeling emotionally vulnerable or out of control. Not only will we be too quick to believe our feelings, but we'll also be far too quick to obey them. And what happens next isn't pretty:

- We feel a sudden craving for a bowl of chocolate ice cream at ten o'clock at night . . . so we head for the freezer and dig in.

- We feel like staying up and watching a late-night movie . . . so we ignore our body's cues to get some rest.

- We don't feel like getting out of bed the next morning . . . so we pull the covers up over our head and call in sick at work.

- We don't feel like cleaning our house . . . so we let it go until the mess is so bad we're *really* depressed.

- We feel the need to blow off steam . . . so we go on a rant and apologize later.

And if we cater to our emotions and let them control our actions in these kinds of daily routines, we'll be even more vulnerable to being controlled by our emotions in the major transitions and difficult seasons of life.

In recent decades, there has been a lot of research and discussion regarding the seasons of a woman's life. Some of this study has increased our understanding of the way that we are "fearfully and wonderfully made" (Ps. 139:14). However, it has also provided some women with an excuse for out-of-control attitudes and behavior.

Who among us hasn't been tempted at times to attribute our negative moods and reactions to where we are in our monthly cycle? This way of thinking almost cost "Marie" her marriage:

*I am fifty-two years old, and I can see how this lie had my heart completely deceived. My husband tried to confront me and help me see the Truth, but I was so deceived and reinforced by the PMS proponents that there was no way I would listen. I had to face the possibility of my husband leaving before my eyes were opened.*

For some women, a difficult pregnancy "explains" erratic mood swings and volatile behavior. I have known other women who seem to be planning ahead to have a breakdown when they hit menopause.

Certainly what happens in our bodies does affect us emotionally, mentally, and even spiritually. We cannot isolate these various dimensions of who we are—they are inseparably intertwined. But we fall into a trap when we justify fleshly, sinful attitudes and responses based on our physical condition or hormonal changes.

I remember an occasion years ago when I was physically and emotionally wrung out from an intense speaking schedule. My attitude and my tongue were on a roll; I was being negative and generally hard to live with. Subconsciously I was justifying myself because of how I was feeling. A friend who happened to be within the radius of my cantankerous spirit looked at me and said simply, "Nancy, don't let tiredness be an excuse for carnality."

I confess that at the moment, I didn't particularly appreciate the rebuke, but it was exactly what I needed to hear—a painful, but necessary, reminder of the Truth.

As with other aspects of nature, God has designed our bodies to function in seasons and cycles. Certainly each season of life has its challenges. One of the consequences of the fall was that childbearing would be accompanied by sorrow and pain. But childbirth is not the only time those consequences are felt. For example, the difficulties some women experience associated with their menstrual cycle are a practical reminder of our fallen condition.

But every monthly cycle is also a reminder that God made us *women* and that with our womanhood comes the capacity for being a bearer and nurturer of life. As a younger woman, I found this to be a regular prompt that He had made me and that my calling was to glorify Him in each season of life.

And now many of my women friends and I are experiencing new challenges that come with the aging process. Some days those changes can be overwhelming, discouraging, and disorienting.

But God made our bodies! He understands (better than we do) how they work. Do we think things like menstrual cycles, hormones, pregnancy, and menopause catch Him off guard?

The psalmist praises God for His watch care and His sovereign plan as it relates to the creation of our physical bodies:

> You formed my inward parts;
>     you knitted me together in my mother's womb.
> I praise you, for I am fearfully and wonderfully made.
>     Wonderful are your works;
>     my soul knows it very well.
> My frame was not hidden from you,
>     when I was being made in secret,
>     intricately woven in the depths of the earth.
> Your eyes saw my unformed substance;
>     in your book were written, every one of them,
>     the days that were formed for me,
>     when as yet there was none of them.
>
> —Psalm 139:13–16

What an incredible thought! Long before you were born, every molecule of your body and every day of your life from conception to the grave was carefully thought through and planned by God. He ordained the day you would start menstruation, when and how many times you would be able to conceive, and exactly when you would stop ovulating. He understands exactly what is taking place in your body through every season and change.

Is it conceivable that this wise, loving Creator would be unaware of our hormone levels at any stage of maturity or would have failed to make provision for every season of life? He does not promise us an easy or trouble-free journey. But He has promised to meet all our needs and to give grace to respond to the challenges and difficulties associated with every stage of life.

He may choose to meet your needs through such means as good nutrition, supplements, and exercise. He may use the wisdom and resources of a medical professional to help. He may surround you with understanding friends who will encourage and walk with you through a difficult season. Or all of the above. Regardless, He will take you safely through each season as you look to Him to be your source, your sustainer, and your Shepherd.

Long before anyone had ever written a book on the subject of menopause or estrogen, Francis de Sales (1567–1622) wrote words of wise counsel for women of every generation—words that are even more meaningful and encouraging to me today as an older woman, than when I included them in the first edition of this book years ago:

> Do not look forward to the changes and chances of this life in fear; rather look to them with full hope that, as they arise, God, whose you are, will deliver you out of them. He has kept you hitherto,—do you but hold fast to His dear hand, and He will lead you safely through all things; and, when you cannot stand, He will bear you in His arms. . . . The same everlasting Father who cares for you today, will take care of you to-morrow, and every day. Either He will shield you from suffering, or He will give you unfailing strength to bear it. Be at peace then, and put aside all anxious thoughts and imaginations.[1]

Paul's prayer at the end of his first letter to the Thessalonians is not just for first-century believers. And it is not just for men. I believe it is a prayer that can be claimed by women in every season of their lives. It is a prayer we can expect God to answer, as we exercise faith and allow Him to do so:

> May the God of peace himself sanctify you completely,
> and may your whole spirit and soul and body be kept blameless
> at the coming of our Lord Jesus Christ.
> He who calls you is faithful; he will surely do it.
>
> —1 Thessalonians 5:23–24

## 40. *"I can't bear being depressed."*

Depression is a real and painful issue for many women I have known personally and for others who have contacted me or our ministry, desperate for help and hope. In fact, twice as many women as men suffer from depression.[2]

Depression comes in different sizes, shapes, and colors. In any form, whether mild or acute, it is life-altering. At the severe end of the spectrum, it can be life-threatening. But no less perilous than the depression itself are the lies (or in some cases, half-truths) the Enemy perpetuates about this condition.

"I can't bear to go on being depressed" is just one of those lies. There are numerous others. For example:

- "Only unspiritual people get depressed."
- "Depression is always rooted in sin."
- "Depression is never rooted in sin."
- "Depression is purely a physiological (or brain or hormonal) issue."
- "Depression is purely a spiritual issue."
- "The answer to depression must first/always be sought in medication and/or therapy."
- "Christians should never treat depression with meds and/or therapy."
- "The physical/emotional effects of depression can be treated effectively apart from dealing with any spiritual/heart issues that may be involved."
- "There's no real hope for those who are depressed."
- "Any Christian who really wants to can be healed from his/her depression."

As is the case with other topics we've considered, the lies about depression—and the corresponding Truth that sets us free—could be the subject of an entire book. But I'd like to shine at least a ray of light into the darkness that is so frequently the companion of depression.

For starters, depression is no respecter of persons, and its presence is not necessarily an indicator of a person's spiritual condition. No less a spiritual giant than the unrivaled nineteenth-century British pastor Charles Spurgeon experienced bouts of severe depression throughout his adult life. He recalled one spell in which "My spirits were sunken so low that I could weep by the hour like a child, and yet I knew not what I wept for."[3]

"As well fight with the mist," said Spurgeon, "as with this shapeless, undefinable, yet all-beclouding hopelessness."[4] Perhaps you are familiar with this "all-beclouding hopelessness."

Depression and anxiety are complex issues, and we still have much to learn about their causes, as well as the long-term effects of various types of treatment. Much research has been done to try to understand the interrelationship between personal experience, genetic predisposition, and various other physiological and psychological factors. (Multiple factors have been identified that likely contributed to Spurgeon's lifelong battle with depression.)

Some people seem to be more susceptible to depression due to genetic factors or general human frailty.

Further, in this broken world, depressing things happen to people—things they did not choose, circumstances over which they have no control, things that are not their "fault." Natural disasters, job loss, chronic physical pain or illness, hunger and starvation, war, the death of loved ones—any of these experiences can trigger bouts of depression. And then there are the blows inflicted on us by the sins of others—rejection, abandonment, physical and verbal abuse, sexual assault, racism, oppression, injustice, and more.

At some level, illness (whether physical, emotional, or mental), pain, and depression are an unavoidable consequence of living in a fallen world.

As the apostle Paul reminds us in Romans 8, the entire creation "groans" under the weight of its sinful condition, longing for our final redemption.

Depression can also be caused or exacerbated by our own sins or by sinful responses to hurtful circumstances or offenses—ingratitude, bitterness, unforgiveness, unbelief, claiming of rights, anger, and self-centeredness. If these issues are not addressed, the consequences will inevitably show up in our bodies and souls, creating very real physical and emotional problems.

In many instances, medication can help alleviate the symptoms of depression. However, if the depression is caused or fueled by something other or more than an organic, physical issue, the medication is unlikely to provide an effective long-term solution.

Properly administered, medication may help a depressed person get stabilized enough to think clearly, providing a window of opportunity to begin dealing with non-physiological issues that have contributed to the problem. But no prescription drug can "cure" the deeper issues of the spirit. If the sufferer does not address those inner heart issues, she is unlikely to experience more than temporary relief.

## DEPRESSION IN THE BIBLE

You may be surprised to learn that numerous individuals in the Bible suffered with depressive tendencies. Their stories provide helpful insight into some (not all) of the contributing causes of depression. In some cases, their struggle was nothing more than the consequence of their own pride, selfishness, and anger.

For example, *King Ahab* became depressed when he couldn't get his own way. When Ahab's neighbor refused to sell him a piece of property he badly wanted, he became "vexed and sullen. . . . And he lay down on his bed and turned away his face and would eat no food" (1 Kings 21:4). Ahab's wife, Jezebel, attempted to pull him out of his depression by promising to help him get what he wanted. She said to him, "Arise and eat bread and let your heart be cheerful; I will give you the vineyard of Naboth the Jezreelite" (1 Kings 21:7).

I confess I sometimes see the spirit of Ahab when I look in the mirror. I may tank emotionally, in response to things not going "my way." Deep down I'm angry, but rather than express that anger outwardly, I sink into an emotional pit, hoping that someone will notice and attempt to make me feel better, as Jezebel did to Ahab.

The story of *Jonah* illustrates how resisting and resenting God's choices can produce depression and suicidal thoughts. When God did not destroy the Ninevites as Jonah felt they deserved, "it displeased Jonah exceedingly, and he was angry. And he prayed to the LORD and said . . . 'O LORD, please take my life from me, for it is better for me to die than to live'" (Jonah 4:1–3). God's response forced Jonah to face up to his anger: "And the LORD said, 'Do you do well to be angry?'" (4:4). The same exchange was repeated a short time later, when Jonah became further depressed after a vine that had provided shade withered up and died. God wanted the prophet to see that it was not his circumstances that were actually causing his depression, but rather his angry response to God's sovereign choices.

*Hannah* was a godly woman who became depressed when she had to deal with a combination of unfulfilled longings and a strained relationship over a prolonged period of time. Her husband loved her dearly, but it was not within his power to fix the issues that plagued her. For reasons known only to the Lord, He had closed Hannah's womb and she was barren. To rub salt into the wound, her husband's other wife, Peninnah, had no difficulty conceiving and bearing children and didn't hesitate to remind Hannah of that fact:

> And her rival used to provoke her grievously to irritate her, because the LORD had closed her womb. So it went on year by year. As often as she went up to the house of the LORD,

she used to provoke her.
Therefore Hannah wept and would not eat.

—1 Samuel 1:6–7

When we fail to see God's hand in our circumstances or when we contend with Him over His choices for our lives, we can, like Hannah, become candidates for emotional and spiritual depression.

In Psalm 32 we learn of the physical and emotional anguish that resulted when *King David* refused to confess his sin in the matter of Bathsheba and Uriah:

When I kept silent, my bones wasted away
through my groaning all day long.
For day and night your hand was heavy upon me;
my strength was dried up as by the heat of summer.

—Psalm 32:3–4

In contrast to the depression he experienced because of his sin, David periodically encountered times of intense emotional darkness that were not directly connected to his own sin. Some of the most honest, heart-wrenching psalms express the depths of his despair:

Attend to me, and answer me;
I am restless in my complaint and I moan. . . .
My heart is in anguish within me;
the terrors of death have fallen upon me.
Fear and trembling come upon me,
and horror overwhelms me. . . .
My tears have been my food
day and night.

—Psalms 55:2, 4–5; 42:3

In such excruciating seasons, David learned the importance of counseling his heart according to the Truth of God's character.

> Why are you cast down, O my soul,
> and why are you in turmoil within me?
> Hope in God; for I shall again praise him,
> my salvation and my God.
> My soul is cast down within me;
> therefore I remember you.
>
> —Psalm 42:5–6

In his classic book *Spiritual Depression*, medical doctor and pastor Martyn Lloyd-Jones applies this psalm to those who find themselves struggling with depression:

> You must say to your soul: "Why art thou cast down"—what business have you to be disquieted? You must . . . exhort yourself, and say to yourself: "Hope thou in God"—instead of muttering in this depressed, unhappy way. And then you must go on to remind yourself of God, Who God is, and what God is and what God has done, and what God has pledged Himself to do.[5]

In the last chapter of the book of James, we find a passage that provides encouragement and practical help for those who have been laid low by depression and feel powerless to press on:

> Is anyone among you suffering? Let him pray.
> Is anyone cheerful? Let him sing praise.
> Is anyone among you sick? Let him call for the elders of the church,
> and let them pray over him, anointing him with oil in the name of
> the Lord. And the prayer of faith will save the one who is sick,
> and the Lord will raise him up.
> And if he has committed sins, he will be forgiven.
> Therefore, confess your sins to one another and pray for one another,

that you may be healed.

The prayer of a righteous person has great power as it is working.

—James 5:13–16

When James speaks here of those who are sick, he's not just talking about a nagging headache or seasonal allergies. Two different Greek words are both translated "sick" in these verses. The first (v. 14) is a word that means "to be weak, feeble, to be without strength, powerless."[6] The second (v. 15) means "to be wearied, sick or faint."[7]

We're talking about more than just a physical ailment, in other words (though physical illness can be emotionally and mentally debilitating). The totality of body, soul, and spirit is affected. You can just picture someone who has been weakened and is bowed down—whether due to the circumstances of life, her own sin, or both. She is depleted, drained, and overwhelmed, and she feels helpless to do anything about her condition. She may be chronically discouraged, or she may be what is known today as clinically depressed.

So what can we glean from this passage when it comes to those who are sick with depression?

## LOOKING UP

The first insight that stands out to me is that *regardless of how we are feeling or what we are going through, our first response should be to turn to the Lord.* Whether we are prospering or suffering, happy or sad, healthy or sick—before we do anything else, we should acknowledge God's presence and ask Him to walk with us through the experience, to direct us in responding to the circumstances and to provide His resources to deal with the situation.

More often than not, however, our first response is to turn to someone or something *other* than the Lord. When we're hurting and in search of comfort, relief, or escape, we're prone to seize upon the most immediate, tangible solutions we can find. We want something that will give us results (the faster the better) and dull the pain—preferably something that doesn't require too much effort.

After all, it's easier to call a friend for support than to get on our knees with an open Bible and listen to what God wants to say to us in our "dark night of the soul." It's easier to try to mask the pain with food, drink, exercise, or sleep than to do the hard work of identifying attitudes or behaviors that may be contributing to our condition. It's easier to numb our feelings with social media or Netflix or planning a dream vacation or throwing ourselves into a hobby than to humble ourselves and acknowledge our ingratitude, unforgiveness, or anger. It's easier to rely on a doctor, a therapist, or antidepressants than to ask God how He might want to use our pain to sanctify us and to bring glory to Himself.

Any of these means may provide a measure of relief. But apart from an infusion of God's grace in our lives, they're likely to be inadequate and short-lived. Nothing less than the "God of all comfort" can meet our deepest needs at such times.

This is not to say that all those other things are wrong or unhelpful. A good night's sleep can make a world of difference in how a beleaguered mom with two preschoolers and a newborn feels. Sometimes a change in diet can greatly affect our physical well-being, which in turn affects our emotional and mental well-being. Physical exercise can be beneficial in dealing with physical symptoms related to depression. A physician may be able to diagnose and treat a physiological problem that is impacting our emotional condition. Friends can provide encouragement, especially if they help point our thinking back to the Truth. And sometimes we need someone with flesh on to take our hand and help us walk to His throne of grace.

But looking *outward* without turning our hearts *upward* for solutions to life's problems—whatever their origin or cause—can leave us feeling hopelessly mired in despair.

## LOOKING OUT

The second Truth James 5 emphasizes is *the importance of the body of Christ in helping hurting people.*

Some have a mindset today that only "professionals" can minister effectively to those with emotional or mental issues. I'm not saying that there's no place for people who have been trained in mental-health fields. I have dear friends who love the Lord and have been greatly helped by wise professionals—particularly those with a Christian, biblical worldview—in dealing with depression and the fallout of abuse and trauma.

However, let's not forget that God has given the body of Christ rich resources to care for desperate, needy people. He has given us His Word and His Spirit. We need to learn how to take the ointment of the Word of God and apply it to the needs of hurting people.

And so, James says, when your suffering has left you weak and sick, let the people of God minister grace in Jesus' name. After you have first prayed yourself, ask God for grace to share your needs with the spiritual leaders of your church, difficult as that may seem. Confess any sin God may have revealed through your suffering. Then let the Lord strengthen, comfort, and encourage you through the prayers and care[8] of these spiritual shepherds.

James holds out the promise of both forgiveness, where needed, and healing for those who are afflicted. That restoration may not be instantaneous or entire in the short term. Just as God does not heal every physical ailment this side of eternity, your emotional or mental affliction may be with you throughout your earthly journey. But you can be assured that however long your suffering may last, He will walk with you, His grace will sustain and sanctify you, and one day the healing will be full and complete.

We have a Savior who cares deeply about those who suffer. He is tender and compassionate toward those who are weak and struggling: "A bruised reed He will not break and a dimly burning wick He will not extinguish" (Isa. 42:3 NASB).

And Scripture urges us to show the same compassion for hurting people: "Comfort the discouraged, help the weak, be patient with everyone" (1 Thess. 5:14 CSB). This is a good word for all of us in the body of Christ, as we seek to extend His heart to those in need.

You cannot "fix" someone else's depression, but you can offer comfort, help, and patience. You can listen without judging. You can check in occasionally to counter the depressed person's tendency toward isolation or offer practical help when she is overwhelmed. Even small gestures of kindness can make a big difference. And yes, helping a depressed person will require you to be patient. She may not have the emotional energy to respond to you or may even lash out, so you will need to learn to extend love and speak truth, all generously seasoned with gentleness and grace. And don't forget that prayer is a powerful form of caring—perhaps the most powerful.

## HELD BY THE SAVIOR

Author Stephen Altrogge speaks out of years of personal experience when he describes depression this way:

> Everywhere you look, things look dark. Bleak. Black. Hopeless. Helpless. The waiting room for depression says, "Abandon hope, all ye who enter here."[9]

But Stephen refuses to give in to hopelessness. He realizes there is no formula to lift the clouds of gloom and despair. Nevertheless, he encourages those who are depressed to fight for faith. Separate your feelings from the truth, he says. Find a faithful friend to help you stay anchored to what is true. And take simple, practical steps to refresh and nurture your body—even if that's the last thing you feel like doing—so you can "think more clearly and see things more accurately" and "more easily process and embrace God's promises."

At the end of the day, Altrogge reminds his fellow sojourners that true hope is found in Christ alone:

> Ultimately, your hope in depression hinges on Jesus. He's holding onto you even when it feels like you're free falling. You may be in the dark, but your Shepherd is walking right beside you. He knows what it's like to be overwhelmed by grief and swallowed by bleakness. Your grip on life may falter, but his grip on you won't.[10]

That's the Truth. The Truth will not eliminate all pain and sadness—at least not in this life. But the Truth will enable you to walk by faith, to persevere in climbing what seventeenth-century writer John Bunyan called the "Hill Difficulty," in his Christian classic, *The Pilgrim's Progress*—knowing that the "Celestial City" lies ahead.[11] There and then, all pain, depression, and tears will be forever banished, eclipsed by the presence of the Savior, who bore all your sorrows and sins as His own, that you might enter into His eternal rest and joy.

When it comes to dealing with even our darkest emotions, we must remember that "feeling good" is not the ultimate objective in the Christian's life. God does not promise that those who walk with Him will be free from all difficult emotions. In fact, as long as we are in these bodies, we will experience varying degrees of pain and distress.

As we will see in the next chapter, the focus of our lives must not be so much on changing or "fixing" things to make ourselves feel better as on the glory of God and His redemptive purposes in the world. Everything else is expendable. True joy comes from abandoning ourselves to that end.

| THE LIE | 37. If I feel something, it must be true. |
|---|---|
| THE TRUTH | • My feelings cannot always be trusted. They often have little to do with reality and can easily deceive me into believing things that are not true. Psalm 119:29–30; Jeremiah 17:9–10 <br><br> • I must choose to reject any feelings that are not consistent with the Truth. Psalms 33:4; 51:6; 56:3–4; Ephesians 4:14–15; Philippians 4:8–9 |
| THE LIE | 38. I can't control my emotions. |
| THE TRUTH | • I do not have to be controlled by my emotions. Psalm 6:1–10; Isaiah 54:10; Matthew 5:44; 28:20; Ephesians 4:26; Philippians 4:4–7; 1 Thessalonians 5:18 <br><br> • I can choose to fix my mind on the Truth, to take every thought captive to the Truth, and to let God control my emotions. Psalm 42:11; Isaiah 26:3; 50:10; John 10:10; 17:17; 2 Corinthians 10:5; Philippians 4:8–9; Colossians 3:1–2 |

| | |
|---|---|
| **THE LIE** | **39. I can't help how I respond when my hormones are out of whack.** |
| **THE TRUTH** | • By God's grace, I can choose to obey Him regardless of how I feel.<br>Philippians 2:12–13; James 4:7<br><br>• There is no excuse for ungodly attitudes, responses, or behavior.<br>1 Thessalonians 5:23–24<br><br>• My physical and emotional cycles and seasons are under the control of the One who made me, cares for me, and has made provision for each stage of my life.<br>Psalm 139:1–18 |
| **THE LIE** | **40. I can't bear being depressed.** |
| **THE TRUTH** | • Physical and emotional symptoms of depression are sometimes the fruit of issues in the spirit that need to be addressed.<br>1 Samuel 1:6–7; 1 Kings 21:4, 7; Psalms 32:3–4; 42:3–8; 55:4–5; Lamentations 3:1–33; Jonah 4:1–4<br><br>• Regardless of how I feel, I can choose to give thanks, to obey God, and to reach out to others.<br>Philippians 4:4–7<br><br>• God has given us powerful resources—His grace, His Spirit, His Word, His promises, the body of Christ—to minister to our emotional needs.<br>Psalm 25:4–5; Romans 8:26; 2 Corinthians 12:9 |

# CHAPTER TEN

# LIES WOMEN BELIEVE...
## ABOUT *Circumstances*

*What a year it's been! We received word that one of Cain's grandsons had a bad fall while working on a building project for his dad. Apparently he was pretty seriously hurt. It's been hard to find out a lot of details, since we have so little communication with Cain and his family. That whole relationship is still strained, and the memories are so painful at times.*

*This year's harvest has been the poorest I can remember. Adam has had to work a ton of extra hours just to get enough food for us to survive. By the time he gets home at the end of the day, he's exhausted and doesn't feel like talking or doing much of anything.*

*I wish I could say I've been an encourager to him through all this, but I've had my own struggles. I just don't have the energy I used to have, and I often feel overwhelmed trying to keep up with things around the house, especially with four children still at home. Our lives are so hectic—it's hard to know how to juggle a husband, kids, grandkids, and housework and still find time for myself.*

*Sometimes the pressure really gets to me, and I find myself being out of sorts with everything and everyone around me. I feel bad about the way I take things out on the kids and Adam. I'm just so tired.*

*It's been too long since Adam and I had time together—just the two of us. I wish we could find a way to get away from it all for a while. Maybe that would help me cope better. I know something's got to change.*

It was one of those days. You've had them—you know, when nothing goes right. You may have read about this particular day in Judith Viorst's classic children's book, *Alexander and the Terrible, Horrible, No Good, Very Bad Day*. It seemed that everything was going wrong for poor Alexander. From start to finish, his day consisted of one irksome experience after another.

Alexander fell asleep with gum in his mouth and woke up with gum in his hair, he had a horrible day at school, a no-good dentist appointment, and a very bad stop at the shoe store. And that wasn't the end of it. Between lima beans for dinner, soap in his eyes during his bath, and having to wear the railroad train pajamas he detested, who can blame the poor boy for sighing at the end of the day, "I think I'll move to Australia!"[1]

Alexander isn't the only one who has felt that way. We've probably all had times when we wished God would call us to the uninhabited regions of the earth!

In fact, that is just what the psalmist prayed on at least one occasion. Everything seemed to be pressing in on him, and apparently he felt he'd had about all he could take:

> Oh, that I had wings like a dove!
> I would fly away and be at rest...
> I would hurry to find a shelter
> from the raging wind and tempest.
>
> —Psalm 55:6, 8

When God first created the earth, He looked at everything He had made and said, "It is good." From the tiniest molecule to the most expansive galaxy in the universe, everything was in perfect order. All existed in perfect harmony. There was no such thing as confusion or heartache or conflict or frustration.

And as we have seen, Adam and Eve enjoyed a perfect environment. Everything worked. Nothing was broken or needed to be fixed. No one was ever late or tired or irritable. No one ever got into debt or had a headache or got sick or died. No one ever got his feelings hurt or said something insensitive or sued anybody.

But all that changed the moment Eve and her husband listened to and acted on Satan's lie. Where once the ground had readily yielded food for the man and woman to eat, now the man had to contend with thorns and thistles to provide for his family. Giving birth was intended to be a joyous, natural experience for the woman, but now she had to endure labor and pain in childbirth.

In addition to thorns and labor pains, the fallen human experience would include

| | |
|---|---|
| *fear, shame, and guilt* | *hurricanes, floods, and earthquakes* |
| *disappointment* | *crime and violence* |
| *arguments and lawsuits* | *poverty, injustice, racism, and war* |
| *tears and temper tantrums* | *arthritis, tumors, and cancer* |

The entrance of deception into the world had far-reaching consequences. Like a drop of food coloring poured into a glass of water, sin tainted everything about human beings and their environment.

And that's what we live with today. Those are our circumstances. God is still with us, but our everyday reality is a fallen world. And Satan still tries to deceive us in regard to these circumstances—resulting in unnecessary disappointment, anger, and despair. How desperately we need God's Truth in order to keep our lives in perspective and hold on to hope!

## 41. *"If my circumstances were different, I would be different."*

I remember talking years ago with a young mother who had a two-year-old child and one-year-old twins. She said with a sigh, "I was never an impatient person—until I had these twins!" This woman believed what most of us have believed at one time or another—that we are the way we are because of our circumstances.

Perhaps you've found yourself saying, as have I, "She made me *so* mad!" In essence, we're saying: "I'm really a kind, gentle, loving, self-controlled, Spirit-filled woman. *But* . . . you can't believe what she did—it's *her* fault I lost my temper!"

Sound familiar? We may insist:

- "I wouldn't have lost my cool if my child hadn't filled the dryer with water and painted the living room furniture with butter!"

- "I wouldn't struggle in my marriage if my parents hadn't made me feel worthless."

- "I wouldn't be so bitter if my husband hadn't run off with that other woman."

What we're really saying is: "Someone or something made me the way I am."

We feel that if our circumstances were different—our upbringing, our environment, the people around us—we would be different. We would be more patient, more loving, more content, easier to live with.

If our circumstances make us what we are, then we are all victims. And that's just what the Enemy wants us to believe. Because if we are victims, then we aren't responsible—we can't help the way we are. But God says we *are* responsible—*not* for the failures of others, but for our own responses and lives.

The Truth is, our circumstances don't make us what we are. They merely reveal what we are. That exasperated mother who believed she had never been an impatient person until she had twins just didn't realize how impatient she was until God brought a set of circumstances into her life to show her what she was really like—so He could change her.

The Enemy convinces us that the only way we can ever be different is if our circumstances change. So we play the "if only" game:

- "If only we didn't have to move . . ."
- "If only we lived closer to my parents . . ."
- "If only we had a bigger house [more closets, more storage] . . ."

- "If only we had more money . . ."
- "If only my husband didn't have to work so many hours . . ."
- "If only I were married . . ."
- "If only I weren't married . . ."
- "If only I were married to someone different . . ."
- "If only I had children . . ."
- "If only I didn't have so many children . . ."
- "If only I hadn't lost that child . . ."
- "If only my husband would communicate . . ."
- "If only my husband were a spiritual leader . . ."

We've been deceived into believing we would be happier if we had a different set of circumstances. But the Truth is, if we're not content within our present circumstances, we're not likely to be happy in another set of circumstances.

When she was in her fifties, nineteenth-century writer Elizabeth Prentiss learned that her husband would be taking a new job that required them to uproot from their home in New York and move to Chicago. The move meant leaving all their friends and posed a danger to her fragile health. In a letter to a friend, she wrote,

> We want to know no will but God's in this question. . . . The experience of the past winter would impress upon me the fact that place and position have next to nothing to do with happiness; that we can be wretched in a palace, radiant in a dungeon. . . . Perhaps this heartbreaking is exactly what we need to remind us . . . that we are pilgrims and strangers on the earth.[2]

George Washington's wife, Martha, expressed the same conviction in a letter written to her friend Mercy Warren:

> I am still determined to be cheerful and happy in whatever situation I may be; for I have also learned from experience that the

greater part of our happiness or misery depends on our dispo-
sitions and not on our circumstances. We carry the seeds of the
one or the other about with us in our minds, wherever we go.[3]

Centuries earlier, the apostle Paul learned that he could rejoice and
be content in any circumstance because his joy and well-being were not
dependent on his circumstances, but on the steadfast love and faithfulness of God and the condition of his relationship with God. That is why
he could say,

> I have learned in whatever situation I am to be content.
> I know how to be brought low, and I know how to abound.
> In any and every circumstance, I have learned the secret
> of facing plenty and hunger, abundance and need.
>
> —Philippians 4:11–12

Elizabeth Prentiss, Martha Washington, and the apostle Paul all
came to understand a life-changing Truth: we might not be able to control our circumstances, but our circumstances don't have to control us.

We can trust a wise, loving, sovereign God to control every circumstance of our lives. Joy, peace, and stability come from believing that every circumstance that touches our lives has first been filtered through
His fingers of love and is part of a great, eternal plan that He is working
out in this world and in our lives.

## 42. *"I shouldn't have to suffer."*

*M*any popular writers and teachers have promised sinners unending peace and joy, a home in heaven, and a prosperous
life between here and there if they will simply come to Jesus.
That kind of preaching, stripped of the call to discipleship, has produced
a generation of "disciples" who have little stomach for the battles of the
Christian life. When their hopes are dashed by the inevitable trials and

tribulations of being a Christ follower, they are easily disillusioned and make a dash for the quickest escape route.

That's exactly what the Enemy wants! By convincing us that our suffering is undeserved or unnecessary, he succeeds in getting us to resent and resist the will and purposes of God.

The message that was preached by the Lord Jesus Himself and by the apostles who followed Him was a call to take up the cross; it was a call to sign up for battle; it was a call to suffer. And the apostle Paul taught that suffering is an essential course in God's curriculum for all believers: "Through many tribulations we must enter the kingdom of God" (Acts 14:22). That's just the opposite of what Satan wants us to believe about suffering.

Arthur Mathews served as a missionary in China from 1938–1949, when the Communists took control. He was one of the last China Inland Mission missionaries to leave China in 1953, after being held under house arrest for four years with his wife and daughter. His writings reflect a commitment to self-denial and a willingness to embrace the plan and purposes of God in suffering:

> We tend to look at the circumstances of life in terms of what they may do to our cherished hopes and convenience, and we shape our decisions and reactions accordingly. When a problem threatens, we rush to God, not to seek his perspective, but to ask him to deflect the trouble. Our self-concern takes priority over whatever it is that God might be trying to do through the trouble. . . .
>
> An escapist generation reads security, prosperity, and physical well-being as evidences of God's blessing. Thus when he puts suffering and affliction into our hands, we misread his signals and misinterpret his intentions.[4]

If we don't trust the heart and intentions of God, we will naturally resist suffering. But, as seventeenth-century Puritan author William Law exhorts us, we must learn to welcome and embrace suffering as a pathway to sanctification and a doorway into greater intimacy with God:

Receive every inward and outward trouble, every disappointment,
pain, uneasiness, temptation, darkness, and desolation, with both
thy hands, as a true opportunity and blessed occasion of dying
to self, and entering into a fuller fellowship with thy self-denying,
suffering Saviour.[5]

The Truth is, God is more intent on our holiness than on our immediate, temporal happiness. He knows that apart from being holy, we can never be truly happy.

The Truth is, it's impossible to be holy apart from suffering. Even Jesus Himself, during His years here on earth, was in some unexplainable way made "perfect through suffering" (Heb. 2:10), and "although he was a son, he learned obedience through what he suffered (Heb. 5:8). If we want to be like Jesus, we can't resist whatever instrument God may choose to fulfill that desire.

All the New Testament authors recognized that there is a redemptive, sanctifying fruit that cannot be produced in our lives except by suffering. In fact, Peter goes so far as to insist that suffering is our calling—not just for some select group of Christian leaders or martyrs, but for every child of God: "For to this you have been called, because Christ also suffered for you, leaving you an example, so that you might follow in his steps" (1 Peter 2:21).

True joy is not the absence of pain but the sanctifying, sustaining presence of the Lord Jesus in the midst of the pain. Through the whole process, whether it be a matter of days, weeks, months, or years, we have His promise:

After you have suffered a little while, the God of all grace,
who has called you to his eternal glory in Christ,
will himself restore, confirm, strengthen, and establish you.

—1 Peter 5:10

### 43. *"My circumstances will never change—this will go on forever."*

This lie imprisons many women in hopelessness and despair.

The Truth is, your pain—be it physical affliction, memories of abuse, a troubled marriage, or a heart broken by a wayward child—may go on for a long time. But it will not last forever. It may go on for all of your life down here on this earth. But even a lifetime is not forever.

The Truth is, a moment or two from now (in the light of eternity), when we are in the presence of the Lord, everything that has taken place in this life will be just a breath—a comma.

A woman called to talk with me about a complicated and difficult situation in her marriage. The situation had been that way for as long as she could remember, and there was no indication of anything changing in the future. In the course of the conversation, I was moved as this dear wife said, "If it goes on for our whole lives, that's okay. I know that time is short and eternity is long. One day this will all be just a blip on the screen."

She spoke not as one who was just resigned to her "fate." She longed for things to be different. But she had a perspective of time and eternity that enabled her to be faithful in the midst of the testing.

Another woman approached me after a conference and said, "I want to thank you for what you said about being faithful to your mate even through hard times." She went on to tell the story of how she had lived for forty years in a marriage to a difficult and ungodly man. She said, "All through those years, many people—including well-meaning Christians—counseled me to get out of this marriage. But somehow God kept drawing me back to that vow I had made, and I did not believe it was right to leave."

After a pause, she continued, "I'm so glad I waited. You see, a year ago my husband finally got saved, and God is truly changing him after all these years. And not only that," she said softly, with tears in her eyes, "you can't believe the incredible changes God has brought about in my life as a result of this journey."

Why is that perspective so hard for us to come by? The problem is, we're so earthbound that to most of us forty years sounds like eternity! We can't fathom enduring anything hard for that long. If we could only see that forty years—or longer—is inconsequential in the light of eternity.

Regardless of how long our suffering may continue here on earth, God's Word assures us that it will not last forever.

So we do not lose heart. Though our outer self is wasting away,
our inner self is being renewed day by day.
For this light momentary affliction is preparing for us
an eternal weight of glory beyond all comparison,
as we look not to the things that are seen but
to the things that are unseen.
For the things that are seen are transient,
but the things that are unseen are eternal.

—2 Corinthians 4:16–18

For I consider that the sufferings of this present time are not
worth comparing with the glory that is to be revealed to us.

—Romans 8:18

Weeping may tarry for the night,
but joy comes with the morning.

—Psalm 30:5

Your night of weeping may go on for months or even years. But if you are a child of God, it will not go on forever. God has determined the exact duration of your suffering, and it will not last one moment longer than He knows is necessary to achieve His holy, eternal purposes in and through your life.

In those cases where there is no relief from pain in this life, we have literally hundreds of promises in God's Word that one day all suffering will

be over, faith will become sight, darkness will be turned to light, and our faithfulness will be rewarded with unending joy. He promises that one day,

The wilderness and the dry land shall be glad;
the desert shall rejoice and blossom like the crocus. . . .
And the ransomed of the LORD shall return
and come to Zion with singing;
everlasting joy shall be upon their heads;
they shall obtain gladness and joy,
and sorrow and sighing shall flee away.

—Isaiah 35:1, 10

Regardless of how powerful the forces of darkness seem to be here and now, the final chapter has been written—and God wins! Believing the Truth about what lies ahead will fill us with hope and enable us to persevere between now and then.

## 44. *"I just can't take any more."*

Here's another lie the Enemy works hard to get us to believe, because he knows if we do, we will live in defeat and hopelessness. One woman wrote and said,

*I have one-year-old twin boys who have been chronically sick with ear infections and colds for two months, causing them to be whiny and irritable constantly. I kept telling myself, my husband, and anyone who would listen, "I can't take it anymore." The lie was a self-fulfilling prophecy, and it was stressing me out. When I finally said, "Yes, by God's grace, I can take it, and He will enable me to do my duty to them," the greatest part of the tension and stress I was feeling dissolved.*

We've all had seasons when we feel we just can't keep going, we just can't take any more. As with every other area of deception, the key to

defeating this lie is to counter it with the Truth. Regardless of what our emotions or our circumstances may tell us, God's Word says, "My grace is sufficient for you" (2 Cor. 12:9). Most of us are familiar with that verse. But, when it comes to the circumstances and trials of our lives, few of us really believe it. What we really believe is . . .

- "I can't take one more sleepless night with this sick child."
- "I can't continue in this marriage."
- "I can't bear to be hurt one more time by my mother-in-law."
- "I can't go on with three teenagers and a mother with dementia living in our home."
- "I just can't take any more."

However, whether we choose to believe it or not, if we are God's children, the Truth is that His grace really *is* sufficient for us. That's assuming, of course, that we haven't taken on ourselves responsibilities He never intended us to carry. If the burden is God-given, we can go on by His grace. His grace is sufficient for every moment, every circumstance, every detail, every need, and every failure of our lives.

That is the Truth with which you and I must perpetually counsel our hearts:

- When I'm exhausted and think I can't possibly face the unfinished tasks that are still before me, *His grace is sufficient for me. [Say it aloud. Say it again. Say it until you believe it.]*
- When I'm having a hard time responding to that family member or that person at the office who really gets under my skin, *His grace is sufficient for me.*
- When I'm tempted to vent my frustration by speaking harsh words, *His grace is sufficient for me.*
- When I've given in to my lust for food for the umpteenth time that day, *His grace is sufficient for me.*

- When I blow it with my family and become uptight and short-tempered, *His grace is sufficient for me.*

- When I don't know which direction to go or what decision to make, *His grace is sufficient for me.*

- When my heart is breaking with an overwhelming sense of loss and grief as I stand by the grave of a loved one, *His grace is sufficient for me.*

What do you need God's grace for? Wayward children? Aching body? Unloving husband? No money in the bank? Struggling to raise three kids without a dad in the home? Don't know where next month's rent is coming from? Lost your job? Just moved to a new city and don't know a soul? Driving hours each week to visit a parent in assisted living? Church going through a split? Desperately lonely? Plagued with guilt? Chemically dependent? Hormones going haywire?

Fill in the blank. Whatever your story, whatever your situation, right now, *His grace is sufficient for you.* His divine resources are available to meet your need—no matter how great.

Dear child of God, your heavenly Father will never lead you anywhere that His grace will not carry you. When the path before you seems hopelessly long, take heart. Lift up your eyes. Look ahead to that day when all suffering will be over. And remember that when you stand before Him, all the tears and sorrows of a lifetime will seem dim in comparison with the beauty and glory of His face. Without a doubt, you will say, "His amazing grace has brought me safely home."

## 45. *"It's all about me."*

### It's all about *you.*

No doubt you've seen this message in various places—from commercials to billboards to bumper stickers to social media.

The philosophy behind those ad campaigns is almost as old as the human race. In effect, it's exactly what the Serpent said to Eve: "It's all about *you*." It's a campaign he has been running effectively ever since.

One writer observed that "to most people the greatest persons in the universe are themselves. Their lives are made up of endless variations on the word 'me.'" [6]

It's true. Our instinctive reaction to life is self-centered: How does this affect *me*? Will this make *me* happy? Why did this have to happen to *me*? What does she think about *me*? It's *my* turn. Nobody cares about *my* ideas. He hurt *my* feelings. I've got to have some time for *me*. I need *my* space. He's not thinking about *my* needs.

It's not enough for us to be the center of our own universe. We want to be the center of everyone else's universe as well—including God's. When others don't devote themselves to promoting our happiness and meeting our needs, we get hurt and start looking for alternate ways to fulfill our self-centered agenda.

You'd think the church would be the one place where things would revolve around God. But that's not necessarily so. In his book *Finding God*, Dr. Larry Crabb offers a penetrating analysis of the extent to which the evangelical church has given in to this deception:

> Helping people to feel loved and worthwhile has become the central mission of the church. We are learning not to worship God in self-denial and costly service, but to embrace our inner child, heal our memories, overcome addictions, lift our depressions, improve our self-images, establish self-preserving boundaries, substitute self-love for self-hatred, and replace shame with an affirming acceptance of who we are.
>
> Recovery from pain is absorbing an increasing share of the church's energy. And that is alarming. . . .
>
> We have become committed to relieving the pain behind our problems rather than using our pain to wrestle more passionately with the character and purpose of God. Feeling better has become more important than finding God. . . .

As a result, we happily camp on biblical ideas that help us feel loved and accepted, and we pass over Scripture that calls us to higher ground. We twist wonderful truths about God's acceptance, his redeeming love, and our new identity in Christ into a basis for honoring ourselves rather than seeing those truths for what they are: the stunning revelation of a God gracious enough to love people who hated him, a God worthy to be honored above everyone and everything else. . . .

We have rearranged things so that God is now worthy of honor because he has honored us. "Worthy is the Lamb," we cry, not in response to his amazing grace, but because he has recovered what we value most: the ability to like ourselves. *We now matter more than God.*[6]

The apostle Paul knew better. He understood that God does not exist for us, but rather, we exist for Him:

> All things were created through him and for him.
> And he is before all things, and in him all things hold together.
> And he is the head of the body, the church.
> He is the beginning, the firstborn from the dead,
> that in everything he might be preeminent.
>
> —Colossians 1:16–18

How was Paul able to sing hymns to God in the middle of the night, his body racked with pain in the bowels of a Roman prison? How could he stay faithful and "rejoice always," while being stoned, shipwrecked, lied about, and rejected by friends and enemies alike? How could he "rejoice always" when he was hungry and tired?

His secret was that he had settled the issue of why he was living. He was not living to please himself or to get his needs fulfilled. From the point of his conversion on the road to Damascus, he had one burning passion: to live for the glory and the pleasure of God. All that mattered to him was knowing Christ and making Him known to others:

> I do not account my life of any value nor as precious to myself,
> if only I may finish my course and the ministry that I received
> from the Lord Jesus, to testify to the gospel of the grace of God.
>
> —Acts 20:24

The bottom line for Paul was: "To live is Christ." Once that was settled, nothing else mattered much.

## CORAM DEO

*Coram Deo* is a Latin phrase that means "in the presence of God." Years ago, a woman sent me a framed piece on which she had written in calligraphy a succinct reminder of what it means to function as our Creator designed us to live:

### Coram Deo

Living all of life
in the presence of God
under the authority of God
and to the glory of God.

I want to close this chapter by introducing you to three women who have exemplified to me what it means to live *coram Deo*.

"Cindy" shared her story with me in a lengthy letter. She got married at the age of eighteen and had three children by the time she was twenty-one. Though she had been baptized as a child, she didn't know what it was to have a personal relationship with Jesus Christ. But when she was in her thirties, as her mother lay in a hospital in a coma, dying of cancer, Cindy picked up a Gideon Bible and cried out to the Lord to help her. "From that moment on," she wrote, "my heart's desire was to know God."

Over the next several years, Cindy's family life became increasingly rocky. Her fourteen-year-old daughter ran away from home, and her two sons were in consistent trouble at school and with the police. At one point Cindy left her husband for two weeks, intending to divorce him.

But through a series of circumstances, God gave her a new compassion for him, and she returned home.

In the midst of all this turmoil, Cindy attended a meeting at a nearby church, where she heard the good news of God's love and how Jesus died to save sinners. She turned to Christ in repentance and faith, and became a new creature.

Things continued to get worse at home. Her children were completely out of control. Her daughter ended up on the streets for a year after her dad wouldn't let her back in the house one day. Subsequently the daughter married and had five children. At the time Cindy wrote me, her daughter was going through a divorce.

One son was dishonorably discharged from the Marines and spent four years in prison. He and his father were estranged and had not spoken in years.

The other son became a drug addict. He was involved in a homicide in a tavern and spent twenty-two years in a penitentiary. Though he made a profession of faith while in prison, he no longer had any interest in spiritual things.

Cindy concluded her letter by sharing her perspective on the whole bleak picture:

> There are no Christmases or Thanksgivings here at home. Will my family ever be healed emotionally and spiritually? Only the Lord knows. But God is my Lord, and I believe He wants to use me to be a testimony and a light for my family. If I don't show them the truth of God's amazing grace, who will? It would be so easy to just walk away and go to some island where there is peace and joy. But God has chosen me to be where I am, to be a testimony to my unsaved husband and to my children.
>
> How can I help my husband see that one day his pride will be taken away and he will have to face Christ? How can I help my daughter see the truth of God's unconditional love? How can I help my eldest son, who has turned his back on God since leaving prison? How can I help my husband reconcile with his other son

*and daughter? Only through God's power, wisdom, and love. So
with all my heart, mind, body, and soul, I say, "Yes, Lord—whatever
You want me to do."*

*Coram Deo.* Even when her family was far from God and she couldn't
glimpse the faintest ray of hope.

*Jennie Thompson's* husband went to be with the Lord after an intense two-year battle with leukemia. In a letter written three months after Robert's homegoing, this young widow with four boys ages seven and
under expressed an extraordinary perspective on the heart and purposes
of God:

> *The Lord has been faithful in holding us up through this time. I
> wouldn't in a million years have chosen this path for my life or the
> lives of my children, but we have learned so much in and through
> our circumstances that we could never have learned another way.
> God has been honored and glorified in a way that never could
> have happened without our circumstances, so I must praise Him
> for those circumstances.*
>
> *God wants to receive the glory that is due Him as our Creator
> and almighty God. Our happiness is the by-product of being
> in and doing His will. That, and only that, is the reason I can be
> weeping at the graveside of my best friend, my husband, and the
> father of my children and still have peace and joy.*

Jennie too lived *Coram Deo.* Even when the path led to her husband's
graveside.

Finally, I remember when my dear friend and prayer partner Janiece
Grissom began to experience numbness and tingling in her hands and
then her arms. After numerous tests and doctor appointments, a neurol-

ogist confirmed that she had Lou Gehrig's disease. Janiece was forty-one years old and the mother of four children, ages four to twelve.

Over the next ten months, the disease took over first one part and then another of her steadily weakening body. Throughout those months, as we had occasion to talk on the phone, Janiece always refused to focus on herself or her prognosis. Invariably, when she would hear my voice, she would say, "Nancy, you've really been on my heart! How can I pray for you?"

In October of that year, I visited with Janiece and her husband, Tim, in their home in Arkansas. By this time she was confined to a recliner. She could not use her arms or legs and could speak only with difficulty because she had lost 50 percent of her lung capacity. Again, I was deeply touched by how God-conscious and God-centered this couple was, even as they faced the ravages of this disease.

I remember Janiece saying over and over that evening, "God has been so good to us!" As the evening drew to a close, several of us surrounded her chair, prayed together, and then sang one of her favorite hymns:

Like a river glorious is God's perfect peace. . . .
Stayed upon Jehovah, hearts are fully blest
Finding, as He promised, perfect peace and rest.[7]

Within the next week, Janiece's physical condition began to deteriorate even more rapidly. Because she was unable to swallow, she was taken to the hospital to have a feeding tube inserted. She never returned home. On the evening of December 13, I called her husband to see how she was doing. Her strength was almost gone, and she could not speak above a whisper. "But the incredible thing," Tim said, "is that she is still spending most of her waking hours praying for other people." Within a matter of hours, Janiece breathed her last and was in the presence of the Lord.

Janiece Grissom died the way she had lived—selflessly loving God and others. In her mind it was never about herself—her health, her comfort, her future. It was all about her God. All that mattered was glorifying Him through saying yes to His purposes for her life. Her sole desire, as expressed by the apostle Paul, was that "now as always Christ will be honored in my body, whether by life or by death" (Phil. 1:20).

In life and in death, *Coram Deo.*

Three lives lived in God's presence. Three women who refused to believe "It's all about me." My friend and author Susan Hunt sums up beautifully the Truth that counters this lie:

> History is the story of redemption. This story is much bigger than I.
> I am not the main character in the drama of redemption. I am not
> the point. But by God's grace I am a part of it. My subplot is integral
> to the whole. It is far more significant to have a small part in this
> story than to star in my own puny production. This is a cosmic story
> that will run throughout eternity. Will I play my part with grace and
> joy, or will I go for the short-run, insignificant story that really has
> no point?[8]

The Truth is, it's not about you. It's not about me. It's all about Him. The Truth may not change your circumstances—at least not here and now—but it will change *you*. The Truth will set you free.

| THE LIE | 41. If my circumstances were different, I would be different. |
|---|---|
| **THE TRUTH** | • My circumstances do not make me what I am; they merely reveal what I am.<br>Matthew 6:21; 15:19; Luke 6:45<br><br>• If I'm not content with my present circumstances, I'm not likely to be happy in another set of circumstances.<br>Philippians 4:11–12<br><br>• I may not be able to control my circumstances, but my circumstances do not have to control me.<br>Hebrews 13:5; James 1:2–5<br><br>• Every circumstance that touches my life has first been filtered through God's fingers of love.<br>Genesis 45:8; 50:20; Job 1:8–12; 14:5; Psalm 139:16; Matthew 10:29–31; Romans 8:28 |
| **THE LIE** | 42. I shouldn't have to suffer. |
| **THE TRUTH** | • It's impossible to become like Jesus apart from suffering. There is redemptive fruit that cannot be produced in our lives apart from suffering.<br>Hebrews 5:8; 1 Peter 4:1<br><br>• Suffering can become a doorway into greater intimacy with God.<br>Acts 14:22; 1 Peter 2:21; 3:9<br><br>• True joy is not the absence of pain, but the presence of Christ in the midst of the pain.<br>Psalm 23:4; Hebrews 2:10, 17–18; 1 Peter 5:10 |

| | |
|---|---|
| **THE LIE** | **43. My circumstances will never change—this will go on forever.** |
| **THE TRUTH** | • My suffering may last a long time, but it will not last forever.<br>Psalm 30:5, 11–12; Romans 8:18; 2 Corinthians 4:8–18<br><br>• My painful circumstances will not last one moment longer than God knows is necessary to achieve His eternal purposes in and through my life.<br>Genesis 21:5–7; 40:23–41:1; John 11:17<br><br>• One day all pain, suffering, and tears will be removed forever.<br>Isaiah 35:1, 10; Revelation 21:1–7 |
| **THE LIE** | **44. I just can't take any more.** |
| **THE TRUTH** | • Whatever my circumstance, whatever my situation, His grace is sufficient for me.<br>Psalm 130:5; 2 Corinthians 12:7–10<br><br>• God will never place more on me than He will give me grace to bear.<br>2 Corinthians 11:22–30 |
| **THE LIE** | **45. It's all about me.** |
| **THE TRUTH** | • God is the beginning and end and center of all things. All things were created by Him and for Him. It's all about Him!<br>Acts 20:24; Colossians 1:16–18 |

# WALKING IN THE Truth

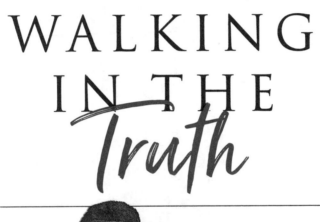

# CHAPTER ELEVEN

# COUNTERING LIES WITH THE *Truth*

e've examined many different lies that are widely believed by Christian women today. However, we've by no means exhausted the lies in the Enemy's arsenal. Deception has endless variations, which Satan tailors to our natural bents. Like a seasoned fisherman, he selects the lure that he knows is most likely to attract his intended prey—the one we're least likely to consider harmful. He doesn't care what we believe, as long as we don't believe the Truth. The Truth causes his kingdom and his control to crumble.

Before we take a final, close-up look at the Truth that counters Satan's lies (chapter 12), let's step back and review the two major points of this book:

**Believing lies places us in bondage.**
**The Truth has the power to set us free.**

We've seen that the progression toward spiritual bondage begins when we *listen* to Satan's lies. We may think it won't hurt to be exposed to ungodly ways of thinking in the movies we watch, the music we listen to, the books and magazines we read, the websites we visit, and the friends we associate with. But we don't realize how subtly those deceptive philosophies can influence our thinking. That's why God promises a special blessing to "the one who does not walk in the advice of the wicked or stand in the pathway with sinners or sit in the company of mockers!" (Ps. 1:1 csb).

Once we permit Satan's lies to gain an entrance into our minds, the progression continues as we *dwell* on those lies. If we don't immediately reject deceptive ways of thinking, but allow ourselves to entertain them in our minds, sooner or later we'll begin to *believe* them. And what we believe inevitably is what we will *act on.*

When we *act* on the lies we've believed, we begin to establish patterns in our lives that ultimately enslave us.

"Shondra's" testimony illustrates how believing things that aren't true keeps us from experiencing freedom in our relationship with God and others.

*Believing that God didn't really love and accept me, and that I was worthless, put me in bondage to perfectionism and seeking approval. In my relationship with God, I felt as though I could only please Him by being a perfect Christian. I believed that if I sinned, He would not accept me. I was defeated in my Christian walk because I knew I was not without sin; my faulty thinking condemned me and put me in bondage.*

*My pride became evident in two ways: (1) I denied my sin—I couldn't bear to admit I had failed to be perfect, because I didn't want God to find me unacceptable. (2) I relied on my own self-fueled attempts to be holy, even though my human effort always resulted in failure—which made me feel even more unacceptable to God. This cycle of effort/failure/sin/guilt kept me from truly experiencing forgiveness, freedom, and joy in my relationship with God.*

*In my relationships with others, I sought to find approval and acceptance in making them happy. I became a people-pleaser and a "yes-woman." Keeping people happy was critical to my feeling worthwhile. My relationships were marked by dishonesty, as I was driven to avoid confrontation or causing disappointment. I masked my real feelings, not wanting to bother anyone with my problems.*

*I felt very alone because no one really knew me, and I became bitter and frustrated toward the people who "used" me (even though I practically sent them an invitation to do so).*

*I could not accept any personal limitations. I viewed any mistake or shortcoming as proof of my worthlessness. I consistently set goals too high to reach and inevitably fell short. I demanded absolute perfection of myself, and criticized myself mercilessly when I couldn't achieve it. The self-imposed pressure I lived under became unbearable and sent me into depression in my midthirties.*

*Recently, I realized I was in bondage and needed to be set free from the tyranny of the lies I was believing. However, I was still hesitant to cry out to the Lord for help, because deep inside, I felt that He would reject me if I admitted my weak and sinful condition.*

Then Shondra attended a local church women's conference where I was speaking on the power of the Truth to set us free. It was like a light went on in her heart; for the first time, she began to have hope:

*During the conference, the Holy Spirit deeply convicted me about my neglect of God's Word. His Word is Truth, and if I am to defeat the stronghold of Satan's lies in my life, I need to saturate my life with God's Word. I really believe that this is my only hope. I cannot make it without consistent time exposing my mind and heart to the Truth of God's Word. I have committed to spending time every day reading and meditating on God's Truth. I realize that renewing my mind will be a process of continually confronting the lies and refuting them with God's Word. I know that the Scripture has supernatural power, and I claim His promise that the Truth will set me free!*

As you've read this book, have you recognized any specific area(s) where you have listened to, believed, and acted on lies? Are there areas of spiritual bondage in your life—areas where you are not walking in freedom before God? These may be major, deeply rooted issues, or they may be matters that seem relatively insignificant. They may be areas where you have been defeated and cried out for deliverance for years. Or they may be issues you are just now recognizing for the first time.

Regardless, as we have seen, the pathway from captivity to freedom involves at least three steps:

1. Identify the area(s) of bondage or sinful behavior.
2. Identify the lie(s) at the root of that bondage or behavior.
3. Replace the lie(s) with the Truth.

*The Truth has the power to overcome every lie.* This is what the Enemy doesn't want you to realize. As long as you believe his lies, he can keep you in bondage. But once you know the Truth and start believing and acting on it, the prison doors will swing open and you will be set free.

*The Truth has the power to set us free* (John 8:32) and to protect our minds and hearts from deceptive thoughts and feelings. There are moments when I feel besieged with emotions or thoughts I know are not of God—angry, irrational, fearful, controlling, or resentful thoughts. That's when I need to run to the Truth for refuge. God's Word promises: "He will cover you with his pinions, and under his wings you will find refuge; his faithfulness is a shield and buckler" (Ps. 91:4).

*The Truth has the power to sanctify us*—to purify our minds, our hearts, and our spirits. Just before He went to the cross, Jesus reminded His disciples about the cleansing power of His Word (John 15:3). Two chapters later, He prayed to the Father, "Sanctify them in the truth; your word is truth" (17:17). Often, as I approach the Scripture, I pray, "Father, please wash me with Your Word. Your Word is Truth. Use the Truth to cleanse my heart, purify my mind, bathe me in Your Word."

## CHOOSING THE PATHWAY OF TRUTH

Each time the Enemy bombards us with lies, we must learn to counsel our hearts according to the Truth and to act on the Truth, regardless of what our human reason or our feelings tell us.

When I find myself giving in to weariness, frustration, or my flesh;

when my mind and emotions are swirling with things I know aren't true, I try to stop and identify the Truth that counters those lies.

I speak the Truth to myself—sometimes aloud and, if necessary, over and over again—until the Truth displaces and replaces the lies I have been believing. I cry out to God for grace to act on what I know to be true. Time after time, I'm amazed at the power of the Truth to calm my turbulent emotions and to restore settledness and sanity to my confused thoughts.

Though it happened a number of years ago, I still remember well, sitting in a meeting where some long-simmering issues came to a full boil. In the course of the discussion, one individual made some statements about me that, from my perspective, were unfounded and extremely damaging. I was devastated.

Over the next several hours, the Enemy began to wreak havoc with my mind and my emotions. All I could think about was how wrong the other person had been, and how deeply I had been wounded. I began to let resentful thoughts take root in my mind, and became obsessed with trying to figure out how to vindicate myself and prove my innocence. My emotions spun out of control and I careened into a downward spiral of anger and self-pity.

Looking back now, I realize I was listening to and believing a number of lies . . . lies like:

- "So-and-so" intended to hurt me.
- I deserve to be treated better; I shouldn't have to go through this.
- The other person was totally at fault. I was totally innocent.
- The damage can't be undone.
- "So-and-so" made me angry.
- I have a right to be angry.
- I have a right to defend myself and to be sure others know the truth.
- I just can't let this go. I can't help the way I feel.

Believing those lies resulted in hours of inner turmoil and struggle.

The next morning, as I opened my Bible and began to read where I had left off the day before, I found myself in Matthew chapters 5 and 6. There I had a head-on collision with the Truth:

> Blessed are the meek. . . .
> Blessed are the merciful . . . .
> Blessed are the peacemakers. . . .
>
> I say to you, Do not resist the one who is evil.
> But if anyone slaps you on the right cheek,
> turn to him the other also. . . .
> Love your enemies and pray for those who persecute you. . . .
>
> For if you forgive others their trespasses,
> your heavenly Father will also forgive you,
> but if you do not forgive others their trespasses,
> neither will your Father forgive your trespasses.
>
> —Matthew 5:5, 7, 9, 39, 44; 6:14–15

Now I had a choice. Would I continue to believe the lies, or would I embrace the Truth? My emotions wanted to hold on to the offense. I wanted to nurse the grudge; I wanted to stay angry; I wanted somehow to hurt the person who had hurt me. But in my heart I knew that choice would not lead to freedom.

As I knelt before the Lord, with the open Bible in front of me, I knew I had to forgive and that I had to relinquish any right to get even or to withhold love from that individual.

I began to counsel my heart according to the Truth. I reminded myself of the consequences of refusing to forgive, of the mercy I would forfeit if I refused to extend mercy to others, and of the blessings I would receive if I was willing to obey His commands.

I knew I couldn't drum up forgiveness or talk myself into a holy response to the person who had wounded me, but I could lift my eyes from my own "suffering" and toward the One who has "borne our grief" and "carried our sorrows" (Isa. 53:4). I could surrender my emotions to the Father's will, because Jesus did the same. I could forgive the one who had offended me, because Christ forgave my offenses against Him. I could lay down my desire to see the other person punished, because Christ went to the cross to take on my punishment and extend grace toward me.

I knew that once I *chose* to obey God and forgive, my emotions would follow. There on my knees, I finally waved the white flag of surrender. I yielded myself and the entire matter to the Lord and agreed, as an act of my will, to forgive the one who had hurt me.

The emotional release didn't come immediately. For a while, I was tempted to give in to resentment or to subtly retaliate. But, by God's grace, I continued to speak the Truth to my heart and to make the choice to act on the Truth. I began to look for ways to rebuild the relationship and invest in the one who had hurt me.

In the weeks that followed, my emotions gradually followed my will. And in time, the Lord shed light on why I had reacted the way I had and showed me some deeper heart issues that I had not realized needed to be addressed. How grateful I am that He loves me enough to orchestrate those kinds of circumstances and experiences to make me more like Jesus.

## THE TRANSFORMING POWER OF TRUTH

Spiritual freedom is the sweet fruit of knowing, believing, and acting on the Truth. And how can we know the Truth? We must remember that the Truth is not merely an idea or a philosophy. The Truth is a Person—the Lord Jesus Christ. He said of Himself, "*I am . . . the truth*" (John 14:6). Jesus didn't point men to a religious system; He pointed them to Himself. To those who claimed to be His followers, He said,

> If you abide in my word, you are truly my disciples,
> and you will know the truth, and the truth will set you free. . . .
> So if the Son sets you free, you will be free indeed.
>
> —John 8:31–32, 36

Abandoning lies and walking in the Truth is not a formulaic, mechanical self-help process. We cannot simply change our minds, chant a few words, and find ourselves walking in freedom. Because of the pervasive and destructive nature of the Enemy's lies, we are all deeply broken by sin, and we are dependent on the Spirit and the Word of God to transform our thinking.

The cross stands as a monument to freedom for sinners of all time. There Jesus took our guilt on Himself and endured the pain of the cross so we could be truly free.

> For freedom Christ has set us free; stand firm therefore,
> and do not submit again to a yoke of slavery.
>
> —Galatians 5:1

Though it may sound elementary at first, it's a revolutionary, liberating truth that because Christ set us free, we can *live* free. He did the heavy lifting to remove the yoke of sin from our shoulders. Because of the cross, freedom really is possible!

That's not to suggest that no effort is required on our part, to truly walk in freedom. We must renew our minds daily (Rom. 12:2) and "fight the good fight of the faith," by taking "hold of the eternal life to which [we] were called" (1 Tim. 6:12). But even our effort is God-initiated, dependent on His grace and power, energized by His Spirit, and effected in us by the power of the cross. Walking in freedom is not a matter of behavior modification, but of letting Christ be our life—depending on Him moment by moment, and responding to the work of His Spirit in our lives.

True freedom is only found in a vital, growing relationship with the Lord Jesus, who has revealed Himself in the Scripture. If we want to know Him, if we want to know the Truth, we must devote ourselves to reading, studying, and meditating on His Word. There is no substitute and there are no shortcuts. The Enemy is constantly confronting us with his lies. In order to combat his deception, our minds and hearts must be filled with Christ and saturated with His Word.

But it's not enough to know the Truth. We must also *surrender* to the Truth. That means we must be willing to change our thinking or our lifestyle in any areas where they don't square with the Word of God.

We can't assume a particular viewpoint is true just because everyone else thinks that way—or because it is what we've always believed, or because a well-known Christian author promotes that position, or because a well-meaning friend or counselor says it's true. Everything we believe and everything we do must be evaluated in the light of God's Word. That is our only absolute authority.

Living according to Truth requires a conscious choice to reject deception and to embrace the Truth. That's why the psalmist prayed, "Remove from me the way of lying. . . . I have chosen the way of truth" (Ps. 119:29–30 NKJV).

Every time we open the Scripture or hear the Word proclaimed, it ought to be with the prayer that God will open our eyes to see any areas where we have been deceived, and with a heart attitude that says, "Lord, Your Word is Truth; I will submit to whatever You say. Whether I like it or not, whether I feel like it or not, whether I agree with it or not, whether it makes sense or not, I choose to place my life under the authority of Your Word—I will obey."

Once we know the Truth and are walking according to the Truth that we know, God wants to make us instruments to point others to the Truth.

> Speaking the truth in love,
> we are to grow up in every way into him
> who is the head, into Christ. . . .
> Therefore, having put away falsehood,
> let each one of you speak the truth with his neighbor,
> for we are members one of another.
>
> —Ephesians 4:15, 25

As I shared in the Introduction, the burden that gave birth to this book was a longing to see women set free through the Truth. That vision is expressed in the last verses of the book of James:

> If anyone among you wanders from the truth
> and someone brings him back,
> let him know that whoever brings back a sinner
> from his wandering
> will save his soul from death
> and will cover a multitude of sins.
>
> —James 5:19–20

The idea of "bringing back" someone who has wandered from the Truth is foreign to most in our day. As deception has inundated our culture, many believers fear being labeled intolerant or narrow-minded. We don't want to rock the boat or be considered judgmental. It seems easier just to "live and let live."

But in Christ and in His Word, we have the Truth that sets people free. That is good news! And there is no other way for those we know and love to be delivered from darkness, deception, and death. If we truly care about them, we will prayerfully and actively seek to restore them to God's way of thinking.

Let's learn the Truth, believe it, surrender to it, and live it out—even when it flies in the face of our culture. Then let's proclaim the Truth with boldness, conviction, and compassion, seeking to bring wandering brothers and sisters back to Christ.

# CHAPTER TWELVE

# THE TRUTH THAT
# SETS US *Free*

*I*n the midst of writing this book, there have been times when I have found myself believing and acting on some of the very lies I was addressing: "I don't have time to do everything I'm supposed to do!" "I can afford to shortcut my time with the Lord this morning." "I can't control my emotions." "I'm acting this way because I'm so tired . . . because I've had so many interruptions . . . because I've got so much to do . . ." And "I just can't take any more!"

Again and again, in hectic, hassled, or hurting moments, God has directed my heart back to the Truth. As I listen to the Truth, meditate on it, believe it, and surrender to it, the Spirit of God sets me free. My mind and emotions are stabilized, and I am able to look at my circumstances from God's perspective. The longer I walk with God, the more I am in awe of the power of the Truth!

We have already looked at many of Satan's lies and the corresponding Truth that counters each lie. In this final chapter, I want to highlight twenty-one Truths that I find myself going back to over and over again. They form a solid foundation and a protective fortress for my mind, will, and emotions. This is the Truth that sets me free—the Truth that will set you free as well.

Rather than skimming through this chapter, let me encourage you to take time to savor these liberating, life-changing Truths. Meditate on them; say them aloud again and again until your thinking becomes aligned with God's way of thinking. You may even want to memorize this list, along with the key Scriptures that correspond to each Truth.

In the days ahead, anytime you realize you are believing lies, go back and review this list. Renew your mind and counsel your heart according to the Truth.

1. *God is good* (Pss. 119:68; 136:1).

When the sun is shining and you have money in the bank and you're healthy and everyone thinks you're wonderful, it's not hard to believe that God is good. But when you lose your job or a loved one is diagnosed with a terminal illness or your church goes through a nasty split or your husband says he doesn't want to be married to you anymore, the Enemy may move in and cause you to question God's goodness.

The Truth is, regardless of the circumstances, regardless of what we feel, regardless of what we think, God *is* good, and everything He does is good.

2. *God loves me and wants me to have His best* (Rom. 8:32, 38–39).

God doesn't love us because we're lovable or worthy, but because He is love. There is absolutely nothing we can do to earn or deserve His love. We cannot comprehend such unconditional love; but if we believe it and receive it, His love will transform our lives.

Because God is good and loves us perfectly, we can be confident that He longs for us to experience all the joy in life He designed us to know. He knows we will only find this true, lasting joy and fulfillment in Him. He loves us so much that He insists we come to Him, the only source of full satisfaction.

3. *I am complete and accepted in Christ* (Eph. 1:4–6).

You may have been rejected by a parent, a mate, a friend, or a child. But if you are in Christ, you are accepted in Him. We don't have to perform to be acceptable to Him. We don't have to jump through a bunch of spiritual hoops. In fact, there is not one thing we can do to make ourselves acceptable to a holy God. Yet we—fallen, condemned, unworthy sinners—can stand before God clean and unashamed, acceptable in His sight. How? Because Jesus—the pure, sinless Son of God—is acceptable to Him, and we stand in Him.

### 4. *God is enough* (Ps. 23:1).

"The LORD is my shepherd; I shall not want." You've probably known that verse since you were a small child. But do you believe it? Do you really believe that He is *your* Shepherd? The Truth is, if we have Him, we have everything we need for our peace and happiness—now and forever.

### 5. *God can be trusted* (Isa. 26:3–4).

God keeps His promises. He has promised never to leave or forsake us (Heb. 13:5). He has promised that those who trust in Him will never be disappointed. When you are tempted to doubt that, it may help to remind yourself: "God has never once let me down—and He's not going to start now!"

### 6. *God doesn't make any mistakes* (Isa. 46:10).

Other people may make serious mistakes that affect our lives. But God is always fulfilling His eternal purposes, and they cannot be thwarted by any human failure. If we are in Christ, our lives are in His hand, and nothing can touch us that has not first been "filtered through His fingers of love." God makes no mistakes with His children's lives. Someone has said, "God's will is exactly what we would choose if we knew what God knows." When we stand in eternity looking back on this earthly existence, we will know by sight what we can only see now by faith: He has done all things well.

**7. *God's grace is sufficient for me*** (2 Cor. 12:9).

As children of God, we will never face a circumstance that exceeds His grace. Where sin abounds, grace abounds much more (Rom. 5:20). When we are weak, He is strong. When we are empty, He is full. When we have no resources of our own left, His resources have not begun to be depleted.

Whatever you are going through right now, His grace is sufficient for you. Whatever you will go through tomorrow—or next year or fifty years from now—His grace will be sufficient for you then.

His grace is sufficient to deal with the memories, wounds, and failures of the most scarred or sordid past. His grace is sufficient for a lifetime of singleness or for a half century of marriage to a difficult man. His grace is sufficient for the single mom trying to raise four children. His grace is sufficient for the mother of three toddlers—or three teenagers—and for the woman who longs to be a mom. His grace is sufficient for the woman caring for her elderly parents, for the empty nester, for the woman going through menopause, for the widow living on Social Security, and for the invalid in a nursing home.

We need to speak this Truth to ourselves; we need to speak it to each other. In every season, in every circumstance, His grace *is* sufficient. It is sufficient for me; it is sufficient for you.

**8. *The blood of Christ is sufficient to cover all my sin*** (1 John 1:7).

There is not a sin you or I have ever committed or a sin we could ever commit that cannot be forgiven and covered by the all-sufficient sacrifice of Jesus' blood. This should not cause us to take sin more lightly. To the contrary, the realization that our sin required the lifeblood of the Lord Jesus should leave us broken and humble in spirit, determined to choose the pathway of obedience by the power of His indwelling Holy Spirit. As the psalmist acknowledged: "If you, O LORD, should mark iniquities, O Lord, who could stand? But with you there is forgiveness, that you may be feared" (Ps. 130:3–4).

9. *The cross of Christ is sufficient to conquer my sinful flesh*
(Rom. 6:6–7).

Through the death of Christ and our union with Him, you and I have been set free from the dominion and power of sin. We are no longer slaves to sin. When we do sin, it's not because we couldn't help ourselves; it is because we chose to yield to our old master. The Truth is, we don't have to sin (Rom. 6:14).

10. *My past does not have to plague me* (1 Cor. 6:9–11).

Paul made this point to the believers in the church of Corinth, some of whom had quite a checkered past. He reminded them that though sin separates us from God, through Christ, the worst of sinners could be made clean and new.

You may have been an adulterer, a murderer, an alcoholic, or a lesbian; you may have aborted a child or been sexually promiscuous; you may have been a slave to lust or anger or food or pride. But if you are in Christ, that is no longer your identity. You are not what you once were. You are not the same person. You have been cleansed by the blood of Jesus, set apart for His holy purposes, and declared righteous in the eyes of God.

The Truth is that the things that happened in our past—our upbringing, the ways we've been wronged, the ways we have wronged others—don't have to be a hindrance. In fact, by God's grace, they can actually become stepping-stones to greater victory and fruitfulness.

11. *God's Word is sufficient to lead me, teach me, and heal me*
(Pss. 19:7; 107:20; 119:105).

It seems that few people in our day really have confidence in the power of the Word of God to radically and lastingly change lives, to deliver people from bondage, and to reveal the will of God for our lives. Too often, the Scripture is viewed as one of a number of valuable resources or as a last resort after everything else has been tried.

The Truth is, the Word of God is alive and powerful; it is medicine for afflicted hearts and peace for plagued minds. It is a lamp for our feet and a light for our path. Whatever our need, whatever our circumstances, the Word of God is sufficient to meet that need and the needs of those we love.

Those around us who are hurting, ashamed, rebellious, or floundering don't need to hear our opinions and suggestions. They need to know what God says. They need to know His commands, His promises, and His ways. We demonstrate our love when we point them to the Truth and humbly and lovingly show them how to apply His Word to their situation.

12. ***Through the power of His Holy Spirit, God will enable me to do anything He commands me to do*** (1 Thess. 5:24; Phil. 2:13). God does not command us to do anything that He doesn't give us the grace to obey, as we depend on Him. That means, for example, that

- there is no one we cannot forgive (Mark 11:25);
- there is no one we cannot love (Matt. 5:44);
- we can give thanks in all things (1 Thess. 5:18);
- we can be content in every circumstance (Heb. 13:5).

The issue is not that we *can't* obey God—that we *can't* forgive that parent who hurt us so deeply, love that difficult colleague, give thanks in the midst of the storm, or be content with our one-bedroom apartment. The real issue is that we *won't* forgive—that we are *unwilling* to love and *refuse* to give thanks and to be content with what God has provided.

By the enabling power of the Holy Spirit, we can *choose* to forgive, *choose* to let Him love others through us, *choose* to give thanks in every circumstance, and *choose* to be content.

**13.** *I am responsible before God for my behavior, responses, and choices* (Ezek. 18:19–22).

We may not be able to control the circumstances that come into our lives—we had no choice about the homes we were born into, our overall physical appearance, our upbringing, and many other factors that have influenced and shaped our lives. But, by God's grace, we do not have to be victims; we can control how we respond to the circumstances He has allowed to come into our lives.

When we begin to assume personal responsibility for our own choices, when we stop blaming other people and circumstances for sinful behaviors or negative patterns in our lives, we will be released from the sense that we are helpless victims. We will be free to obey God regardless of our circumstances.

**14.** *I will reap whatever I sow* (Gal. 6:7–8).

The choices you and I make today will have consequences down the road. Every selfish, sinful, or indulgent choice we make today is sowing a seed that will reap a harvest of sin and pain, not only in our own lives, but in the lives of others, potentially for generations to come. And every act of obedience is a seed that will produce a multiplied harvest of blessing. The harvest is rarely immediate. But it will come.

**15.** *The pathway to true joy is to relinquish control* (Matt. 16:25; Luke 1:38; 1 Peter 5:7).

The only way for any of us to experience true freedom and peace is to let go of the reins—to relinquish control to God, believing that He can be trusted to manage all that concerns us.

I once found myself battling resentment toward a colleague who had disappointed me. As we are sometimes prone to do, I mulled the situation over and over in my mind. I finally called a friend and asked her to pray for me. As we prepared to hang up, she said, "Nancy, I don't quite know how to say this, but remember . . . *you're not God.*" Ouch.

Why is it so hard to let God be God? Why is it so hard to turn over to Him the management of the universe? The Truth is, He *is* in control. He loves us, and He isn't going to fall asleep on the job or let something slip by His notice. The pathway to freedom is to relinquish control of ourselves, and all that concerns us, to Him. Not until then will we see Him do what only He can do.

### 16. *Submission to God-ordained authority honors God and brings blessing* (Rom. 13:1; 1 Peter 3:1–6).

When we submit to God-ordained authority, we reveal to the world the goodness of God's created order, we express that our hope is in Him, we release Him to work in the lives of those in authority over us, we proclaim His right to rule over the universe, Satan is defeated in his attempts to dethrone God, and we cooperate with God in establishing His kingdom.

### 17. *Personal holiness is more important than any temporal pleasure* (Eph. 5:26–27).

Contrary to the world's way of thinking, happiness here and now is not the highest good.

God did not save us to make us happy in a merely temporal sense. He saved us to "redeem us from all lawlessness and to purify for himself a people for his own possession who are zealous for good works" (Titus 2:14). The Lord Jesus left His home in heaven, came down to this earth, and gave His life not so we could live for ourselves and our own pleasure, but so we could be free to live for the One for whose pleasure we were created.

To choose the pathway of holiness will sometimes require sacrificing our personal comfort and convenience. But any sacrifice we make is temporary and cannot be compared with the joy and fulfillment we will gain in time and eternity.

18. *God is more concerned about changing me and glorifying Himself than about solving all my immediate problems* (Rom. 8:29).

   What matters most to God is that every created being reflect His glory. His agenda is to do whatever is necessary to conform us to His image. Some of the problems that cause us to chafe the most are actually instruments He has designed to fulfill His ultimate purpose in our lives. To demand a solution or an escape from that impossible boss, that financial situation, that health problem, or that messy marriage may cause us to forfeit a far higher good that He is seeking to bring about in our lives. How unwise and shortsighted it is to resist problems that may be the very means He has designed to mold us into the image of His Son.

19. *Properly responded to, suffering will produce sweet fruit in my life.* (1 Peter 5:10).

   Suffering takes on a whole different perspective when we realize that it is an essential tool in the hand of God to make us holy and conform us to the image of Jesus.

   In the book of Jeremiah, we find a vivid picture of what happens if we don't allow suffering to do its purifying work in our lives:

   > Moab has been at ease from his youth
   > and has settled on his dregs;
   > he has not been emptied from vessel to vessel,
   > nor has he gone into exile;
   > so his taste remains in him, and his scent is not changed.
   >
   > —Jeremiah 48:11

   In the process of making wine in Jeremiah's day, the juice from the grapes was poured into a wineskin and left to sit for several weeks, until the bitter dregs or sediment settled onto the bottom. Then it was poured into another wineskin so more dregs could be separated.

This process was repeated again and again, until all the dregs had been removed and the wine was pure and sweet.

Jeremiah used this process as a metaphor for the nation of Moab, which had a history of relative ease and comfort. Moab had not been through the purifying process of being "poured" from suffering to suffering. As a result, the thick, bitter dregs of sin remained in the nation—its people were "unchanged."

Suffering is God's means of pouring us from one jar to another—of unsettling us so the dregs of self and sin can be separated out and the pure, sweet wine of His Spirit will be all that remains.

**20. *My suffering will not last forever*** (2 Cor. 4:17–18).

When it seems that we are constantly in the fire, repeatedly being "poured" from one jar to another, our emotions tell us this will go on forever. That is when we need to remind ourselves that God has a specific objective in mind for our suffering. He knows exactly the intensity and the duration that are needed to fulfill His purposes. He will not allow our suffering to last any longer or to be any more severe than is necessary to accomplish His will.

God has promised that one day "there will be no more death or mourning or crying or pain" (Rev. 21:4 NIV). So, my dear sister, when your eyes are filled with tears and you're tempted to throw in the towel, take courage. Lift up your head, cry out for grace, press on, give thanks, and know that it will not be long before your faith will be rewarded with the sight of the One who has promised to be with you to the end.

**21. *It's not about me; it's all about Him*** (Col. 1:16–18; Rev. 4:11).

We all need regular reminders that the world doesn't revolve around us! The entire universe—including you and me—was created to orbit around the One who is high and lifted up and seated on His throne.

Before we can respond in a godly way to the circumstances of life, we must first settle this basic issue: What is my purpose in life? If our goal in life is to be happy or accepted or loved or successful in the eyes of others, then anything that threatens our well-being will be an enemy, an obstacle to fulfilling our objective.

On the other hand, once we agree with God that we exist for His pleasure and His glory, we can accept whatever comes into our lives as part of His sovereign will and purpose. We will not resent or resist the hard things, but embrace them as friends, sovereignly designed by God to make us like Jesus and to bring glory to Himself. We will be able to look into His face and say, "It's not about me. It's about You. If it pleases You, it pleases me. All that matters is that You are glorified."

One of our great-grandsons, Kenan, stopped by today with his wife and two of their daughters to bring us some fresh fruits and veggies from their garden. Our family has been so good to us, especially now that we're older and experiencing more physical limitations.

My eyes continue to deteriorate. Yet, in many ways, I believe I am just now beginning to really see. The fact is, years ago, when my eyes were young and strong, I was so very blind. I didn't see how foolish I was to believe the Serpent. I didn't see the heartache that one wrong choice would bring into our lives. I didn't see the pain our children would reap. Although I know God holds Adam ultimately responsible for our first sin and the curse that resulted, I still feel the weight of yielding to the Serpent's lies.

All I could see at the time was something I wanted very badly—something I thought I needed. I got what I wanted, but I never could have imagined all that would come with it. That one moment of indulgence brought such pain and regret.

Only now, after years of running and hiding and hurting, can I see how much God loves us and how He has always had our best interests at heart. I see clearly now how perfect His ways are and why it's so important to listen to Him and to do things His way. I only wish I hadn't wasted so many years believing things that weren't true.

When I think back, it's amazing how merciful God has been to us. After that awful day, He could have written us off forever, but He has never stopped pursuing a relationship with us. After we lost our two sons, God gave us Seth—and then four more sons and daughters. Seth, in particular, represents the restoration and joy God has brought to our lives.

God also promised that one day there will be another Son. The Serpent will attack and wound Him, as he did us. Then the Son will strike back and deal a final, fatal blow to the Serpent.

It was I, as a woman, along with my husband, who brought this fallen condition on us all those years ago. I can never undo the damage I've done. But—what grace!—God has said that He will use a woman to bring this Son into the world. Through Him all the effects of my sin will be reversed. Even though I resisted God's will, He has not rejected me; He has made provision for my forgiveness, and He still has a plan to use my life and make me fruitful. He truly is a redeeming God.

I don't know when or how all His promises will be fulfilled. But I do know that I believe His Word. Whatever days I have left on this earth I want to spend walking in Truth, obeying Him, and influencing those I love to do the same.

Believing a lie once brought ruin to my life and family.

But now, by the power of His Truth, I have been set free!

# THANK *You!*

Many dear friends and colleagues (also friends!) have labored with me to make this refreshed, expanded book a reality. I am especially indebted to:

*My friends at Moody Publishers.* You were the first to have the vision for publishing this message nearly two decades ago. Without your encouragement, this book might never have been written. And you have continued to steward this message. With over one million copies in print, only eternity will reveal how many women have been set free by the Truth as a result. Special thanks to Judy Dunagan, Connor Sterchi, Erik Peterson, Randall Payleitner, and Ashley Torres for pouring yourselves into this new edition.

*Erin Davis.* You dove headfirst into this project—assembling a review team, compiling their input, carving the book into a bajillion pieces, and valiantly taking the first pass at putting it all back together again. Thank you! I love your heart for this message.

*The review team.* Erin Davis, Judy Dunagan, Dannah Gresh, Andrea Hogue, Mary Kassian, and Carolyn McCulley—your thoughtful, honest, vigorous critique made my life a ton harder for several months, but it made this book a ton better. Color me grateful.

*Anne Buchanan.* You are an editor's editor. Having your fresh eyes and keen mind applied to this manuscript in its final stages was a tremendous help.

*Team Revive Our Hearts.* You're the best! In countless ways, day after day, mostly behind the scenes, you quietly give of yourselves to help call women to freedom, fullness, and fruitfulness in Christ. Special thanks to Martin Jones, Mike Neises, Sandy Bixel, and Hannah Kurtz for your world-class admin support, which makes it possible for me to hunker down in these writing seasons, and to Dawn Wilson for your research assistance.

*Erik Wolgemuth and the Wolgemuth & Associates team.* Your kind assistance with so many of the moving parts of this project has been a great gift.

*Sweet friends (you know who you are)* who checked in regularly while I was in lockdown, asked how it was going, brought groceries and home-cooked meals, sent encouraging texts and emails, and patiently bore with Robert and me having to turn down one invitation after another to get together. We're looking forward to seeing you again!

*My dear praying friends.* What a blessing you are! Thank you for surrounding and undergirding Robert and me in this writing season because you believe in the need for this message. Your prayers have been wind in our sails.

*My precious husband.* What can I say? We won't soon forget the summer of 2017—spectacular weather, the secret garden, bird choirs, the cicada chorus, sunsets over the river, working side by side on the deck (built with your own hands), you writing *Lies Men Believe* while I revised *Lies Women Believe.* You have been at my side every step of this long journey: praying morning, noon, and night; helping me come up with good verbs; graciously bearing with late night and weekend writing sessions; getting me out for "mini vacations" when my brain needed to be oxygenated; raising my flagging spirits; cheering all the way to the finish line . . . I've never been loved this way before.

Finally, eternity will not be long enough to express my gratitude to You, Lord Jesus. You are the Truth that has set me free, and I love You with all my heart!

**PREFACE**

1. Nancy DeMoss Wolgemuth, *Adorned: Living Out the Beauty of the Gospel Together* (Chicago: Moody, 2017).

2. Nancy DeMoss Wolgemuth, *Lies Women Believe Study Guide,* rev. ed. (Chicago: Moody, 2018). Please note that an older version of this guide, called *The Companion Guide to Lies Women Believe,* may still be available. The older version does not cover every aspect of this new edition of *Lies Women Believe,* so be sure and look for the Study Guide, not the Companion Guide.

3. Nancy DeMoss Wolgemuth and Dannah Gresh, *Lies Young Women Believe: And the Truth That Sets Them Free* (Chicago: Moody, 2008); Dannah Gresh, *Lies Girls Believe* and *A Mom's Guide for Lies Girls Believe* (Chicago: Moody, 2018); Robert Wolgemuth, *Lies Men Believe: And the Truth That Sets Them Free* (Chicago: Moody, 2018).

**CHAPTER 1: Truth . . . or Consequences**

1. Thomas Brooks, *Smooth Stones Taken from Ancient Brooks: Collected Sayings of Thomas Brooks,* comp. C. H. Spurgeon (Morgan, PA: Soli Deo Gloria, 1996, orig. pub. 1860), 93.

**CHAPTER 2: Lies Women Believe . . . About God**

1. A. W. Tozer, *The Knowledge of the Holy* (New York: HarperCollins, 1961), 1.

2. Pat Barrett and Anthony Brown, "Good Good Father," © 2014 Common Hymnal Digital (BMI) Housefires Sounds (ASCAP), Tony Brown Publishing Designee (BMI), worshiptogether.com Songs, sixsteps Music (ASCAP), Vamos Publishing (ASCAP), Capitol CMG Paragon (BMI) (adm. at CapitolCMGPublishing.com). All rights reserved. Used by permission. International copyright secured. All rights reserved. Used by permission.

3. Matt Maher, "Your Grace Is Enough," © Thankyou Music (PRS) (adm. worldwide at CapitolCMGPublishing.com excluding Europe which is adm. by Integrity Music, part of the David C. Cook family, Songs@integritymusic.com) / Spiritand song.Com Pub (BMI). All rights reserved. Used by permission. International copyright secured. All rights reserved. Used by permission. (50% control) CapitolCMG. © 2003, [2008] Thankyou Music (PRS) (administered worldwide at CapitolCMG Publishing.com excluding Europe which is administered by Kingswaysongs) and Matt Maher. Published by Spirit & Song®, a division of OCP. All rights reserved. Used by permission (50% control) OCP..

4. Stuart Townend and Keith Getty, "In Christ Alone," © 2002 Thankyou Music (PRS) (adm. worldwide at CapitolCMGPublishing.com excluding Europe, which is adm. by Integrity Music, part of the David C. Cook family. Songs@integritymusic.com). All rights reserved. Used by permission. International copyright secured. All rights reserved. Used by permission.

5. G. Campbell Morgan, *Exposition of the Whole Bible: Chapter by Chapter in One Volume*, G. Campbell Morgan Reprint Series (Eugene, OR: Wipf & Stock, 2010, orig. pub. 1959), 36.

6. Helen H. Lemmel, "Turn Your Eyes Upon Jesus" (1922).

### CHAPTER 3: Lies Women Believe . . . About Themselves

1. "Meg Ryan: What She Really Thinks of Herself," *Ladies' Home Journal*, July 1999, 98.

2. W. E. Vine, *The Expanded Vine's Expository Dictionary of New Testament Words*, ed. John R. Kohlenberger III with James A. Swanson (Minneapolis: Bethany, 1984, orig. pub. 1940), 751.

3. Elisabeth Elliot, *A Lamp unto My Feet: The Bible's Light for Daily Living* (Ada, MI: Revell, 2004), Day 28, 83–84.

### CHAPTER 4: Lies Women Believe . . . About Sin

1. Amy Bloom, *Self*, April 1999, 40.

2. Arthur Bennett, ed., *The Valley of Vision: A Collection of Puritan Prayers & Devotions* (Carlisle, PA.: Banner of Truth, 1975, 2002 edition), 124, 143.

3. Robert Lowry, "Nothing but the Blood" (1876).

4. John Alexander, "And That's That: Sin, Salvation, and Woody Allen," *The Other Side*, January/February 1993, 55.

5. Bennett, ed., *Valley of Vision*, 137.

### CHAPTER 5: Lies Women Believe . . . About Priorities

1. Cited in *Seasons of the Heart: A Year of Devotions from One Generation of Women to Another*, compiled by Donna Kelderman (Grand Rapids: Reformation Heritage Books, 2013), June 24. Language has been lightly updated from the original.

2. Nancy Leigh DeMoss, *A Place of Quiet Rest* (Chicago: Moody, 2000).

3. Some of the material in this section has been adapted from chapter 10 of Nancy DeMoss Wolgemuth, *Adorned: Living Out the Beauty of the Gospel Together* (Chicago: Moody, 2017), 209–214.

### CHAPTER 6: Lies Women Believe . . . About Sexuality

1. Mary Kassian, *Girls Gone Wise in a World Gone Wild* (Chicago: Moody, 2010), 135–136.

2. Nicole Braddock Bromley, *Hush: Moving from Silence to Healing after Childhood Sexual Abuse* (Chicago: Moody, 2008).

3. "Nicole Braddock Bromley," OneVOICE (website), http://iamonevoice.org/nicole.

4. Bobbi Dempsey, *The Everything Tantric Sex Book: Learn Meditative, Spontaneous, and Intimate Lovemaking* (Avon, MA: F+W Media, 2007), 157.

5. Sheena McKenzie, "Mona Lisa: The Theft That Created a Legend," CNN (website), updated November 19, 2013, http://www.cnn.com/2013/11/18/world/europe/mona-lisa-the-theft/index.html. See also Sidonie Sawyer, "The Mona Lisa Stolen by Museum Worker," *Huffpost*, May 26, 2015, https://www.huffingtonpost.com/sidonie-sawyer/the-mona-lisa-stolen-by-museum-worker_b_7432448.html.

6. "Rosaria Butterfield on Sexuality," video uploaded by The Gospel Coalition on August 13, 2015, transcribed by the author, https://vimeo.com/136256875.

7. Ibid.

8. Juli Slattery with Abby Ludvigson and Chelsey Nugteren, *Sex and the Single Girl* (Chicago: Moody, 2017), 40.

9. These "two commitments" listed on pages 148–49 are adapted from Slattery, *Sex and the Single Girl*, 42.

10. This list is adapted from one quoted in Juli Slattery and Dannah Gresh, *Pulling Back the Shades: Erotica, Intimacy, and the Longings of a Woman's Heart* (Chicago: Moody, 2014), 61–63.

11. John R. Kohlenberger III and James A. Swanson, *The Hebrew English Concordance to the Old Testament* (Grand Rapids: Zondervan, 1998), word #3359.

12. Strong's Concordance and Thayer's Lexicon accessed through Bible Hub, s.v. *enechō* (Strong's #1758), http://biblehub.com/greek/1758.htm.

13. Carolyn McCulley, "Sex and the Single Woman," in John Piper and Justin Taylor, eds., *Sex and the Supremacy of Christ* (Wheaton, IL: Crossway, 2005), 186–87.

## CHAPTER 7: Lies Women Believe . . . About Marriage

1. Amanda Marcotte, "Think Today's Couples Split Household Chores? Think Again," *Los Angeles Times*, December 13, 2016, http://www.latimes.com/opinion/op-ed/la-oe-0512-marcotte-housework-men-20150512-story.html.

2. Kelly Wallace, "Sheryl Sandberg Teams Up with LeBron James to Get Men to #LeanIn," CNN, March 5, 2015, http://www.cnn.com/2015/03/05/living/feat-sheryl-sandberg-lebron-james-men-lean-in/.

3. Joan C. Williams, "Why Men Work So Many Hours," *Harvard Business Review*, May 29, 2013, https://hbr.org/2013/05/why-men-work-so-many-hours.

4. Gordon J. Wenham, *Genesis 1–15*, vol. 1 of *Word Biblical Commentary*, gen. eds. David A. Hubbard and Glenn W. Barker (Dallas, TX: Word, 1987), 68.

5. Brian C. Howell, *In the Eyes of God: A Metaphorical Approach to Biblical Anthropomorphic Language* (Eugene, OR: Pickwick Publications, 2013), 124.

6. Kenneth A. Mathews, *Genesis 1-11:26,* vol. 1A of *New American Commentary: An Exegetical and Theological Exposition of Holy Scripture,* gen. ed. E. Ray Clendenen (Nashville: B&H, 1996), 214.

7. For a more extensive study of Genesis and an explanation of male and female roles, see Mary A. Kassian and Nancy Leigh DeMoss, *True Woman 101: Divine Design: An Eight-Week Study on Biblical Womanhood* (Chicago: Moody, 2012).

8. Southern Baptist Convention, "Baptist Faith and Message," article 18 ("The Family"), rev. June 2000, http://www.sbc.net/bfm2000/bfm2000.asp.

9. Nancy DeMoss Wolgemuth, *Adorned: Living Out the Beauty of the Gospel Together* (Chicago: Moody, 2017), 268.

10. Dave Dunham, "A Word About Polite Abusers," Pastor Dave Online, June 30, 2016, https://pastordaveonline.org/2016/06/30/a-word-about-polite-abusers.

11. Susan Hunt, *The True Woman: The Beauty and Strength of a Godly Woman* (Wheaton, IL: Crossway, 1997), 218, 223.

12. For a fuller treatment of the consequences of the fall as it relates to male/female roles, see Raymond C. Ortlund Jr., "Male-Female Equality and Male Headship: Genesis 1–3," in *Recovering Biblical Manhood and Womanhood: A Response to Evangelical Feminism,* ed. John Piper and Wayne Grudem (Wheaton, IL: Crossway, 1991), 95–112.

**CHAPTER 8: Lies Women Believe . . . About Children**

1. Nancy Leigh DeMoss and Mary A. Kassian, *True Woman 101: Divine Design—An Eight Week Study on Biblical Womanhood* (Chicago: Moody, 2012); Mary A. Kassian and Nancy Leigh DeMoss, *True Woman 201: Interior Design—Ten Elements of Biblical Womanhood* (Chicago: Moody, 2012).

2. Margaret Sanger, *Woman and the New Race* (n.p: Figgy Tree, 2016, orig. pub. 1920), 64.

3. Laura Enriquez, "10 Eye-Opening Quotes from Planned Parenthood Founder Margaret Sanger," Life News, March 11, 2013, http://www.lifenews.com/2013/03/11/10-eye-opening-quotes-from-planned-parenthood-founder-margaret-sanger.

4. Adapted from Planned Parenthood Federation of America, "Margaret Sanger—20th Century Hero," report issued August 2009, https://www.plannedparenthood.org/files/7513/9611/6635/Margaret_Sanger_Hero_1009.pdf.

5. "What Does the Bible Say about Family Planning?," GotQuestions.org, https://www.gotquestions.org/family-planning.html.

6. Holly Elliff with Bill Elliff, *Turning the Tide: Having More Children Who Follow Christ* (Niles, MI: Revive Our Hearts, 2008), 4–5.

7. Albert Mohler, "Can Christians Use Birth Control," Albert Mohler (website), June 5, 2012, http://www.albertmohler.com/2012/06/05/can-christians-use-birth-control-4/.

8. Donna Christiano, "Fertility Treatment Options," *Parents*, 2011, http://www.parents .com/getting-pregnant/infertility/treatments/guide-to-fertility-methods, accessed November 19, 2017.

9. Laura Bell, "The Fate of Frozen Embryos," Parenting (website), http://www.parenting .com/article/the-fate-of-frozen-embryos, accessed November 10, 2017.

10. Elliff, *Turning the Tide*, 14–15.

11. Mark Lino, "How Much Will It Cost to Raise a Child?" United States Department of Agriculture (website). August 18, 2014, http://blogs.usda.gov/2014/08/18/how-much-will-it-cost-to-raise-a-child.

12. Lauren Sandler, "The Childfree Life: When Having It All Means Not Having Children," *Time*, August 12, 2013, http://content.time.com/time/subscriber/ article/0,33009,2148636-1,00.html.

13. Sandler, "The Childfree Life," *Time*, http://content.time.com/time/subscriber/ article/0,33009,2148636-3,00.html.

14. Amy Julia Becker, "How Many Kids Should We Have?" *Christianity Today*, July 2010, http://www.christianitytoday.com/women/2010/july/how-many-kids-should-we-have.html.

15. First Timothy 2:15 has the same grammatical construction as Paul's admonition to Timothy in chapter 4, verse 16: "Keep a close watch your yourself and on the teaching. Persist in this, for by so doing you will save both yourself and your hearers." Paul is saying that preaching was Timothy's role and that perseverance in his calling would accompany genuine conversion. Preaching was not a means of Timothy's salvation, but a necessary fruit of it.

16. Nancy Pearcey, *Finding Truth: Five Principles for Unmasking Atheism, Secularism, and Other God Substitutes* (Colorado Springs, CO: David C. Cook, 2015), 36.

17. John Piper, *Seeing and Savoring Jesus Christ* (Wheaton, IL: Crossway Books, 2004), 15.

18. Robert Mounce, *Romans*, vol. 27 of *New American Commentary: An Exegetical and Theological Exposition of Holy Scripture*, gen. ed. E. Ray Clendenen (Nashville: B&H, 1995), 256.

## CHAPTER 9: Lies Women Believe . . . About Emotions

1. Francis de Sales, cited in *Daily Strength for Daily Needs*, ed. Mary W. Tileston (Boston: Little, Brown, 1899), 29.

2. "Depression in Women: Understanding the Gender Gap, Mayo Clinic (website), http://www.mayoclinic.org/diseases-conditions/depression/in-depth/depression/ art-20047725, accessed November 11, 2017.

3. "Spurgeon on Depression," Plentiful Redemption (website), May 16, 2013, https://plentifulredeemer.wordpress.com/2013/05/16/spurgeon-on-depression/.

4. Ibid.

5. D. Martyn Lloyd-Jones, *Spiritual Depression: Its Causes and Cure* (Grand Rapids: Eerdmans, 1965), 21.

6. Blue Letter Bible, s.v. asthene ("sick"), https://www.blueletterbible.org/lang/lexicon/lexicon.cfm?t=ESV&strongs=g770.

7. Blue Letter Bible, s.v. kamn ("sick"), https://www.blueletterbible.org/lang/lexicon/lexicon.cfm?Strongs=G2577&t=ESV.

8. John MacArthur addresses the meaning of "anointing him with oil" in James 5:14: "Lit., 'rubbing him with oil': 1) possibly this is a reference to ceremonial anointing (see notes on Lev. 14:18; Mark 6:13); 2) on the other hand, James may have had in mind medical treatment of believers physically bruised and battered by persecution. Perhaps it is better to understand the anointing in a metaphorical sense of the elders' encouraging, comforting, and strengthening the believer." *The MacArthur Study Bible, New King James Version* (Nashville: Word Bibles, 1997), 1934.

9. Stephen Altrogge, "How to Fight for Faith in the Dark: Three Lessons for Depression," Desiring God (website), http://www.desiringgod.org/articles/how-to-fight-for-faith-in-the-dark.

10. Ibid.

11. John Bunyan, *The Pilgrim's Progress,* in *John Bunyan,* Legacy of Faith Library (Nashville: B&H, 2017), 191.

## CHAPTER 10: Lies Women Believe . . . About Circumstances

1. Judith Viorst, *Alexander and the Terrible, Horrible, No Good, Very Bad Day* (New York: Atheneum; Simon & Schuster, 1972).

2. George Lewis Prentiss, ed., *More Love to Thee: The Life and Letters of Elizabeth Prentiss* (Amityville, NY: Calvary, 1994), 374.

3. Harry C. Green and Mary W. Green, "The Pioneer Mothers of America," 1912, cited in Verna M. Hall, comp., *The Christian History of the American Revolution: Consider and Ponder* (San Francisco: Foundation of American Christian Education, 1988), 76.

4. R. Arthur Mathews, *Ready for Battle: 31 Studies in Christian Discipleship* (Wheaton, IL: Harold Shaw, 1993), 123, 71.

5. William Law, cited in *Daily Strength for Daily Needs,* ed. Mary W. Tileston (Boston: Little, Brown, 1899), 17.

6. Larry Crabb, *Finding God* (Grand Rapids: Zondervan, 1993), 17–18.

7. Frances R. Havergal, "Like a River Glorious" (1874).

8. Susan Hunt, *The True Woman: The Beauty and Strength of a Godly Woman* (Wheaton, IL: Crossway, 1997), 75.

# Revive Our Hearts™

Through its various outreaches and the teaching ministry of Nancy DeMoss Wolgemuth, *Revive Our Hearts* is calling women around the world to freedom, fullness, and fruitfulness in Christ.

**Offering sound, biblical teaching and encouragement for women through . . .**

 *Books & Resources* Nancy's books, True Woman Books, and a wide range of audio/video

 *Broadcasting* Two daily, nationally syndicated broadcasts (*Revive Our Hearts* and *Seeking Him*) reaching over one million listeners a week

 *Events & Training* True Woman Conferences and events designed to equip women's ministry leaders and pastors' wives

 *Internet* ReviveOurHearts.com, TrueWoman.com, and LiesYoungWomenBelieve.com; daily blogs, and a large, searchable collection of electronic resources for women in every season of life

**Believing God for a grassroots movement of authentic revival and biblical womanhood . . .**

**Encouraging women to:**

- Discover and embrace God's design and mission for their lives.
- Reflect the beauty and heart of Jesus Christ to their world.
- Intentionally pass on the baton of truth to the next generation.
- Pray earnestly for an outpouring of God's Spirit in their families, churches, nation, and world.

Visit us at **ReviveOurHearts.com.** We'd love to hear from you!

# Go online for more lie-breaking resources

LIESWOMENBELIEVE.COM

And to explore more books helping readers
counter lies with the Truth, please visit

**LIESBOOKS.COM**

# Go deeper in exposing the lies with the Truth!

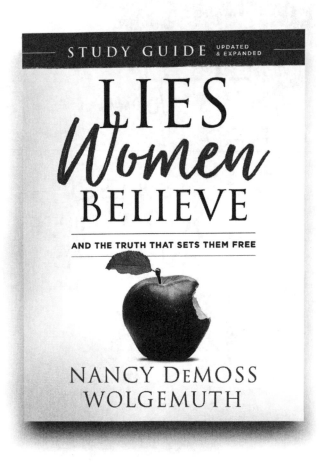

# Women mentoring women the Titus 2 way

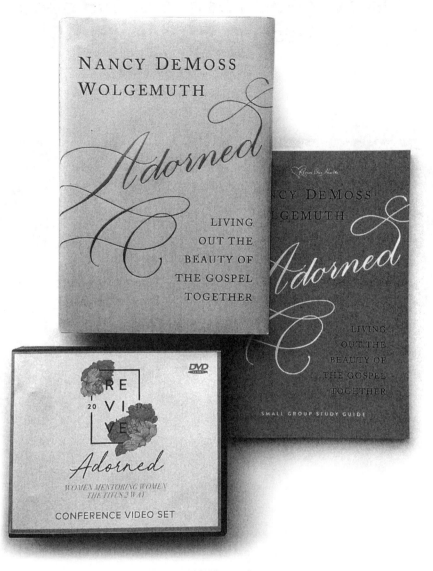

**MOODY**
**Publishers®**

*From the Word to Life®*

A fresh look at the Titus 2 model of older women living out the gospel and training younger women to do the same. The *Adorned Small Group Study Guide* is a 14-session guide through Nancy's book and can be used alongside the DVD set: teaching sessions and dramatic vignettes filmed at the Revive 2017 conference.

BOOK 978-0-8024-1259-1 | ALSO AVAILABLE AS AN EBOOK

STUDY GUIDE 978-0-8024-1865-4

DVD SET 978-0-8024-1886-1

# Discover God's beautiful and good design for women